The effects of the employment of foreign workers

with an introductory note ...

by

W.R. BÖHNING

Centre for Research in the Social Services
University of Kent

and

D. MAILLAT

Professor at the University of Neuchâtel

*with an introductory note
by the Secretariat*

ORGANISATION FOR ECONOMIC CO-OPERATION AND DEVELOPMENT

The opinions expressed and arguments employed in this publication
are the responsibility of the authors
and do not necessarily represent those of the OECD.

CONTENTS

INTRODUCTORY NOTE BY THE SECRETARIAT

THE ECONOMIC EFFECTS OF THE EMPLOYMENT OF FOREIGN WORKERS: WITH SPECIAL REFERENCE TO THE LABOUR MARKETS OF WESTERN EUROPE'S POST INDUSTRIAL COUNTRIES

by

W.R. Böhning

THE ECONOMIC EFFECTS OF THE EMPLOYMENT OF
FOREIGN WORKERS: THE CASE OF SWITZERLAND

by

Denis Maillat

<u>INTRODUCTORY BY THE SECRETARIAT</u>

<u>RESEARCH INTO THE ECONOMIC EFFECTS OF
THE EMPLOYMENT OF FOREIGN WORKERS</u>

BACKGROUND

1.   Ever since its establishment one of the principal preoccupa-
tions of the Working Party on Migration has been to study the
causes and economic consequences of the employment of foreign
manpower in the more industrialised countries of Europe. Considering the aim of O.E.C.D. to be the encouragement of its
Members to follow active and innovatory employment policies, the
Group decided that one of its tasks consisted in:

a) drawing the attention of the immigration countries to
    the role played by foreign manpower in growth and
    employment and

b) recommending these countries to take account of this
    potential when formulating strategies and measures
    designed to influence labour supply and demand.

2.   The first reflections and consultations made, from 1973
onwards, on the possibility of elaborating theory and its
accompanying models within O.E.C.D. proved to be disappointing.
On the one hand the experience and documentation available at
the time seemed insufficient and on the other, at macro-economic
level, the contribution towards policy formulation which could
be expected from the concepts which the accepted doctrine was
able to supply appeared to be small. As W.R. Böhning notes in
his report (paragraph 1), it was only when pressure groups began
to call the massive migratory movements into question that the
interest of the economists was awakened. The contributions of
economists such as, e.g., V. Lutz and L.P. Kindelberger
represent merely exceptions which confirm the rule. In particular it was not possible to grasp and quantify in a satisfactory manner the benefits and costs of immigration for the
receiving countries.

3.   Recognising these constraints, the Working Party on
Migration selected an approach by localised studies. This was
to provide some grasp of concrete situations (which differed
markedly according to region and country) and to discern those
factors hidden by national averages (which often conceal regional

phenomena, where these are contradictory and at different
stages of development). This approach had moreover the advantage of being able to lead simultaneously to similar research
in the countries of origin of the migrants, by means of inter-
locking studies. These were summarised in a report by Bernard
Kayser entitled "Manpower Migration and Labour Markets" (published in 1971). In spite of its limitations this report gave
quite precise indications as to the consequences of immigration
within certain geographically restricted labour markets (in the
broad sense). It was followed by a document on "Cyclically
determined Homeward Flows of Migrant Workers" (published in
1972). These studies led to the formulation of principles which
have enjoyed a certain currency outside O.E.C.D.. They cleared
the ground of some simplified generalisations concerning e.g.
advantages and disadvantages, competition between national and
foreign work forces, the educational role of migration, the
links between migration and development, and the accelerator
function exercised by foreign manpower; namely a series of
generalisations which shared the defect of attributing a homogeneous character to differing groups of migrant workers.
4.   Nevertheless it may well be asked whether such studies
enabled a response to be given to the fundamental question which
the group had posed, namely, the integration of foreign manpower
policy within national employment policies. This question had
been in the mind of the Working Party, which had envisaged that
such research should be complemented by studies on the place of
foreigners within the occupational structures of the industrialised countries. The improvement in both factual and analytical
knowledge which has been observed recently in certain Member
countries (the literature cited by Messrs. Böhning and Maillat
is an example), has led the O.E.C.D. to bypass the documentary
stage and to start on a policy-oriented study capable of leading
with some rapidity to a certain number of conclusions, provisional certainly, but of use for the formulation of a policy line.
5.   It was agreed that this study would comprise both an
historical and descriptive part and an analytical part. The
latter should notably:

    a) analyse the relationship between the forms in which
        the foreign work force is utilised and the functioning
        of the labour market; and,

b) assess certain consequences of the employment of foreign workers on the economic system.

The research would be conceived in such a manner as to enable it to be related to the parallel research on the functioning of the labour market and the behaviour of the economic agents on that market. /The first results of this research are to be found in two contributions prepared by Jean Vincens and Derek Robinson7. W.R. Böhning, a research associate at the Centre for Research in Social Science of the University of Kent, Canterbury, was entrusted with the preparation of the study.

THE PREPARATION OF THE RESEARCH

6. A first version of Mr. Böhning's report was examined by a meeting of experts held on the 28th and 29th June, 1972. At the invitation of the Secretariat, certain participants had presented written contributions outlining their thinking on the questions to be studied or concerning the results of their own research. Notably:

a) a report on the Swiss situation by D. Maillat, Professor at the University of Neuchâtel;

b) a synthesis of a study by Adriana Marshall (Social Science Faculty of the Netherlands Economic Institute) on the Immigration of Manpower into the Netherlands, prepared by the author(1);

c) a note on the utilisation of a systems approach in studying the effects of immigration, by J.L. Reiffers, Dean of the Faculty of Economics, University of Aix-Marseille II(2);

---

1) This study was published in 1973 by the Rotterdam University Press under the title "The import of Labour. The case of the Netherlands".

2) The approach Mr. Reiffers recommends consists in (a) assessing the changes brought about by immigration in the fundamental economic structure (effect of immigration on the parameters), examining the role of immigration in the short-term adjustment of economies (effects on the values of constant-parameter variables) and (b) studying the relationship between the short- and long-term effects. Research in the latter direction should enable short-term reception policy in particular to be linked with the fundamental aims of structural policy.

d) a note concerning the utilisation of statistics in
    the study of migration by G. Tapinos, Economic
    Activity Research Service of the National Foundation
    for Political Science, Paris(1);

e) a summary of a study by Eskil Wadensjö of the
    University of Lünd, on Economic Aspects of
    Immigration into Sweden, prepared by the author(2);

f) a note concerning the model adopted by the O.E.C.D.
    Development Centre within the framework of a study
    concerning cost and benefit of migration as opposed
    to the transfer of capital (document prepared by
    G. Gallais-Hommono and F. Bourguignon, consultants at
    the Centre)(3).

7.   The discussion on Mr. Böhning's report and the other
contributions gave rise to a debate of some depth both on the
basic questions and on the possible types of approach. As a
result of that discussion and of written observations sent
subsequently to the Secretariat, Mr. Böhning was able to prepare
a second version of his study. At the same time the Secretariat
asked M. Maillat to rework his report; thus O.E.C.D. finally
had available two studies, one fairly general in character, the
other concerning more specifically the Swiss case.

---

1) According to Mr. Tapinos the statistics on migration have not
   generally gone beyond the stage of administrative observation.
   These statistics may therefore answer the internal needs of
   government departments but have no connection on the face of
   it with the variables explaining this phenomenon. Their use
   in the absence of any theory may lead to erroneous conclusions, if not to an impasse. In fact, the theoretical
   hypothesis should precede statistical observation; it is the
   former which should determine the type and quantity of
   information to be collected. It is first necessary, therefore, to consider the state of development of the problem
   and hence the nature of the available observations in order
   to decide next whether the statistics can be used.

2) This study was published in 1973 by Stüdentlitteratur, Lund
   1973, under the title "Immigration och samhällsekonomi" by
   Eskil Wadensjö.

3) The aim of this study is to analyse the relationship between manpower migration from developing countries and
   direct investment in these countries particularly from the
   respective standpoints of the social benefits and costs.

THE CONCEPTUAL FRAMEWORK - GENERAL

8.   Far from opposing one another, these two studies are
complementary. The theses proposed by Böhning are to a large
extent confirmed in the more specific research of Maillat.
Moreover, both studies reject a formalised approach to follow
in preference an interpretation of observed fact and behaviour.
Thus Böhning adopts as his conceptual framework the process of
"self-feeding" immigration and Maillat attempts to integrate
immigration into the development of the Swiss labour market and
production apparatus.

Böhning's concept

Böhning's reasoning may be summed up as follows:

i) the rise in living standards, education and aspirations
   of the former working class in the industrialised
   countries has not been accompanied by any profound and
   generalised change in the job structure, the consequence
   of which has been the continued existence of an extremely
   important group of jobs which are socially undesirable
   or relatively badly paid. Aided by economic expansion
   and full employment, the workers of the country, and
   especially the young, incline more and more towards
   jobs which are socially more desirable, leaving the
   others unoccupied. Confronted with this situation the
   simplest alternative, and the one which permits the
   social, productive and employment structures to be
   retained substantially intact, is the "temporary"
   immigration of foreign workers. Such immigration
   should also enable a response to the movement of the
   economic cycle;

ii) the employment of foreigners spreads progressively from
    primitive pockets of poverty to other jobs. This
    extension is determined by complementarity between un-
    skilled and skilled jobs. Foreign workers seem wholly
    suitable for filling jobs which demand neither a true
    occupational training nor a knowledge of the national
    language. Large manufacturing enterprises realise also
    that foreigners are easily utilisable in mass production
    or in jobs which can be heavily fragmented. These un-
    attractive employments (although relatively well paid)

which the workers of the country tend if possible to avoid, thus finally create new work opportunities for the foreigners.

iii) Up to this point the self-feeding process of immigration does not seem apparent. There would seem rather to be a propagation phenomenon, rendered possible by the availability of foreign workers, complementarity of jobs and growth in the production of goods and services. But this consideration does not take into account e.g. the fact that the demand for consumer goods and social capital represented by the foreigners necessarily creates an additional demand for manpower. Taking his inspiration partly from the Dutch study by the "Centraal Planbureau", Böhning arrives at the conclusion that the satisfaction of manpower demand by immigration may well be largely illusory. The employment of each foreign worker tends to lead to a requirement for another. (Paragraph 31). ⟦In the latter case this is only the extreme situation. Policies followed in respect of admission, stay and employment of foreign workers and of their families on the one hand, and the external turnover rate (paragraph 67) on the other, limit the multiplier effect on the demand for new foreign manpower. It will be noted that while putting this argument forward Böhning nevertheless subjects it to many conditions (cf. similarly paragraph 128)⟧.

iv) These observations, which concern more particularly the relationship between the labour market and immigration, are completed by a sociological view. Böhning introduces in this respect the notion of "maturity" in the migratory flow. He distinguishes four stages of maturity. The first corresponds to the recruitment of male workers (generally young, quite well-qualified and well-selected) to occupy a limited number of places. These workers envisage only a short stay in the host country. The problem of family immigration does not arise. In the course of the second stage (which may be defined as one of transition), the characteristics of the immigrants show signs of change, the length of stay rises and the rate of returns diminishes. But it is during the third stage that immigration begins to present those characteristics which the majority of observers are in agreement in discerning in it. Recruitment spreads to new regions and becomes less selective, at least from the point of view of occupation. The longest-standing immigrants begin to bring their families to join them and their activity rates diminish in consequence. (This is not necessarily the result of the presence of the wives, who often find work themselves, but rather of the immigration of younger children). The duration of stay in the immigration country becomes longer and the rate of returns continues to diminish.

v) In the course of this third stage, which corresponds roughly to the phase of propagation in the employment of foreigners (see point (iii) above) the increased number of immigrants begins to represent a quite significant demand for durable and non-durable consumer goods. This process is gradual and the additional annual demand appears limited. Moreover, it may be satisfied by an increase in productivity. Nevertheless, over the years, the effects are cumulative and are liable to produce results on employment in the consumer goods, equipment and distribution services industries. It is thus probable that a growing proportion, although still restricted, of foreign workers will end up by being utilised in satisfying the needs of the immigrant population. The immigrant population (active and non-active) similarly expresses needs for social infrastructure. Here again the additional annual demand may appear limited, but it is in this area (administration, social services and similarly schools and housing) that the limits of a more intensive use of existing capacity will be felt more quickly and more strongly. This will have important consequences on the additional demand for labour and on the volume of immigration.

vi) In the fourth stage, the increase of the length of stay, the heightened re-assembling of families, and natural growth contribute to a still further enlargement of the foreign population. An economic, social, cultural and religious infrastructure develops, composed for the most part of people who belong to the same ethnic groups as the migrants. This additional presence of foreigners reinforces the demand for consumer goods and social capital (and consequently for manpower) beyond the limits which would have been reached by the mere pursuit of importing workers. It is at this stage (200,000 to 300,000 migrants belonging to the same ethnic group) that reaction appears on the part of the native population. The intervention of the authorities may then go beyond labour market control and take on the aspect of limitative measures in immigration.

10. This résumé produces only the essential part of Böhning's conceptual framework (paragraphs 13-52). It is nevertheless sufficient to enable us to ask whether it is a valid key to the interpretation of the processes of immigration and whether it adheres to factual reality. Böhning (paragraph 12) underlines that in the event he is merely creating a typology and that the factual situation in different countries may deviate more or less from his model. This observation should be considered as a warning against any eventual mechanical interpretation of this same model. Indeed the phenomena which Böhning describes can be found in all countries, but they often overlap and do not always present themselves in reality in the logical and temporal order which the author would propose to us. This is the price to be paid for any attempt at theorising in an extremely complicated process, such as that of present-day migration, for which moreover we have very few conceptual instruments provided by the doctrines of general economics and those of the labour market. The information which Böhning possesses is very rich (although not complete in the case of certain countries); his intellectual scruples lead him to exploit it to the maximum and to introduce into his reasoning an important number of variables. This necessarily weighs down the exposé and calls for a very attentive reading of the text. It may be asked at this point if recourse to a formal model would not have been an advantage. The reply can only be negative for two different reasons: one of substance, the other concerning the objectives of the research and the role of the Working Party on migration. Econometrics and the instruments of so-called formal logic are equally of undeniable utility in the representation of a simple, or simplified, reality capable of being discerned from numerous data; such is not always the case in our field. On the other hand, the objective of this research is rather to present to the Working party a statement of the problems which is as complete, objective and intelligible as possible thus enabling it to draw conclusions for policy at O.E.C.D. level; it is not

to produce work of an absolute scientific value. Now the conceptual framework of Böhning's report responds sufficiently well to this requirement. On the one hand, it is sufficiently eclectic and hardly ideological at all, and on the other hand, it elaborates and develops notions (notably that of the self-feeding process of immigration) which enable it to give reasonable explanations of a certain number of facts and problems. These considerations do not exclude that in the future the study of certain specific themes may be tackled by using a more formalised approach. What can be learnt from the research at present in progress within the O.E.C.D. Development Centre may well be very useful in this respect. Equally, in seeking a deeper understanding of the relationship between immigration and the economy and society of the reception country the undeniable importance should be noted of the utilisation of a systems approach as recommended by J.L. Reiffers. The report by D. Maillat, (page 1) already represents an attempt to integrate the phenomenon of immigration within the process of the functioning of a given economic system.

Maillat's approach

The study by Maillat would appear to have been facilitated by his being able to concentrate on a country like Switzerland which possesses a reasonably satisfactory statistical cover and where the problems of foreign manpower have been fully debated. Nevertheless, this advantage requires a supplementary effort insofar as the very richness of the documentation obliged the rapporteur to undertake a fairly fine analysis of the functioning of the Swiss labour market, of the dynamics of immigration and of the effects of policies. Switzerland is without doubt the country where the employment of foreigners has had the most obvious repercussions. On the one hand, immigration has quickly taken on a structural character and, on the other, as Maillat notes, immigration policy has been practically the sole instrument at the disposal of the Federal Government for direct intervention in economic activity. It must be recalled in this connection that Switzerland does not possess the instruments of a medium-term and conjunctural policy available, to a greater or lesser degree, to the other countries of Western Europe. It is through the admission and more or less strict regulation of the immigration and employment of foreigners that the Federal Authorities have been able to act indirectly on the labour market and on wages and to do without a conjunctural policy. Moreover since 1970 (that is to say since the adoption of very restrictive measures which resulted practically in putting a stop to new immigration) an increasingly pressing need has been felt to give the Federal Government other means of intervention in the regulation of growth (in accordance with O.E.C.D. recommendations). Modifications in immigration policy and the volume of entry flows have been made in response to the requirements of conjunctural development without too great a concern for long-term consequences. It was only after 1963, when the cost to the community of the increasing flow and ever-growing number of permanent settlements became obvious, that the authorities (who were moreover subjected to strong political pressures) began to modify their attitude. The phenomenon of immigration, and Swiss policy in the matter, thus develops through a certain number of phases linked to short-term evolution of the economy and the labour market. These are the phases which Maillat distinguishes and utilises as reference points, enabling him to avoid traps of theorisation and to provide us with an interpretation which adheres very closely to the facts. Nevertheless this study contains certain elements which would confirm the theses of Böhning relating to stages of maturity in immigration. This initiative permits an explanation of:

a) how, during a period from roughly 1945 to 1960, immigration evolved to the point of rendering obsolete the basic idea which had inspired the first admissions after the war, that is to say that the employment of foreign manpower ought to have a strictly temporary character.

b) the reasons invoked for the adoption, from 1963 onwards, of measures limiting the admission and the employment of foreigners.

c) the different phases of these measures and their scope.

d) the difficulties in which the authorities have found themselves when faced with pressures in a contrary sense, between which they had to arbitrate.

e) the effects of the trade-offs carried out.

f) the orientation at present followed (assimilation of foreigners who live for long periods in Switzerland, and special regimes for certain categories which enable

a certain flexibility in the labour market to be
assured).

RESULTS OF THE RESEARCH

Immigration and employment - the problem of competition

12.   Concern to avoid competition between national and foreign
manpower has been at the base of traditional measures of a
regulatory nature designed:

a) to subordinate the employment of foreigners to the non-
availability of the appropriate national manpower;

b) to limit their utilisation to a given occupation,
employer or locality; and,

c) to guarantee that the treatment of foreigners as
concerns conditions of remuneration and/or employment
would not be inferior to that of national workers.

The degree of application of the measures evoked under (a)
and (b) has varied from one country to another with the development of employment, of the functioning of the administrative
services, of the attitude of the unions, and of public opinion.
It cannot be denied that in countries such as Switzerland, this
juridical framework served efficiently during an initial period
to guide foreigners towards jobs in which shortages of national
manpower had been established. However, these measures were
generally conceived as a response to the need for an administrative control of an immigration limited in volume and not generally extending beyond the economic cycle. When the employment
of foreigners becomes massive and takes on a structural
character, these measures lose much of their effectiveness, the
more so as it is at that moment that the application of another
series of standards intervenes designed to assure mobility of
employment (partial or total) to the original immigrants. It
is thus legitimate to wonder if competition phenomena in employment between national workers and foreigners can reveal themselves.

13.   Böhning develops this theme in paragraphs 59-73 of his
study. He excludes the contention that introduction of foreign
labour might be a cause of unemployment for workers of the
country on the grounds that it is the response to a demand.
This would appear an intuitively correct statement when it is

placed - as Böhning does - at a global level in a context of
full employment. It would appear to be confirmed by factual
studies carried out by O.E.C.D. in the past (cf. paragraph 3
above). It can be accepted therefore without need of any
specific demonstration. The rapporteur believes however that
the presence of foreign manpower on the labour market may cause
the competitive position of certain groups of native workers to
deteriorate. He attempts to take this possible phenomenon into
account with the aid of three tables /3(a), 3(b), 3(c)7, drawn
up on the basis of the conjectured elasticities of substitution
of D. Collard. The first of these tables is at one and the
same time an illustration of the logical pattern followed by
the author and the qualitative representation of the numerical
results obtained by the two others.

14. In spite of the simplifications which Böhning has found it
necessary to apply (for example, division of workers into the
three traditional broad categories, which now retain little
real significance, and utilisation of a somewhat global series
of German statistics), the results of this scheme may be considered acceptable enough providing they are not used as an
absolute rule allowing no exceptions. At the same time, there
will be retained as a potential subject for further research,
the conclusion that the general body of foreign workers -
whether skilled or not - would represent a very competitive
element in relation to the unskilled national workers. This
question is important: it goes beyond the strict limit of
competition to raise the more general question of the optimal
allocation of foreign workers and of the reciprocal and complementary relations which may be established between immigration,
job structures and the behaviour of enterprises and labour.
Another question worthy of consideration concerns possible
competition between different groups of foreigners.

Foreign manpower and mobility mechanisms

15. It has become almost commonplace to say that foreign manpower, besides its role as "a conjunctural shock absorber"
introduces into the economic system and the labour market a
practically permanent element of flexibility, which the native
workers are no longer able to ensure. The value of the foreign
worker would consist precisely in his playing this role and
compensating for stagnant or declining mobility on the part of
the native manpower. Böhning supports this thesis in paragraphs

64-67. He tries, moreover, to present in an Annex a numerical illustration of the additional flexibility which immigration grants to the system, thanks largely to the amount of external turnover, that is to say to entries and quits by the foreign work force on the labour market of the immigration country. This argument may be developed concretely noting that it is precisely this turnover which provides enterprises with a practically limitless availability of adequate manpower (particularly the young in good physical condition). It may be observed nevertheless that this model is liable to more or less sharp modifications as the period of stay of an important proportion of the migrants increases. Moreover, quantitative and qualitative changes in the supply and demand, or crucial political action, may, in the long-term change certain fundamental data and put the survival of this "industrial reserve army" in jeopardy. This is a question worthy of specific research which would take account, interalia, of new trends which may be discerned in the field of job restructuring.

16. The possibility of opposing the development of immigration by active mobility policies for national manpower is rejected by Böhning as unrealistic, (paragraphs 68-73). Concerning mobility between occupations and between sectors, he repeats his favourite argument, that it is the wage restraints (and one may add models of life-style) characteristic of the economies and societies of the Western countries which impede any movement towards less well paid or socially undesirable jobs (and encourage the abandonment of these jobs). This is the theme shared by many observers and expounded by Böhning throughout the whole length of his study. It does not call for any particular comment.

17. As concerns movement from inactivity to active life (that is to say participation in the labour market by so-called secondary or special groups), the reporter utilises a psycho-sociological argument which consists in saying that, in a society enjoying a high standard of living, inactivity becomes not only tolerable but also desirable when confronted by the very limited attractions exercised by the jobs which the secondary workers might be able to fill. Without denying the truth of this statement it may be observed that it covers only a part of the real situation. The secondary groups (married women, students, the handicapped, and older workers) differ from the migrants not only in their motivation but also with

regard to their occupational and personal qualities and
opportunities for using them. In other words, the jobs which
these people can fill do not usually coincide with the jobs
filled by the migrants, at least from the viewpoint of the
enterprises (whose choices are decisive in economies where
decision-making is decentralised) and the work organisation
which they adopt. There would not therefore be any possible
substitution between one group and the other. Proof of this
statement is rather complicated (it would require, interalia,
a comparison between each sub-group of migrants and each sub-
group of possible secondary workers); it would nonetheless be
very useful if only to avoid certain arbitrary comparisons of
which some studies are not wholly guiltless. It is probably
necessary to distinguish the case of married women, who may in
theory be recovered by the labour market, from that of those
women, generally younger, who may be observed in increasing
numbers in production jobs within certain industries. The
latter is a form of manpower which in principle may be regarded
as in competition with that of migrant masculine labour. This
increased participation on the part of women would represent
one of the principal characteristics of the labour market of
the near future. In certain countries - for example France -
this may lead to some reduction (at least initially) of the
volume of foreign immigration flows. In other countries it
may lead rather to a change in the composition of these flows.
18. Similar observations may be made with regard to the
existence of an alternative between immigration and policies of
increased aid to geographical mobility and regional development.
Here the rapporteur solves the problem by a declaration which
he makes substantially in the following form: foreign manpower
does not slow down structural change, indeed on the contrary,
by the flexibility which it affords the labour market, it
mitigates the negative effects of all kinds which these same
changes might have for the native worker. This theme is
perfectly in accord with, first, the arguments which Böhning
develops in a more diffused manner in other parts of his report,
second, the general inclination of that document and third,
the idea that one should not base one's reasoning, at the risk
of falling into utopia on a model which pre-supposes total
mobility, both occupational and geographical. However, since,
in the event, the purpose is to make the most objective judgement possible about policies which might constitute alternatives

to immigration, but might also be complementary to it, a
certain number of precise questions might be formulated, if
only to verify the soundness of this foundation. For example:

a) if in certain countries and given sets of circumstances
   there is a real alternative (either partial or total)
   between immigration and geographical mobility, i.e. if
   the foreign work force and that part of the national
   manpower theoretically interested in mobility enjoy
   similar opportunities for employment;

b) if initiatives in regional development (aimed mainly
   at decentralising and diversifying the apparatus of
   production or at assuring a better balance between
   urban and rural milieux) may be taken in certain
   countries without having recourse to foreign labour,
   just as much during the phase of infrastructure creation
   as during the operational period proper.

It will be evident that a reply to these kinds of questions
can in the last analysis only be given by detailed specific
studies or, in the extreme case, national ones, but a simple
indication of their existence may serve to open a fruitful
debate upon these little known subjects.

Relationship between immigration and mobility -
lessons to be drawn from Swiss experience

19. The study by Maillat (notably chapters 1 and 3) shows
clearly how the powerful mobility which was characteristic of
the Swiss labour market until 1963 (that is to say before
restrictive measures were adopted) would rarely have been
possible without immigration. Immigration put Switzerland in
a situation comparable to that of countries with a limitless
labour supply. On the other hand, because of control over
entry and employment, the foreigners were not allotted to
branches or professions at random. Thus the native workers were
able to spread themselves without much competition (aided by a
differential development in wages) over the total economy. This
provided quite a satisfactory allocation of the available manpower, both national and foreign.
20. Although a great part of the foreign manpower was subject
to continual renewal, it was not possible to prevent an ever
greater number of foreigners (both active and non-active) from

appearing in Switzerland. This provoked quite strong reactions of a socio-political character accompanied by negative attitudes as to the long-term effects of employing foreigners. The measures adopted from 1963 onwards to respond to these reactions ended up by aggravating the difficulties of the labour market, on which tensions increased. Besides their limitative character these measures have the defects:

  a) of not being selective;

  b) of not constituting any encouragement to structural reform of the productive mechanisms and of jobs - but was that possible? - and above all;

  c) of rendering change of job by foreigners even more difficult and thus restraining mobility.

21. After undergoing changes of varying importance, the system was radically transformed from 1970 onwards. The main features of the present scheme are:(1)

  i) the aim of stabilising the number of active foreigners holding annual permits and settlement permits at 600,000, which means that new entries can only be in exchange for registered departures (such as leaving the country and death, for example, but also, it will be noted, naturalisation);

  ii) an important relaxation of the restrictions concerning the mobility of workers on annual permit, permitting them to change their employer after one year's stay and their canton or occupation after three years;

  iii) allocation of newly admitted workers by canton and responsibility by the same cantons for the redistribution of labour amongst enterprises;

  iv) an allotment of seasonal workers, the number of which is fixed annually;

  v) a number of frontier workers which is in theory unlimited but which can be subjected to indirect restrictions through redefinition of that category by the authorities.

---

1) For further details see "L'Arrêtés du Conseil fédéral" du 6 juillet, 1973.

In spite of the rigidity of fixing of an overall maximum, the authorities thus have a range of instruments which should enable them to refine their actions. Moreover, new relaxations are foreseen, concerning, inter alia, the mobility of workers on annual permit. Nevertheless, the important thing at this time is not to predict the future effect of the sum of these measures (which to be effective must in any case be accompanied by a general structural policy and an active manpower policy applicable to native workers as well as to foreigners); it is rather to note that Swiss experience has brought into prominence the function which immigration can exercise within the field of distributive mobility and demonstrated the profoundly contra-dictory aspect of measures which aim at the same time at limiting the volume of foreign manpower and maintaining - or even accentuating - the obstacles to its mobility. The change of attitude on the part of the Swiss authorities on the subject of this mobility is extremely significant.

22. In the absence of an active labour market policy and a formulation, even though only indicative, of orders of priority within the economy, allocation of manpower in Switzerland has occurred through machinery whose principal component parts have been, according to Maillat, elasticity in the labour supply, an increase in employment capacity, and change in the range of wages across industries. Given continual growth, these elements would have acted with perfect interdependence. In particular, the fluidity of the labour market (due to immigration and the tendency towards mobility of the native workers) would have enabled enterprises to increase their employment capacity. As the latter developed, the mobility of Swiss workers would have increased, and the distribution of manpower would have been effected as a result, principally though not exclusively, of the development of a range of salaries across industries. By using the official statistics, Maillat is able to provide a quite convincing proof of this hypothesis. He demonstrates for example the substitution role played by foreigners in low wage industries and in the metal and machinery industry (which is not a low wage industry but one whose work environment may well be considered unsatisfactory by the workers of the country) and the progressive orientation of the Swiss themselves towards high wage industries (which are precisely those where the capacity for employment has increased the most) and towards apparently more prestigious employment in the tertiary or near

tertiary sectors. In this connection a declaration by the
rapporteur (paragraph 3.2.3.) deserves to be made the subject
of debate: "immigration has played the role normally ascribed
to technical progress by facilitating the passage of the Swiss
towards the tertiary sector.... In normal conditions, movement towards the tertiary sector is due to lack of jobs in the
secondary sector resulting from the recessive nature of technical progress upon employment. In Switzerland it has been a
voluntary movement favoured by immigration which has stimulated
mobility.... The development noted in Switzerland is somewhat
abnormal, for the employment structure of the productive
apparatus. This explains why foreign manpower has become
structurally necessary".

The role of the salary range

23. One question which merits discussion in detail is that of
the allocation role played by wages. Of course, it is to be
examined within the special framework of this macro-economic
research on the consequences of immigration, without entering
into the often artificial debate dividing the quantitivists
from those who favour an interpretation based largely on psycho-
sociological elements. Especially in movement between jobs by
workers, the role of salary differentials would have been para-
mount in Switzerland (qualitative elements, psychosociological,
institutional and occupational, would tend moreover in the same
direction). In conformity with his analytical method, Maillat
examines this question in dynamic terms, that is to say as a
function of the economic and political situation (compare
paragraph 3.2.4.).

24. The results of this analysis can be summarised thus:

     1) During the period 1949 to 1959, factors allied to the
market (for example, profits) produced within a group of
industries a rapid expansion of employment capacity and
naturally an above-average rise in wages. The important movement of Swiss workers towards this group (group I following
Maillat's classification) nevertheless prevented excessive
wage claims. By recovering the skilled and semi-skilled manpower, enterprises likewise avoided excessive training costs or
recourse to the practice known as "over-qualification". This
same movement did not hinder the activity of the industries in
the other group (group II) who were able to replace their
losses in national manpower, and even increase their volume of

total manpower, by engaging foreign workers who were ready to work at the wage rates in force (and moreover generally confined within these industries by legal constraints and by the recruitment policy of the enterprises in Group I). In conclusion, differential salary rises were produced according to which of these two categories of persons the industrial branch in question was exploiting. The inter-industrial wage range broadened, but, thanks to this abundant supply both of Swiss and of foreigners, the labour market experienced a remarkable flexibility.

2) During the period 1959 to 1964, the increase in the global demand led to increasing employment capacity in Swiss industry as a whole. The industries of Group II gradually lost their national manpower but as they could not afford to lose it completely and wishing equally to remain attractive to foreign workers they reacted by accelerating their wage rises. The Swiss workers showed a tendency to move towards the tertiary sector. Policies aiming at increasing participation in the labour market by potential workers (the secondary groups according to Böhning's terminology) were revealed as clearly insufficient. The industries of Group I did not therefore reach the position of satisfying their manpower needs (for practical purposes the number of Swiss workers increased only in the printing trades and chemicals). Thus powerful tension on the labour market resulted, with the need to have recourse to new immigration less selective than in the past. Foreign workers were from then on recruited into all branches, without however, the principles governing their mobility being changed. It was during this period that the phenomenon of self-feeding immigration began to make itself felt. Some of the manpower must, according to Maillat, have been withdrawn from the machinery of industrial production in order to satisfy needs in infrastructure, especially for housing, of the immigrants themselves, whose families were arriving in greater numbers. It is probable that in spite of the closure of the inter-industrial salary range, due to catching up by the industries in Group II, an important wage drift was produced within the enterprises. This is confirmed by the fact that enterprises concluded between themselves agreements designed to combat poaching of labour. The period is of special interest for study of the relationship between wages and manpower mobility. It will be noted finally that the period is characterised by strong inflationary pressure; it was

then that the Swiss began to speak of a causal link between
immigration and inflation. More recent (and more reliable)
analyses have put paid to this thesis: nevertheless it retains
a certain importance insofar as it represents one of the arguments invoked in 1963 for the restraint of immigration.

3) The restrictions on the admission of foreigners adopted
in 1963 reinforced the tensions on the employment market and
provoked a closing up of the wage range to the point where the
dispersion appeared weaker than in 1949. Nevertheless, these
tensions were mitigated in that foreigners could still
replace Swiss who left certain branches. From 1965 onwards,
the new measures (which maintained the preceding embargo on an
increase in the total numbers of personnel by firm and introduced a special ceiling with regard to foreign labour) reduced
the supply of new manpower sharply. In these conditions wages
manifest a saw-tooth development: as soon as rises take place
in certain branches and the range opens out, a re-adaptation
movement by the other branches is observed. The result of
this process is a general increase in salaries which is higher
than before.

25. As concerns the period since 1970, Maillat cannot offer us
precise observations. He confines himself to quoting the
economic report of O.E.C.D. in 1972 which draws attention to an
increased general mobility; thus confirming the salutary effect
of measures adopted to facilitate (within the framework of the
so-called "global" limitation) movement of the foreigners.
Given the rigidity of the national manpower supply and the fact
that the foreign manpower has from now on become a structural
element, the distributive mobility of the labour force will
depend especially, within the near future, on the propensity
towards mobility of those foreign workers who have been in
Switzerland for more than one year (that is to say of those
who, according to the most recent regulations, will be legally
entitled to move around). This propensity will be affected
essentially by wage levels. In the short-term one can thus
expect wage rises of some importance. In the longer term, the
movement of salaries and manpower mobility will depend upon the
degree of change in the production apparatus. If this modification reduces manpower needs, mobility, according to Maillat,
may undergo a braking effect and (competitive) rises in wages
may well be reduced.

26. This is, nevertheless, a very complex development and it
will be difficult for it to operate in the most effective
direction for the system merely by liberalisation of foreign
manpower movements. The interpretation of this development
brings back into play the more general question of future
policies for growth, for structure and for manpower. In this
field, Maillat (compare similarly 4.1.) does not give us any
true forecast. (He nevertheless discusses a certain number of
assumptions in the part devoted to production ensembles - 4.3. -
and in the conclusion of the study). He was probably not able
to do so given that the responsible authorities and the enterprises themselves seem to be still hesitating in front of the
fundamental choices.

Effect of immigration on income distribution: an attempt at
interpretation by Böhning

27. The conceptions of Böhning in the field of the dynamic of
wages (paragraphs 74 and 75) seem, at first sight, to be inspired much more by a socio-structural interpretation than by
a purely factual one. Nevertheless, as he penetrates further
into the specific subject of the relationship between immigration
and wage growth (paragraphs 76 to 86) his reasoning becomes
more positive and he finishes by reaching conclusions not far
removed from those obtained by Maillat from an empirical examination and a different approach.

        For Böhning, salary differences between the three major
occupational classes (skilled, semi-skilled and unskilled
workers) would remain rigid for practical purposes, while inter-
sectoral differences would show a certain flexibility. This
would be the result of interplay between the Unions on the one
side, seeking to maintain differences between occupations while
attempting at the same time to improve the position of their
members at sector level, and the employers on the other side
finding it more normal to accept differential rises in various
industries rather than to provoke a general disturbance of
established hierarchies. As a corollary, Böhning adds that the
high wages which characterise industries where profits are high
would occur independently of the labour demand concerning the
different occupations. /See also B.C. Roberts, General Report
on the O.E.C.D. Wage Determination Conference, provisional text,
July 1973.

28. Within this framework, the employment of foreign workers
(even when spread throughout all sectors) would have practically
no braking effect on growth of wages in the more dynamic
industries (where the relationship between salary development
and manpower demand would be weak). On the contrary the elimination of bottle-necks in low salary industries, made possible
by emigration, would have certain consequences at sector level
even though these may be limited globally. Here everything
depends, according to Böhning, on the development of the labour
market: if the labour demand remains constant, the employment
of foreigners will have quite a strong braking effect on the
tendency towards wage rises, but if the labour demand grows
more and more, this effect will tend to dissolve. When the
economy is turning at full strength, Böhning concludes, it is
not bottlenecks which induce salary pressure but rather the
action of the Unions, who attempt to recover their position by
demanding a yet bigger slice of the bigger cake. In the course
of the third stage of maturity, when the consequences of
immigration seem to be showing themselves more clearly, the
presence of foreigners enables stronger growth of the economy
not only because of what the immigrants produce, but also by
the additional demand for consumer goods and social capital
which they express. At micro-economic level, braking effects
on salary are visible but it is legitimate to wonder whether,
globally, immigration does not end up by producing a general
rise in remuneration which would not occur in its absence. The
reply of Böhning is affirmative; it could not be otherwise given
the premises which he seems to adopt, namely that immigration
produces higher profits which must nevertheless be divided
(even though unequally) between the enterprises and the working
class. /It will be recalled that the majority of those economists who have treated manpower immigration have attributed to
the employment of foreigners a depressive role on monetary
salaries (cf. for Germany: T. Bain and A. Pauga, in Kyklos,
1972, 4, pages 820 to 824). Cost inflation would be thus
countermanded by immigration. Finally a translation of the
Phillips curve would operate, in the sense of an attenuation of
the relationship between prices and rate of unemployment (work
in course at the University of Aix-Marseille, directed by J.L.
Reiffers, would seem to confirm this observation as concerns
France.) Böhning does not question the validity of these observations. He thinks, however, that this depressive role will

only apply in the immediate future. In the long-term, immigration will have quite the opposite effect .

29. It will be noted that Böhning's theses can probably be
confirmed by the empirical observations of Maillat on Switzerland.
Böhning likewise has found confirmation for it in other countries
(paragraph 84 of the report). Nevertheless, this sum of case
studies does not satisfy him completely. For that reason he
bases his conclusions to some extent on an argument "a contrario",
that is to say by imagining, through a sort of exercise in in-
formal simulation, what would be the probable development in
the absence of immigration (paragraphs 82 and 83). Without
immigration, tensions on the labour market would probably have
led to wage rises so strong that employers would have been
obliged to carry out labour saving investments to contain their
manpower needs. This would in the long-term have checked the
growth of wages. In those jobs where this operation was not
possible, salary rises would eventually have caused and pro-
pagated such pronounced inflation that severe restrictive
measures would have become necessary, having cumulative effects
on the economic system. The demand for labour would thus have
been reduced and hence the progressive rise in wages.

30. Finally, Böhning arrives at the stage of pronouncing
judgements on the distribution of income (paragraphs 87 to 90)
similar to those expressed by observers who have tackled the
problem without too great an ideological reserve or doctrinaire
alignment.

1) the initial restraint imposed by immigration on wage
growth (that is to say the desequilibrum, in terms of relative
profit, which national workers may suffer in comparison with
capital) is later (notably the third stage of maturity) largely
compensated for by an increase in real income per head produced
by immigration /In the absence of immigration the initial advantages won by the workers will be quickly eliminated by an
increase in prices or a reduction in investment - compare
paragraph 897.

2) however, the additional prosperity which immigration
renders possible is more profitable to capital than to labour
because of the unequal distribution of revenue which is inherent in our type of society (paragraph 87).

3) the mobility of national workers towards better
remunerated or more prestigious jobs, is at the origin of
immigration. However, immigration by reproducing itself

sustains and multiplies this movement. In other terms, the effect (immigration) is retroactive on the cause (mobility) in a system of reciprocal relationship. It may thus be claimed that in fact immigration enables the individual rise of the national workers without altering the social structure.

4) by contributing to an increase in enterprise profits, immigration contributes equally to an enlargement of the fiscal take on these profits. On the other hand, immigrants are themselves taxpayers. However, while they contribute to taxes and social security approximately in the same proportions as the national population, immigrants receive, according to Böhning, much less than the average of social expenditure per capita. Logically this phenomenon should produce, on the whole, favourable consequences for the national population. Although he presents an extremely interesting framework for reflection (cf. paragraph 88, footnotes nos. 84, 85, 87, 88 and notably 118 et seq.). Böhning is not able to give that detailed examination which the importance of the subject would require. This framework must thus be widened at some future stage of specific research. The latter would enable important lessons to be discerned on policies relating to "reception structures" for the immigrants, which practically everyone is in accord in saying are at the same time inadequate and costly. If it could be effectively demonstrated that immigrants receive proportionately less than they give, many of the practical and psychological blocks which oppose an improvement in these structures could be eliminated.

Is immigration a cause of inflation?

31. In asking the two rapporteurs this question we were aware of the difficulty of answering it and this for three reasons: first, because the causes of modern inflation are imperfectly known; secondly, because these causes have similarly an international component which escapes appreciation in terms of the national economy, and finally because immigration varies in volume and in role according to country and time and is able therefore to exercise only a variable effect on economic equilibrium or disequilibrium. It is a question rather of confronting the traditional opinion - according to which immigration would put a brake on inflation insofar as it would assure the fluidity of the labour market or the immigrants would retain their spartan consumption habits - with a more recent thesis -

according to which the immigrants would end up having a limited effect on the restraint of salary costs /note the contrary opinions quoted in paragraph 28_7 and express (notably when accompanied by their families) a by no means negligible demand for consumer goods and equipment reflected in prices and wages; they would also have in particular a marginal productivity well below that of the native people and of the capital invested in labour saving devices. It will be added that it is a question of confronting two opinions, not in order to pronounce in favour of one or the other but rather to give some elements of reflection to those responsible for national policies when they meet at O.E.C.D.

32. Böhning has provided us with a good number of elements of reflection. The analysis which he carries out (paragraphs 91 to 99) leads him to conclude that, even at the third stage of maturity /the study is centred principally on this stage_7 immigration exercises a sure deflationary effect:

1) it would have practically no significant consequences in inflationary terms for factor cost /the elements which enter into account here would be the continued restraint on salaries exercised by immigration and the wage pressures induced by the immigrants. The variable rate of external turnover (defined throughout as the difference between rate of entry and rate of departure) would act naturally on these two element_s7.

2) it would maintain a noticeable deflationary effect on the price of consumer goods and indirectly on the price of investment goods, Böhning bases his reasoning essentially on the propensity to save, family composition, and the role played by remittances (of which the net deflationary effect is however more limited than might be imagined, given the possibility that these remittances may turn back on the market of the immigration country in the form of consumer demand). Of course an essential role would equally be played by the variable rate of external turnover.

33. One would have expected an important specific development of this theme by Maillat, since it is precisely in Switzerland that there has most frequently been invoked (notably to justify the first restrictive measures) a direct causal link between immigration and inflation (cf. paragraph 24.3 above). On the contrary Maillat (Chapter 4, paragraph 2) tackles this subject with a certain prudence and confines himself essentially to reiterating the opinions of Rossi and Thomas (No. 41 of his

bibliography). Without concealing other competing causes
(notably monetary flows) these authors attribute substantially
the acceleration in inflation rates which occurred in Switzerland
towards the end of the 50's to a cumulative process (or better
a revolving one): a vicious circle in which, at a given moment,
the self-feeding process of immigration would have played an
important role. In particular the growth in the population
(caused notably by the immigration of both active and inactive
persons) would have brought in its train an increase in global
demand which in turn would have led to pressure on wages and
prices and thus a growing demand for manpower. This last would
have rendered a new immigration necessary... and so on and so on.
Naturally in the course of this process immigration would have
had a restraining effect on wages and thus exercised an immediate
anti-inflationary role which would not have been manifest in
its absence.

34. The question then moves (as Rossi and Thomas do) rather in
the direction of productivity theory and, thence, towards the
theory of the structure of the production apparatus (cf. Maillat)
and of the ends and means of the economic system. At the end
of this attempt at dismantling and re-assembling other peoples'
thoughts, one may conclude with Maillat "that it is appropriate
to beware of too direct a causal link between immigration and
inflation. Indeed, the migratory flow and its volume are only
a reflection of a long process which has influenced the
apparatus of production". (Chapter 4.2. last paragraph but one).

The productive apparatus and immigration

35. Growth in global demand would, according to Maillat, have
shattered the manpower allocation system, thus dismantling the
implicit wages policy (a differentiated policy resulting from
immigration) which had functioned throughout the 50's. "It was
then that the inadequacy of our productive units and most
probably of our scale of production appeared..." (Chapter 4.2.
last paragraph). Switzerland is a borderline case, of course,
and one must beware of applying to other countries Maillat's
views on the relation between immigration and the productive
mechanisms (Chapter 4.3.). It is nonetheless true that this
examination brings into focus relations and interdependencies
which may well reappear elsewhere (and which would not perhaps
be quite so clearly discernible elsewhere.) This examination
helps us, in short, to formulate a nucleus of general ideas

without obliging us to elaborate a more or less imaginary
model.

36. The determinant elements of the fundamental development
have been, on the one hand, the structure of the Swiss economy
(small and medium-sized enterprises) which is congenial to
"capital-saving" investment and to "generalised sub-contracting",
and on the other hand, the (growing) volume and type of demand
to which Swiss production has responded (a demand with a large
international component). This type of demand requires a high
degree of flexibility and tends to the avoidance of too great
an investment in fixed capital. If in addition (a) the investment decisions were probably taken before 1950 (that is to say
at a time where, at least in Switzerland, the future appeared
uncertain), (b) confronted with an unexpected growth in the
economy the manpower supply (thanks to immigration) has been
abundant, the reasons which led Swiss entrepreneurs to maintain
(during a practically uninterrupted sequence of favourable
economic conjunctures) somewhat traditional productive mechanisms
and scales of production will easily be understood. Indeed the
combination appeared at the time natural, profitable and certain.

37. Maillat does not restrict himself to describing this
development. His examination is rich in observations of a more
general importance. We will retain some of them:

1) immigration has been a "considerable encouragement" to
the maintenance of the structure of the productive apparatus,
not only from the technical point of view, but also in the
sense of maintaining the type of ownership and the method of
management. This point, adds Maillat, is important, for
immigration has made it possible to avoid earlier recourse to
a modification of production scales (which generally implies
structural change).

2) incentive to substitute capital for labour was weak
in Switzerland until 1963. It is only after that date that the
increase in wages, which had become more marked, has caused
substitution movement. But the replacement of manpower by
capital within the framework of existing productive structures
has only enabled a limited increase in productivity. This
increase is essentially due to technical progress and to
economies of scale, for these are the two main elements which
permit simultaneous saving of the various factor costs. Now,
it was precisely these elements (which are moreover inter-
dependent) which were lacking the most in the Swiss productive

apparatus, given that their introduction was retarded by the
abundance of manpower consequent upon immigration. /As Maillat
recalls, a Swiss author, F. Schaller, expresses a contrary
opinion as concerns notably the utilisation of technical progress.
This author bases his thesis on two arguments: (a) it is only
possible to draw maximum advantage from technical progress where
one can count on a more numerous population, (b) Switzerland
is an under-populated country in relation to the present condition and potential development of production techniques.
"Ergo", concludes this author in substance, Switzerland needs
more immigration. It is possible that Schaller's premises /in
particular those under (b)7 are wrong. It is nevertheless
possible that these two theses are not as contradictory as
would appear at first sight. Maillat speaks rather of the past
and Schaller seems more concerned with the future. Maillat
puts his emphasis on the enterprise and manpower aspect and
Schaller (if we have well understood him) on the population and
economic-system aspect. It seems to us in particular that
Schaller conceives a more reasoned system able to profit from
technical process through an increase in that element which is
most lacking, namely human resources (Schaller refers expressly
to Sauvy). Of course - it may be added - reality has proved
quite different, but this is because in Switzerland immigration
has been inserted into a predetermined framework not particularly
favourable towards innovation. It could not therefore contribute
to a rationality which was non-existent either in peoples'
minds or in the course of events. It may well be, moreover,
that once reconversion on a bigger scale has been effected and
all the necessary technical progress incorporated, the Swiss
economy will need abundant new immigration (assuming that
public opinion permits it). In Germany, where a fresh start
was made, the abundance of manpower supply (ensured first by
refugees from the East and later by immigrants) seems rather
to have favoured economy of scale (as to technical progress,
the question remains to be seen). Böhning (paragraph 102)
seems to have the German example in mind when he states that
"imported labour helps to realize economies of scale, at least
in the short-run".
38. Böhning's contribution on the subject must now be examined
(paragraphs 100 to 117). Böhning does not deal "ex professo"
with the role of technical progress and economies of scale.
As concerns the latter, he restricts himself to affirming that

immigration contributes to their realisation, at least in the
short-term (paragraph 102). His contribution consists notably
in refuting the thesis according to which immigration, by
holding back intensive employment of capital i.e. capital
deepening, impedes those elements which determine real economic
growth in the long-term. To this thesis, which he qualifies as
"deductive theory", may be opposed empirical observations which
demonstrate the existence of productivity gains in immigration
countries. Böhning's arguments are based essentially on two
points: (a) the decisions of the entrepreneur (aimed throughout at profit maximisation and in principle taking the labour
market situation into secondary account only) see paragraphs
101 and 107; (b) flexibility in the supply and in the means of
utilisation of manpower (made possible by immigration, thus
ensuring great flexibility in the productive apparatus) see
paragraphs 103, 108, 109 and 110. Immigration also assures
full utilisation of new installations, which are eventually
labour saving (see paragraph 110). Through the increase in the
population and in income per head, immigration has (indirect)
consequences on the propensity to invest (paragraph 105) thereby
causing indifferently operations of capital widening and capital
deepening (paragraph 106). In any case immigration enables the
full employment of available productive capital, which would
not be so in its absence (paragraphs 112 to 114).

Demand on social capital

39. Immigrants express a demand on "social capital" (i.e. for
material social infrastructure and social services in the
widest sense), but this demand is altogether less than that of
the national population (Böhning, paragraph 118). Immigrants
also help to finance social resources, to a greater extent
proportionally than the national population (paragraphs 118
and 126 in particular). /As regards this point, Böhning refers
essentially to the framework he gave when discussing the distribution of income (paragraph 30.4 above). This chapter
could nevertheless represent an example of the type of problem
which might be examined in detail.7 The rapporteur discusses
these matters with reference to stages of maturity, but excludes
the fourth stage. /See paragraph 9.6. above for this concept.7
During the first and second stages (paragraphs 119 and 120),
demand almost exclusively concerns housing, but immigrants are
not responsible for an additional demand. It is naturally in

the third stage that the picture changes appreciably, but in different proportions according to the different components of demand.

1) The impact on housing (paragraph 121) is, according to Böhning, more apparent than real since the type of replacement which takes place on this market is similar to that observed on the labour market, i.e. foreigners occupy the districts and accommodation abandoned by the local population. This assertion is no doubt interesting, but it may well be asked whether it has the value of a general rule. If steps were taken to provide decent housing for foreigners, allowance should also be made for the repercussions on the demand for work. Böhning supports his statement by some very interesting comments by K. Jones and A.D. Smith (footnote No. 142), but the situation referred to is typically British.

2) Immigration might have some effects (a) on the rate of mental disease (but the proof is by no means certain according to Böhning), (b) on the rate of other possible diseases not detected when the migrant was admitted (but these are more likely to be individual cases) and (c) on the industrial accident rate. Böhning admits the influence of immigration on the rise in the latter. However, this phenomenon mainly occurs during the first period of immigration and tends to disappear as soon as adjustment to work is complete. On the whole, immigrants, who are generally young and healthy, make a smaller demand on the health service than the national average (paragraph 123). As regards social security benefits in the strict sense, actual demand by migrants is overall less than that of nationals.

3) With regard to school and pre-school education (paragraph 124), Böhning thinks that the demand from immigrants and nationals should balance out (leaving aside the saving made by the country of immigration as regards the schooling of adult immigrants). Böhning expounds on this subject coherently but somewhat too briefly to permit a discussion based on definite data.
40. Böhning's list is almost complete (for other items, see paragraph 122). However, we have noted that no thought, even summary, has been given to adult vocational training. Böhning cannot be blamed for this omission since demand is very small (immigrants do not appear to be motivated) and supply (although apparently greater than demand) is also small. In any event, serious examination of this subject is not within the context of the present research. The interest (not only theoretical)

of studying the alternative of "internalisation" or "externalisation" of training costs (financing of migrants' training by
the employer or by the public authorities) should be noted.
41.   Examination of the alternative of cost "internalisation"
or "externalisation" may also concern other components of the
demand on social capital (for example, housing). This examination requires that some attempt be made to interpret the
nature of the service given by migrant workers. Since firms
are the first to benefit from these workers, it is logical that
they should bear a good proportion of such costs. However, in
view of the benefits brought by this manpower to the community
at large in terms of growth and the labour market, it is quite
fair that there should be public participation in these costs.
This distinction has already been made empirically in a few
countries of immigration, but it requires trimming and further
thought in the course of future research in the light of (a)
the more and more pressing demand for reception structures, (b)
the migrant's position as a taxpayer and (c) the concepts adopted
in the country of employment with regard to income transfer and
social services.
42.   The external rotation variable also plays a decisive role
in the field of social capital in the sense that it lowers
theoretical demand (paragraph 125 and 126). Böhning puts forward some estimated figures with regard to the effect of this
phenomenon on the two major groups of migrants (with or without
their families) and these figures are quite plausible but can
obviously vary from one country to another. In any event, what
should be noted is the comment that rotation, which mainly
concerns unaccompanied immigrants, partly restores the balance
of demand resulting from family immigration. Another interesting
comment concerns the flexibility of the material infrastructure
(such flexibility being both objective and subjective). Lastly,
the examination of the immigration-mobility of nationals
alternative will be noted (paragraph 127). In view of the
different requirements of foreigners and nationals, the latter
alternative is more expensive. This alternative is rather
theoretical, however, when it is remembered that it cannot be
subjected to proof by the facts (see paragraph 26 above).

CONCLUSIONS

43.   The opinions of the two rapporteurs on present day
immigration in Europe (Böhning, paragraphs 129 to 138, Maillat,

Chapter 5) finally coincide in the statement that this
phenomenon has made the economies of the countries concerned
sufficiently flexible to meet the solicitations of demand
smoothly. The result has been a high economic growth rate and
eventually a higher rise in real per capita incomes than without
immigration. According to Böhning, immigrants provide more
goods and services than they consume. He qualifies his favourable opinion when he states that the benefits derive essentially
from external rotation (paragraph 130) and that when immigration
becomes permanent immigrants' needs tend to be inversely
proportional to their economic profitability (paragraph 131).
However, the advantages tend generally to exceed the disadvantages (paragraphs 131 and 136). Maillat /who quotes J.L.
Reiffers, see No. 39 in his bibliography7 agrees that the
calculations (generally too theoretical) of migrants' cost and
the traditional investment they give rise to cannot change the
overall favourable balance: "these costs will be of very little
weight when opposed to the indirect advantages of immigration
permitting the rupture of the principal restraints acting upon
an economy in over-employment" and a society whose principal
aspiration is the increase of its general well-being.
44. Looking to the future, the conclusions of both rapporteurs
appear to be similar in substance in spite of the different
aims of their respective researches. For Böhning (paragraph
138), employment possibilities for migrants are far from exhausted since the economies and societies of Western Europe
cannot very quickly change the features they have acquired in
the recent past. For Maillat the restrictions adopted in
Switzerland have created a situation whose only real alternative
is a fairly thorough review of the productive apparatus, investment decisions, economic policy targets and the representation
and behaviour standards of micro-units, groups and institutions.
This is tantamount to saying that when a society has considerable
recourse to immigration in order to feed its growth and follow
the neo-capitalist patterns of expansion, consumption and social
progress, it can only put a stop to such immigration under pain
of being obliged to review its own essential aims.
45. We could very well abide by these observations, especially
as a number of current phenomena which contribute towards
immigration (declining interest for manual work, reduction in
the duration of working life and working hours, complementary
nature of highly-skilled and unskilled jobs and of highly

technological and more traditional industries) should continue
and even become more marked. However, it would be rather super-
ficial to do so and would indicate that we did not know how to
make prospective use of certain information the rapporteurs
give us. We would point out in this respect that Böhning does
not merely refer to immigration and migrants but nearly always
qualifies these words by speaking of "multi-annual migration"
and "target workers". Furthermore, he concentrates his examination on the "third stage of maturity" and gives an essential
role to the external rotation variable. He concludes by reducing his positive balance in favour of immigration when he
refers to settled migrants. It is therefore feasible to ask
whether the extended residence (and settlement of a good number)
of migrants and their families, the ageing of a considerable
proportion of these workers and the adoption on their behalf
of more effective and more comprehensive social measures will
not in the future weigh the balance rather towards the economic
disadvantages and induce the Western European countries to put
a brake on the entry of foreign workers. It would not in that
event be only a matter of stopping immigration by means of
regulations but of gradually creating alternatives for it, for
example (a) by reforming work organisation in firms and certain
job structures, (b) by revaluing these jobs from the point of
view of pay, social prestige and working conditions, (c) by
encouraging more frequent recourse to labour-saving investment,
(d) by restoring "true prices", i.e. by passing on to employers
a substantial proportion of the costs due to migrants' demand
on social capital (see paragraph 41 above), and (e) by encouraging the abandonment of certain lines of production and encouraging the export of capital with a view to creating jobs in the
workers' countries of origin. This type of action would involve
changes in structure and in behaviour which should be borne in
mind before taking any important decisions for the future.
46. The findings of Böhning and Maillat could nevertheless be
used as a starting point for thinking by those responsible for
defining an immigration policy, to enable them to appreciate
its effects better, to discuss them with the social partners
and to inform public opinion.
47. For an organisation like the O.E.C.D., which seeks to
encourage co-operation and development, this kind of study
should not overlook the legitimate interests of the countries
of emigration, for whom the problem also arises in terms of

alternatives, with the qualification that their development (alternative to emigration) implies by definition greater participation by their economic and political partners.

<u>THE ECONOMIC EFFECTS OF THE EMPLOYMENT OF FOREIGN</u>
<u>WORKERS WITH SPECIAL REFERENCE TO THE LABOUR</u>
<u>MARKETS OF WESTERN EUROPE'S POST-INDUSTRIAL COUNTRIES</u>

by W. R. Böhning

Centre for Research in the Social Sciences
University of Kent at Canterbury

I   INTRODUCTION: The Importance of Asking the Right Question

> "It would be ridiculous to attempt to show whether
> the effects of immigration are a 'good thing' or a
> 'bad thing' . . .   There can be no peremptory conclu-
> sion to a controversy in which there are so many
> factors and so many intermingled and conflicting
> interests.   For whom are the effects good or bad?
> What are the effects good for?   The labour market,
> social relations, an improvement in the workers'
> status?   There is not a single one of the advantages
> . . . which has not its counterpart in the form of a
> disadvantage or a prejudice of some kind . . .   The
> problem of immigration is either bound up with or
> leads to an involved controversy."   M. Allefresde,
> "Forms and Effects of Foreign Immigration in the
> Lyons Region", Working Party on Migration,
> MS/M/404/305, p.87.

1.   International migration is one of the least explored areas of economic
theory and research.   It was only when social and political forces questioned
the desirability of massive migratory movements into Europe's developed
countries during the 1960's that the economists' interest was kindled.   But
instead of detached and realistic analyses from a non-involved economic viewpoint, the ensuing discussions reflected only too often the a priori pro or
contra attitudes which the participants held on social or political grounds.

2.   This paper is a first attempt to rectify this state of affairs.   This
is done not by pitching a new formalised model against the others but by
leaving aside the most restrictive assumptions and by broadening the perspective to take into account the self-generating dynamics of immigration streams.
The existing formalised models are highly unsatisfactory,[1] and their sophisti-
cation cannot gloss over the limitations imposed by assumptions generally
selected to "prove" one's point.   The fault here lies largely in the
insufficient disaggregation of the labour market.   Moreover, in substituting
rigid deductive reasoning for close observation of the facts, many models
suggest structural changes in cases where the immigration really does no more than
influence the time-path of economic variables; or they suggest tremendous
quantitative changes where the immigration adds at most 1-2% to the indigenous
labour force.   Barring unlikely constellations, a 1-2% increase in the labour
force is certain not to create macro-economic effects greatly exceeding that
order of magnitude, though a constant addition of this size can of course have
a cumulative impact.

3.   Furthermore, evaluations of the economic effects of labour immigration
often proceed as if there were no return migration and no net emigration by
national employees.   Economic effects of labour import on the labour market
or the economy as a whole can in a relevant macro-economic framework be

---

[1] See also G. Schiller (1970), pp. 70-88

assessed only if there is a surplus of immigrants over emigrants in persons
of comparable characteristics or if it is possible to pin down the differential effects created by migration streams with differing characteristics.
For example, if during any one year the net emigration of indigenous workers
amounted to 50,000 and the net immigration of foreign workers to the same
number and if the individual, familial, and occupational characteristics
of both streams were comparable, the economic effect would be nil.   On the
other hand, if the net emigration of those 50,000 indigenous workers was
composed of "brain drain" categories with nuclear families, and the net
immigration consisted of unskilled categories with extended families, the
economic effects might be quite considerable, albeit difficult to pin down
exactly.   It is as well to bear in mind that all European countries importing foreign labour on a noticeable scale experience some degree of net
emigration by their indigenous populations.   For Britain, Germany, the
Netherlands, and Switzerland the net loss of indigenous workers during the
post-war period was quite marked[2] - in the case of Britain the loss of
indigenous population was so great that apart from a few years at the end
of the fifties and beginning of the sixties its overall balance of labour
migration was more often than not in the negative or at least in balance.
This question assumes a considerable significance if, as indicated, the
macro-economic effects of labour import are likely to be relatively small;
for the smaller the net balance of migration, the smaller will be the small
effects of foreign immigration.   In the continental labour importing
countries the overall net balance was mainly positive during the 1960's and
may be estimated to have averaged between 20% and 50% of the gross inflow of
non-seasonal workers.

4.   The external balance acquires an additional internal dimension if one
considers the decreasing birth rates and increasing life expectancy.   The
birth rate of some European populations has recently dropped below reproduc-
tion levels (in Sweden and Denmark in 1968 and Germany in 1969), and although
this does not signify an immediate end of the natural increase, it could in
the long run lead to stagnating or decreasing populations where the economically active have to bear an increasing burden of inactive people.[3]   The
labour market, however, is to some degree affected by the falling number of
births immediately.   Lower absolute numbers of births are in part caused by
retardations of demographic growth which lie some 20 years back.   These
earlier retardations mean lower numbers of school-leavers.   On top of the
absolute decrease comes the relative fall of birth rates occasioned by longer
schooling and higher living standards, both of which entail lower activity
rates.   While, for example, the "total population of the EEC increased on
average by 1% per annum during the period 1958-1968, the population of working age (15-64 years) increased on average by 0.6% and the economically
active population by only 0.1%".[4]   Given the technological constraints of our
age and the unabating demand for economic growth - which has to finance the
increasing social burden of inactivity - it is not difficult to see why demographic factors are beginning to reinforce what in most European countries
was originally a purely economic cause of immigration.

---

[2] Authentic figures for the Netherlands are given in Centraal Planbureau
(1972), Annex III table 3.

[3] Cf. H. Wander (1971).

[4] Ph. van Praag (1971), p.126.   See also W.R. Böhning (1972b), pp. 97-114.

5.   In effect, if we look at present-day Europe, we find that while there are practically no restrictions on the emigration and return of nationals, there is no freedom of movement for workers outside the EEC and Nordic Labour Market.[5]   All European countries have established an immigration system largely or exclusively related to economic needs, i.e. needs as expressed in the micro-economic decisions of employers.   This means that any inflow of foreign workers presupposes a demand for them.   This relationship is given formal effect in the general rule that foreign workers are not to be engaged if national workers are available and is administered through work permit requirements, border controls, and "regularizations".[6]   For Germany, which is perhaps the most typical labour importing country of contemporary Europe, a regression showed that the variations in the inflow of non-German employees were to 96% explained by the variations in German labour demand over the period 1957-1968.[7]   France's more "open" immigration system is also strongly governed by the economy, so that the volume of non-seasonal immigration is closely in line with the state of the French economy.[8]   Even for the Britain-Commonwealth situation under the "open door" policy of the fifties and early sixties it was found that the immigration of West Indian workers, for example, was predominantly determined by the state of the British economy rather than any external "push" factors.[9]   For present-day Europe it can be generalized that the volume of labour import is determined by the "pull" of the receiving country, more specifically by its quantitative and qualitative demand for labour.   Under conditions of economic migration control, "push" factors assume no significance unless there is at the same time a specific "pull".   The former is not sufficient in itself,[10] whereas the latter is a necessary and sufficient factor.[11]   Variations in the nationality composition of the inflow, on the other hand, are at given levels of demand more likely to be related to the prevailing conditions in the different sending countries

---

[5] From an economic point of view, Italians in Germany or Norwegians in Sweden are not foreign workers but the expression of a more productive distribution of labour within a regional labour market.

[6] Regularizations were prevalent in France during the 1960's.   Switzerland also experienced a high degree of "tourist" immigration before it intervened in the working of the labour market, cf. R. Braun (1970), p.77.

[7] W.R. Böhning (1970b).

[8] See e.g. G. and S. Castles (1971), J.R. McDonald (1969), and the annual reports in Population (Paris).

[9] C. Peach (1965).

[10] There is apparently one exception to this rule and that is what M. Allefresde calls the "blind" immigration of Portuguese into France.   See Allefresde (1969), p.19 et seq. and 30 et seq. This exception, however, owes its existence as much to permissiveness and laxity on the part of the French administration as to Portuguese "push" factors.

[11] Which is best exemplified by the German situation at the beginning of the seventies, when 1 million Turks were on the waiting list for employment in Germany where almost the same number of vacancies remained unfilled month after month.

(and other immigration countries) than to conditions in the receiving country. "At varying levels of demand for labour, the receiving country's selectivity becomes more important and effects fluctuations in the shares of different nationalities which are related to the stage in the development of the sending countries. As the skill level of a labour force rises in line with the level of development, and as migration streams generally reflect the skill composition of the population at source, the receiving country is likely to admit proportionately more immigrants from developed countries during periods of economic recessions because low-skill jobs are not in demand."[12]

6. What are the goals the European countries hope to attain through labour import? - and what are the criteria, therefore, with which this paper will have to be concerned? Surely, the economic needs of a country as defined by the micro-economic decisions of employers cannot be the relevant criterion. Macro-economically, marginal social productivity overrides marginal private productivity[13]. Given the focus of this paper on the labour markets of receiving countries, we shall have to look first of all at the effects of labour import on employment and unemployment in these countries. As the labour market is a part-determinant of a host of other factors contributing to a nation's economic development and well-being, such as internal and external currency stability, income distribution, and growth, the influence on these variables will also have to be considered. The politician's overall evaluation is likely to extend to the economic effects in the sending countries and to take into account the non-economic aspects of labour import both in his own country and in the field of international relations - evaluations which may dwarf the economic effects considered here. The former Deputy Director of the OECD Manpower and Social Affairs Directorate postulated, furthermore, that "knowledge of the human gains and disadvantages must become an integral part of the fund of information required for policy making so that appropriate weight may be assigned to the value systems other than economic in reaching final decisions respecting national policies".[14]

7. In order to obtain political relevancy, the economist must also answer the following three questions which a politician has to pose when faced with a decision-making situation. Firstly, if labour import is beneficial/detrimental to the attainment of goals A, B, C, what is its effect on goals D, E, F? Are there important goal conflicts or trade-offs? Secondly, if labour import is beneficial/detrimental to A, etc., in a given or assumed situation, how does its effect change over time in an ongoing process of economic development? Thirdly, if labour import is beneficial/detrimental to A, etc., what is the most plausible and likely effect on A, etc., of not importing labour? In other words, what are the policy alternatives and what effects are they likely to have?

8. Given the fact that in contemporary Europe countries have resorted to the import of foreign labour at times of full employment and rising living standards, and have done so for economic reasons, the temptation is irresistible to cut through the maze of economic detail with the apparently innocuous question, "What effect has the import of labour on

---

[12] W.R. Böhning (1972b), p.38.

[13] See B. Thomas (1968), p.298, in relation to international migration.

[14] S. Barkin (1968), p.496.

the living standards of the population here and now?" Such a question - on what would by most people be considered the ultimate aim of economics - seemingly abstracts from goal conflicts (the first of our aforementioned points). Moreover, it looks at an arbitrarily selected point of time and disregards possible dynamic developments which may show up that point of time as transitory (our second point). And in this context it would invite the common mistake of equating the standard of living with all momentarily consumable goods and services. By inferring full employment levels and full capacity utilization the argumentation would follow from the assumption: additional foreign labour would require new capital investment, which presupposes foregone consumption on the part of the national population, thereby reducing the amount of momentarily consumable goods and services in relative if not absolute terms. As will be shown later, such simplified assumptions hinder understanding more than they help. Finally, this kind of question conveniently does not ask what happens if labour is not imported, for in that case the assumed capital widening would presumably be replaced by capital deepening which would probably be even more costly in terms of foregone consumption and would logically reduce momentarily consumable goods and services even further.

9. However, "it must be doubted whether the standard of living defined as momentarily consumable goods (and services) is a sensible yardstick for judging economic policy. This yardstick suggests that the optimal measure for the maximisation of the standard of living would be one which minimises foregone consumption and, in turn, investment. The aim of a rational economic policy must be, however, to take care of the future by investments which will be able to cover the growing needs over time through the expansion of production."[15] Whether capital widening or capital deepening serves this end better in a given situation cannot be determined a priori. Moreover, the question of living standards must not be seen solely in relation to abstract income levels. K. Jones and A.D. Smith write: "Certainly it seems improbable that, as some have feared, immigration has restrained indigenous living standards below the level which, in its absence, they might have attained. Among other evidence which points to this conclusion, special mention should be made of those sections of the study that indicate demands on the social services below those of the indigenous population, and an impact on the housing market which may well have helped, marginally, to raise the standards at which the indigenous population, on average, lives".[16]

10. One should be aware of another pitfall in this context. The "foregone consumption" argument is of course never applied in relation to the growth of the indigenous population. One of its leading proponents said: "In such cases it is unnecessary to refer to foregone consumption. One does not visualize this as a sacrifice or as questionable . . ."[17] When asked what difference there was from an economic point of view between foregoing consumption for one's own later advantage by investing in work places for one's own children and by investing in work places for foreign labour, the same author revealingly replied: "Economically there is no difference at all. It is, if you like a matter of emotion."[18] We are

---

[15] U. Harms (1966), p.278; see also K. Kaiser (1971), p.102.

[16] K. Jones and A.D. Smith (1970), p.161.

[17] H.-J. Rüstow (1965), p.633

[18] H.-J. Rüstow (1966), p.108 (discussion). See also in this connection K. H. Hornhues (1970), pp.143-7.

not denying that it is legitimate to ask _politically_ what short term or
long-term effect labour import has on the _national_ population or some
part of it.   But it must be stressed that _if the question is posed in
economic terms,_ the economic reasoning must not be subject to social or
political prejudice.[19]

11.   Lastly, some of the broad assumptions underlying this paper require
explanation.   First of all we speak of polyannual or target worker
migration.   This derives from the fact that in contemporary Europe most
migrants are **considered and see themselves as people who go abroad with the**
intention of earning as much money as possible as quickly as possible in
order to return home.   Seasonal and frontier workers as well as trainees
are analytically not part of this category, though they are difficult to
disentangle empirically.   Emigrants in the traditional sense of the
word, i.e. people who go abroad with the intention of staying there at
least until the end of their active life, are few and far between and may
be neglected for all practical purposes.[20]   Polyannual or target worker
migration is the most typical and numerous variety today, but we will
have to discover the full reality of this widely mis-used concept.
Secondly, we speak of post-industrial societies.   This relates to the
development which characterizes European countries as economies with a
relatively small and declining agricultural sector, a large semi-automated
industrial sector which tends to decline in relative importance as far as
    manpower is concerned, and an equally large tertiary sector which
expands in these terms.   Thirdly, we speak of capitalist societies.
Apart from the truism that we are looking at societies structured by the
private ownership of capital, "capitalist" as used here **means no more**
than that the relationship between demand and supply on the labour market
is governed predominantly by narrowly economic criteria reinforced by
traditional norms of proper reward, that is, a reward structure which
assigns the highest pecuniary and social rewards to the social elite and
the lowest pecuniary and social reward to the unskilled manual worker
regardless of the true social or historical value of the work performed.
Similar structures can also be found in Eastern Europe's "socialist"
economies - and it is therefore not surprising that there are pockets
of large-scale employment of foreigners, for instance of Poles and
Hungarians in the German Democratic Republic and of Egyptian bricklayers
in Czechoslovakia and Bulgaria.   Still, we are only concerned here with
the typically capitalist relationships in Western European countries.

12.   The conceptualisation in the following section is conducted in
terms of "ideal types" in order to facilitate understanding of the basic
determinants of the matter.   The actual situation in different countries
may, of course, deviate to a greater or lesser extent from the ideal-
typical model.

[19] A.N.E. Jolley (1971), p.48, comes dangerously near to this in "associating"
    immigration with pollution without asking for cause and effect.

[20] See W.R. Böhning (1972a), pp.182-7, and R. Braun (1970), pp. 79, 473 and
    488.   Incidentally, even the presumed settlement migration of coloured
    Commonwealth citizens into Britain is at root a polyannual migration,
    as the following letter of a West Indian to Mr. E. Powell exemplifies.
    "The majority of us, educated and illiterate alike, came to this, our
    'mother' country, with one aim in view and this to better ourselves and
    then return home (I stress return home); to show our people that we
    have achieved something by going away.   Alas, I dare say the majority
    of us, including myself, have been disillusioned and cannot even -
    though we're working every day - find the fare to return home."
    Quoted in _The Times_, 18 November 1971.

II   CONCEPTUAL FRAMEWORK: The Self-Feeding Process of Polyannual

Migration from Low-Wage to Post-Industrial Countries with a

Liberal Capitalist Structure [21]

13. When Europe's industrialised countries made their transition from industrial to post-industrial economies under the conditions of expanding international trade after World War II and while being committed to full employment policies, their working classes experienced a fast and sustained increase in living standards. This increase was achieved with the tradi-tional social job structure, that is, the structure developed during the first stages of industrialisation with socially undesirable and low-wage jobs at the bottom. Under conditions of full employment a noticeable increase in the standard of living has the following two effects.

14. Firstly, it induces a growing gap between the rising expectations and qualifications that go with an increase in the standard of living and better and longer schooling, on the one side, and the undesirability of certain jobs in terms of status, physical hardship, and pecuniary reward, on the other.[22] In effect, non-pecuniary considerations become independ-ent determinants of occupational choice, i.e. independent of wages paid,[23] and the school population from which low-skilled workers are traditionally drawn becomes depleted.[24]

---

[21] This concept was first developed in W.R. Böhning (1972b), Ch.4; for further empirical evidence, see ibid.

[22] L.E. Davis (1971), p.31, gives a pertinent example: "A few years ago the Norwegian government decided to extend the school-leaving age of children by one year . . . Very soon, Norway's important maritime industry was seriously threatened by an inability to recruit new workers. Before the school-leaving age was extended, about 80% of the boys were willing to go to sea; afterwards, only 15% sought sea-faring careers. They wanted a different kind of life because the extra schooling had had an impact on them". For Germany cf. V. Merx (1969), p.98.

[23] See the well documented research in Amsterdam and Rotterdam by P.J.A. ter Hoeven (1964), pp.23, 32-5, and P. van Berkel (1968), p.123 et passim. A related development is the attraction of low paid service work compared with manual work, see e.g. E.W. Hofstee (1968), p.100. D. Maillat's report (1972a) is somewhat contradictory in first relating the mobility of Swiss workers to wage differentials without, it seems testing for other independent factors or spurious correlations (p.11) and then stating that social position and standing also played a "decisive" part (p.16). Even in the notorious employ-ment conditions of the United States it has been found that workers "are not only concerned with wages but with working conditions as well", P.B. Doeringer and M.J. Piore (1971), p.80, see also ibid, pp.86-8.

[24] See e.g. P. van Berkel (1968), p.124.

15. Secondly, it gives workers, especially young workers, the opportunity to leave undesirable jobs for socially more acceptable and better paid jobs without fear of becoming more than temporarily unemployed. This may take the form of inter-firm mobility or, on labour markets characterised by internal labour markets and ports of entry,[25] of promotion within the firm. When workers begin to drift into job openings which are more likely to fulfil their aspirations in respect of status and pay, there opens up a partial labour shortage in socially undesirable jobs.

16. These first endemic labour shortages are commonly accredited to the hitherto unknown strength and length of the economic boom and are generally expected to disappear under more "normal" conditions. However, this view overlooks the fact that such endemic labour shortages hide a <u>structural</u> maladjustment of the labour market. The appearance of a partial labour shortage in socially undesirable jobs in any one sector of the economy signals an impending general labour shortage in all such jobs throughout the economy: there are low-status and low-paid jobs everwhere, and the two tend to go together.

17. A post-industrial capitalist society facing the first instances of endemic labour shortages has two options open to it. Firstly, it could pursue a strongly reformist manpower policy by adapting its social job structure to post-industrial requirements, i.e. to pay a social or historical wage for undesirable jobs[26] - considering the fact that market forces are partly inapplicable to the labour "market" anyway in that wage structures are determined socio-politically by the structure of capitalist societies and considering in particular that competitive forces are the more strongly diluted the higher the status and pay of a job.[27] Secondly, it could fill these jobs with foreign workers admitted not for settlement but for the specific purpose of filling the supposedly temporary gaps on the labour market.

18. The alternative to the first option, namely, to permit large-scale unemployment and a considerable drop, if not reversal, in the real growth of the economy in order to stop the flight from socially undesirable jobs, is politically not feasible. It would probably not be very efficient either at times when unemployment benefits are far above subsistence levels and often not very different from the wages paid in undesirable jobs. The idea of bringing productive capital to the workers in the foreign countries is not a realistic alternative at this stage. The original pockets of labour scarcity in domestic service, tourism, refuse disposal, agriculture, mining, hospitals, and so on, are fixed to their given locations. As a matter of principle, the idea meets with a luke-warm reception from both employers and the general public. Automation

---

25 Cf. P.B. Doeringer and M.J. Piore (1971). Incidentally, it is at the ports of entry, i.e. at the bottom of the internal labour markets, where narrowly economic criteria are most effective and responsive to market conditions.

26 The official Dutch study (Centraal Planbureau (1972), p.41-2) realises that this is the only means to prevent further immigration into the Netherlands at this late stage of the process.

27 Or the further it is from a port of entry, see P.B. Doeringer and M.J. Piore (1971), p.86 et seq. The authors clearly see the chain of causation running from exogenously determined status to status determined wage levels.

is seen not to be a panacea either.   First of all, many of the jobs
involved are not amenable to thoroughgoing automation (hotel and catering
industry, for example).   Also, as we shall see later, the profitability of
automating is more often than not questionable, at least in the short term.
And last but not least, automation - in industry in particular - creates
more highly skilled jobs as well as more semi-skilled jobs in place of a
continuous skill structure.   Semi-skilled activities, however, are the
very activities from which the indigenous population tends to withdraw
because they are boring and frustrating, i.e. undesirable in personal
terms.[28]

19.   The alternative to the second option, i.e. settlement immigration, is
politically indigestible in nation states which are not countries of
immigration on non-economic grounds.

20.   The first option, however, does not commend itself to the political
decision makers on socio-political grounds.   A drastic rearrangement of
the social structure of jobs might require, for example, to pay a dustman
as much or more than an accountant or to give an agricultural labourer the
same status as a research assistant.   Needless to say, our capitalist
societies are neither willing nor able to do this on the scale required in
view of the social consequences anticipated.   (It was instructive to hear
the middle class outcry in April 1971 following British Leyland's decision
to give lavatory attendants at the Longbridge works an annual salary of
£1,500.)

21.   Employers hit by the initial labour shortages naturally seek redress
from their governments.   They present their demands for importing foreign
labour with a high degree of plausibility, given the capitalist context in
which they are made, as in the "national interest" - or certainly as in the
interest of the governing party at the next elections.   Their profitability-
productivity situation is obviously too precarious to sustain pay rises
sufficient to attract indigenous labour, which means that sooner or later
they will have to go out of business with consequential drastic setbacks
to the regional and national economy.   Foreign workers, however, would
surely be prepared to do the jobs at the prevailing wage rates, and if and
when the vagaries of the business cycle should hit the industry in question,
one would incur few social problems by dismissing them.   Thus, the
Konjunkturpuffer approach is born.

22.   Governments usually consent to the import of labour on broadly
economic grounds long before full employment levels are reached in macro-
economic quantitative terms.   Once the political decision has gone in favour
of the foreign worker or Konjunkturpuffer approach, the self-feeding process
of migration from the chosen labour surplus areas into the labour shortage
jobs commences, and it cannot be reversed except by a political decision. It
is incomparably more difficult to take such a decision - because of the increased
internal and additional international constraints - than it would have been to
adopt a strongly reformist manpower policy when the first gaps in the labour
market appeared.

23.   There are two sides to this self-feeding process.   One, as already
implied, relates to the structure of post-industrial societies and the other
to the migratory process itself.   These will now be examined in turn.

---

28 "Industrial work characterized by monotony and social isolation (frequently
   mechanical work such as light assembly work) is accorded a negative evaluation by almost all workers", P. van Berkel (1968), p.130.

(a)   The Economics of Self-Feeding Migration

24. The import of workers from labour surplus countries, which generally
means from less developed countries with a low wage level, does not cure
the ill of structural maladjustment, for it deals with the symptoms but
not the source of the problem.   It serves to preserve the existing social
structure of jobs (though not necessarily the economic structure of jobs).
It may even reinforce it in that at the outset a stigma may become attached
to the jobs involved - which may animate some indigenous workers to leave
them - and when this process gathers momentum all jobs of this kind may
attract an unfavourable image on social and ethnic grounds as well.   A
further reinforcement is provided by institutionalised discrimination:
foreign workers are, at least for the first years, under the control of
labour market authorities which seek to tie them to the jobs for which
they were originally engaged.   Prejudice and discrimination therefore
tend to create non-competing groups.   In some countries this kind of
labour market control is exercised very strictly, but generally the
economic pressures break it down to some degree and, as we shall see, the
concept of non-competing groups becomes more or less inapplicable.

25. Given these circumstances it is not surprising that the employment
of foreigners in originally isolated pockets of low-wage industries soon
spreads to socially undesirable jobs in other sectors of the economy.
Yesterday one saw a foreign cleaner in the hotel and catering industry
or domestic service, tomorrow one finds him in the large and profitable
plants of manufacturing industry, where higher wages are paid right across
the board irrespective of the demand conditions for different grades of
labour.   The complementarity of low-skilled/low-paid and highly-skilled/
highly-paid jobs can be found to a greater or lesser extent in every
sector of the economy.   And the desperate and willing target worker can
be engaged on any job which does not require extensive vocational training
or intensive use of the language of the receiving country.   He is "much
nearer to the economist's ideal of economic man"[29] than the indigenous
worker who finds himself less constrained in his choice of jobs.

26. The extent to which this complementarity aspect of the self-feeding
process contributes to the growth of the foreign work force should not
be underestimated.   It is not only domestic service and parts of the
hotel and catering industry which become large-scale employers of
foreigners in this way.[30]   Probably the greater part of the foreign
foundry workers, textile workers, warehousemen, workers in public services,
bricklayers, and so on,[31] owe their immigration to the interdependence of
dirty, heavy, low-skilled and low-paid jobs with socially more desirable
jobs.

---

[29] B.G. Cohen and P.J. Jenner (1968), p.55.

[30] Domestic service does perhaps not belong into this category of complementary jobs, but all its other characteristics make it convenient to
include it here.

[31] See the exemplification of the complementarity hypothesis for the
German construction industry in V. Merx (1969), p.119 et seq, and
from the same author (1972), p.33 et seq.; also generally ibid.,
p.43, and concerning seasonal workers, ibid., p.124.

27. While this aspect of the self-feeding process proceeds, employers
in the large manufacturing firms, who also feel the draught of the
general scarcity of labour accompanying full employment, begin to realise
that foreigners are just as easily employable in mass production processes
as in auxiliary positions and that in terms of Taylorism there is really
little difference between employing local peasants and foreign peasants.
In some cases a slight re-design of the production process may be called
for and skilled tasks are further subdivided into simple components which
can readily be taught to foreigners who have never before stood at an
assembly line and who do not speak the language of the host country.
Employers are also plagued by the realisation that high frequency
repetitive jobs and, sometimes, the shift work associated with modern
manufacturing processes are creating a kind of fatigue on the side of the
indigenous worker which economic incentives do not always overcome at times
of full employment, so that indigenous workers begin to withdraw from these
highly paid jobs as well, in smaller proportions perhaps but still noticeably. Thus, the economic pressures towards greater productivity and
quicker amortization of equipment, which produce more job **fragmentation**
and continuous working, also produce the type of work place for which
target workers are well suited. It is generally the large firms in
manufacturing which start to hire foreign workers of all backgrounds and
levels of literacy and teach them in a week or two how to turn a screw or
operate a lever.[32] Often the production process is already so **fragmented**
that no further redesigning is required - the car industry being an example.
In other cases employers may completely redesign their production process
to adjust it to the only kind of labour available which promises profitability, i.e. immigrant labour - the wool industry in the West Riding of
Yorkshire being a specific example.[33] Here we find that the pattern of labour
demand at the bottom grades of semi-automated industries changes to a
greater or lesser extent towards the skills (or lack of them) available.

28. This does not necessarily mean that the overall structure of demand
changes, i.e. the proportions between different grades of skill. The
modern manufacturing process constantly creates new kinds of highly skilled
tasks which cannot be broken down into simple components. It is into these
jobs that the indigenous worker moves, leaving behind the gaps at the lower
skill levels for which foreigners are then sought. In individual industries
or even in industry as a whole one might possibly find that unskilled categ-
ries increase disproportionately,[34] but in this case one would probably find
that native workers have moved out of manual jobs or industry altogether
into higher status jobs in administration or services.

---

[32] Figures on the length of vocational induction or training for foreign
workers in Germany are given by U. **Mehrländer** (1969), p.30 ff. According
to her sample of male workers still at the workplaces for which they
were originally engaged, 61% of the construction workers from Italy,
Greece, Spain and Turkey, had received no vocational induction whatsoever.
In metal goods this proportion amounted to 25%, and here 32% had received
up to one week's training, 12% up to two weeks, and 27% four weeks and
over.

[33] Cf. B.G. Cohen and P.J. Jenner (1968). A similar development seems to
have taken place in the French wool industry according to A. Gorgeu,
Les facteurs d'évolution de l'emploi dans l'industrie du textile
française 1950-1969, Thèse ronéotypée, Paris 1971 (private communication
by Jeanne Singer-Kerel to OECD, 27.7.1972).

[34] Cf. V. Merx (1972), p.32 et passim.

29. It should also be borne in mind that in our post-industrial societies
it is semi-automation which predominates and not full automation.   While
both types are labour saving, the former is certainly much less so than
the latter.   Moreover, the rate of decline of industrial jobs due to semi-
automation is likely to be overcompensated by the rate of withdrawal of
native workers as well as by the prevailing rate of increase in final
demand for goods.   Under conditions of constant final demand the foreign
work force in manufacturing industries may therefore steadily increase
while the labour force as a whole slowly declines.   With increasing demand
the former trend will accelerate and the latter will be halted or reversed.[35]

30. In manufacturing industries the complementarity of jobs and the adjust-
ability of production processes coincide to a very high degree and the
resulting concentration of foreign workers in such jobs is no surprise:
over 20% of Switzerland's foreign workers are employed in metal goods and
over 20% in other manufacturing industries; over one third of the foreign
workers in both the Netherlands and Germany are employed in metal goods, and
manufacturing industries as a whole absorb about two thirds of the foreign
work-force in both countries.   The complementarity of jobs on its own, i.e.
without the additional factor of adaptable mass-production processes, comes
to the fore in the construction industry: one third of Luxembourg's foreign
workers are employed in construction and the proportion is as high as a
quarter for Switzerland and stood at that level in Germany during the first
half of the sixties but it has now fallen to one sixth.

31. It could be said at this stage that in economic terms there is nothing
directly "self-feeding" about this process and that it is the mere availability
of foreign labour which makes its use more widespread via the ubiquitous
complementarity of jobs and the selective introduction into assembly-type
work.   Once these possibilities are exhausted - assuming they can be exhausted
or run into exogenous limitations- there must come an end to labour immigration.
Given a finite amount of demand for labour an equivalent amount of labour
import will satisfy it and no further foreign workers are required.   However,
this argumentation overlooks the fact that the consumer demand of foreign
workers and their social capital requirements create additional demand for
labour.   While we can leave the detailed examination of this aspect of the
self-feeding process to later sections of this report, a few figures might
suggest the order of magnitude of the effective macro-economic satisfaction
of labour demand.   The Dutch Central Planning Office estimated[36] that an
annual addition of foreign workers in the region of 1% of the total labour

---

[35] The analysis has been taken a step further by V. Merx (1972), p.17 et seq.,
who examined the extent to which foreign workers carried the expansion of
manual employment in various industrial sectors, carried both expansion
and replacement in the same sector, or carried only replacement functions
in stagnating or declining sectors.   In this part of his analysis, however,
the notion of replacement is a formal one.   For example, in sectors where
foreign employment increased while German employment also increased (or
where German employment declined while the sector as a whole still increased)
the inter-grade replacement of Germans by foreigners is not caught by the
broad category "employees".   It would be wrong, therefore, to imply that
no replacement process has taken place there.

[36] See Centraal Planbureau (1972), especially tables 7, 8 and 13.   See also
W.R. Böhning (1970b), note 2 p.199, who found that the satisfaction of
excess demand of labour relative to frictional demand through labour
import was very small indeed.

force would satisfy three fifths of this 1% labour shortage after one year year (0.63% cumulatively after five years) if all workers were single; but far from satisfying demand it would actually create a further labour shortage amounting to one quarter of the original shortage · after one year (though only to 0.11% cumulatively after five years) if all workers were married with a family size corresponding to the Dutch population and requiring a commensurate amount of public expenditure. If, as we shall see later, the foreign labour force tends to approach the marital composition of the non-migrant labour force with a married portion of 60-70% and if about half of the married foreigners are sooner or later joined by their families, one could estimate the real impact of demand satisfaction on the Dutch lines by equating two thirds of the labour force addition of 1% with effects pertaining to single workers and one third with effects pertaining to family immigration. This would mean in static terms that approximately one quarter of the original labour shortage would be satisfied; or in dynamic terms that the net addition to the total labour force would have to be of the order of 4% in order to satisfy a labour scarcity of the order of 1%; or in terms of final demand that an autonomous increase in the demand for goods and services (i.e. unrelated to the immigration of workers and its repercussions) of the order of 0.25% would suffice to wipe out the effective satisfaction of labour demand. This does not mean that labour import is detrimental in macro-economic terms, it simply means that the satisfaction of existing demand through import of labour is largely illusory, i.e. to 75% under the assumptions of the Dutch calculation. If we may anticipate later findings in this paper which show that a foreign work force of the assumed composition is indeed macro-economically beneficial, especially in terms of comparative advantage, one can easily see that the sum of the private and public consumer effects plus the beneficial production effects tends to nullify the desired satisfaction of labour demand and that each foreign worker induces demand for another one. In this sense economic migration is truly self-feeding until interrupted by exogenous factors.

32. Our reasoning may be summarised as follows. The originally localised import of labour - due to the structural causes and subject to the economic dynamics indicated - quickly extends to all sectors of the economy and turns out to be a generalised need for blue-collar workers in unskilled and semi-skilled positions. The need is neither as widespread in comparable white-collar positions, because indigenous workers are still entering them regardless of unfavourable wages, nor is it as easy to engage foreigners there because of their language and training limitations.[37] Neither the ongoing process of automation nor the real but presumably minute satisfaction of labour demand effectively reduce the need for foreign workers.

33. Satisfactory statistics for the verification of this process are not available, especially as regards its two-dimensional aspect. One must therefore look at one dimension at a time. Table 1 provides some empirical evidence for the social job structure-complementarity hypothesis.[38] It reveals an increasing replacement of German workers by unskilled and semi-skilled foreigners. The male German blue-collar force declined by about 5% between 1961 (when the social upgrading process had been under way for a number of years) and 1968, while the structure of male blue-collar

---

[37] Cf. V. Merx (1972), p.18, and S. Bullinger et al. (1972), p.87 et seq.

[38] See also M. Allefresde's report (1969), p.51 et seq. for French data.

employment only showed a drop of about 3%.   During the same period, both the total and the German white-collar and civil service employment increased by 5%, while the foreign proportion actually fell.   More refined statistics would make this replacement process clearer.

Table 1:   The socio-economic composition of employees over the age of 15 resident in Germany in June 1961 and in Autumn 1968.

	MALES						FEMALES					
	Total		German		Foreign		Total		German		Foreign	
	1961	1968	1961	1968	1961	1968	1961	1968	1961	1968	1961	1968
Blue-collar w.	63.4	60[a]	62.8	58[a]	86.8	90	49.2	43[a]	49.0	41[a]	69.6	86
of which (=100%) Skilled	–	57	–	60	–	22	–	6	–	6	–	4
Semi-sk.	–	32	–	31	–	40	–	47	–	48	–	35
Unskilled	–	12	–	9	–	38	–	48	–	46	–	62
Apprentices	6.5	6	6.6	6	2.7	2	7.7	7	7.8	7	5.4	–
White-collar w.	22.0	26[b]	22.3	27[b]	10.5	8	40.9	48[b]	41.1	49[b]	24.9	12
Civil servants	8.0	9	8.3	9	0.0	0	2.2	3	2.2	3	0.0	0
Overall	99.9	101[b]	100.0	100[b]	100.0	100	100.0	101[b]	100.1	100[a]	99.9	98

Source: Statistisches Jahrbuch für die Bundesrepublik Deutschland; Amtliche Nachrichten;   Volks- und Berufszählung vom 6. Juni 1961; EWG, Sozialstatistik;   and own computations

a = decreasing absolute numbers

b = increasing absolute numbers (all foreign categories experienced an absolute increase between 1961 and 1968).

34.   The following tables provide empirical support for the occupational or industrial dimension of this process, i.e. for the spreading of foreign employment from originally isolated pockets through the whole of the economy due to the ubiquitous existence of socially undesirable jobs and the adaptation of labour demand under shortage conditions in manufacturing industries in particular.   Table 2a measures the process at source, as it were, by examining the occupational composition of workers recruited by official German agencies after the first inter-country recruitment agreement had been concluded in 1956 - with Italy, in order to satisfy a critical labour shortage in Bavarian agriculture.   The recruited new entrants are

Table 2a: The occupational distribution of foreign workers recruited for
Germany in Mediterranean countries (and of the total inflow of
foreign workers), 1956-1964

	Agric. lab.	Miners & Quarrm.	Constr. workers	Prod.-Proc. workers	Others[a]	Total	Number in thousands
1956	56.5%	15.6%	24.9%	1.9%	1.2%	100.1%	10
1957	42.4%	35.8%	17.5%	1.3%	3.1%	100.1%	8
1958	24.4%	26.6%	43.2%	2.9%	2.9%	100.0%	10
1959	10.4%	7.5%	52.3%	1.0%	28.7%	99.9%	15
1960	3.7%	8.6%	34.6%	36.2%	16.9%	100.0%	112
1961	3.1%	12.7%	35.9%	32.1%	16.2%	100.0%	156
(61)	(2.3%)	(8.3%)	(28.0%)	(43.3%)	(18.2%)	(100.1%)	(323)
1962	2.4%	11.4%	17.1%	34.2%	35.0%	100.1%	156
(62)	(1.8%)	(6.9%)	(23.3%)	(41.9%)	(26.0%)	(99.9%)	(358)
1963	2.3%	12.8%	13.9%	38.1%	32.9%	100.0%	131
(63)	(1.9%)	(7.5%)	(23.4%)	(42.9%)	(24.3%)	(100.0%)	(338)
1964	1.6%	11.6%	20.0%	46.9%	19.8%	99.9%	169
(64)	(1.5%)	(7.2%)	(22.3%)	(47.8%)	(21.2%)	(100.0%)	(419)

Index 1961 = 100[b]

1956	118	8	5	0	0	7
1957	67	14	2	0	1	5
1958	48	13	7	1	1	6
1959	53	9	23	1	28	16
1960	84	48	69	81	75	71
1961	100	100	100	100	100	100
(61)	(100)	(100)	(100)	(100)	(100)	(100)
1962	76	89	47	106	216	100
(62)	(89)	(93)	(92)	(107)	(159)	(111)
1963	63	84	32	100	170	84
(63)	(89)	(94)	(87)	(103)	(140)	(104)
1964	57	98	60	158	132	108
(64)	(86)	(112)	(103)	(143)	(151)	(129)

Source: Amtliche Nachrichten and supplement (Erfahrungsbericht)
Excluding Berlin 1956-1962. The bracketed figures on the total
number of newly entering foreigners exclude frontier workers

a = Service workers and unskilled labourers not elsewhere classified

b = Index is based on the original absolute figures

fairly representative for the total inflow of foreign workers. Over half the total number of admitted foreigners were recruited at the end of the fifties compared with about two fifths in later years. At any rate, table 2a shows that most foreigners were originally engaged for agricultural work and only a minute proportion in either industrial or service work. After agriculture it was the building sector and then mining and quarrying which first engaged foreign workers, and finally foreign employment found its way into manufacturing and services. The service figures are certainly inflated by a rather large number of unskilled labourers who would presumably have to be distributed proportionately over all sectors.

35. Table 2b measures the process as a derivative by looking at the occupational and industrial distribution of employed foreigners in Germany.[39] The comparison is not invalidated by the change of the classification system, because the categories have been made comparable as far as possible; because the dispersion of agricultural workers, miners and quarrymen, and construction workers over other sectors than their own is very small; and because the broad categories eliminate some of the possible distortions. Here the development is seemingly not as dramatic during the early years; but this is due largely to the existence of a stock of foreign workers, mainly of Dutch and Austrian frontier workers, who had been there long before labour shortages became acute and partly for historical or personal reasons. They were predominantly employed in manufacturing and services. When the deliberate engagement of foreigners commenced, first agriculture, then construction and mining and quarrying increased their share of the total while manufacturing temporarily lost its dominant position until the deliberate employment of foreign workers also spread into this sector at the turn of the decade. Inter-industrial mobility also played a role here.[40] Ten years after Germany had started to look for foreigners to work in agriculture, the foreign labour force there had been eclipsed by the much larger secondary and tertiary sectors. Foreign labourers in agriculture were of course still needed: in 1970 about the same number of foreigners were recruited for declining agriculture as in 1956, i.e. 5,800, and the absolute number of employed foreigners was still rising as the index shows; but while in 1956 almost all recruited foreigners had been destined for agriculture, the share had sunk to 2% in 1970.[41]

---

39 For data on Switzerland, see e.g. T. Keller (1963), p.351, and D. Maillat (1972b), p.15, both of whom indicate the intra-industrial replacement of Swiss workers in low wage industries by foreigners. For Britain, see K. Jones and A. Smith (1970), pp.56 et seq. and 73 et seq. Their method of measuring minimises the real differentials and their surprise at finding a scaling effect is partly determined by one-dimensional data (industrial and occupational) and partly by looking at a situation where foreign employment had already spread through the whole of the economy.

40 R. Braun (1970), p.53 et seq., gives some interesting figures on the inter-sectoral mobility of Italians in Switzerland. For example, 8.5% of his sample first worked in agriculture but only 0.3% were employed there at the time of the interview.

41 In Switzerland a similar development can be seen in domestic service which was one of the original sectors of foreign employment. In 1950 and in 1960, 30,000 foreigners were working there with a limited permit, and 25,000 in 1970. The latter year's figure would probably reach 30,000 if both foreigners subject to control and established foreigners with unlimited residence permits could be accounted for.

Table 2b: The occupational/industrial distribution of the foreign
           workforce in Germany, 1956-61, 1966 and 1970[a]

	Agric. lab.	Miners & Quarrm.	Constr. workers	Prod.-Proc. workers	Service workers	Total	Number in thousands
1956	5.9%	9.0%	12.7%	42.6%	29.8%	100.0%	88
1957	7.5%	11.0%	12.2%	38.3%	30.9%	99.9%	105
1958	5.7%	13.5%	14.3%	36.4%	30.1%	100.0%	123
1959	4.7%	10.5%	21.9%	38.7%	24.3%	100.0%	163
	Agric.	Ming.	Constr.	Manuf.	Services		
1960	3.1%	7.8%	25.6%	45.2%	18.3%	100.0%	279
1961	1.9%	7.3%	23.3%	51.0%	16.5%	100.0%	549
1966	1.1%	4.7%	18.2%	59.7%	16.2%	99.9%	1,313
1970	0.9%	3.3%	16.7%	62.7%	16.4%	100.0%	1,949
Index 1961 = 100[b]							
1956	50	20	9	13	29	16	
1957	76	29	10	14	36	19	
1958	67	42	14	16	41	22	
1959	74	43	28	23	44	30	
1960	83	55	56	45	57	51	
1961	100	100	100	100	100	100	
1966	144	155	187	280	236	239	
1970	175	161	254	436	353	355	

Source: Amtliche Nachrichten, and supplement (Erfahrungsbericht)
         Excluding Berlin 1956-1959

   a = Mid-year data for 1956-60; end of September data for 1961,
       1966 and 1970

   b = Index is based on the original absolute figures

36. A similar picture could be painted for the relatively small mining
and building sectors, and in order to take the structural development of
the economy into account table 2c shows the share of foreign workers in
the number of employees (i.e. excluding self-employed and family workers)
in each sector.   Data for the crucial early years and a more detailed
breakdown are unfortunately not available, and the index minimises the
changes that occur.   Nevertheless, this table indicates the strength of
the replacement effect still obtaining in agriculture and construction
over ten years after foreigners were first employed there.   It also
indicates the pronounced spreading of foreign employment into industry
compared with services.

Table 2c: The share of the foreign workforce in the total number of
employees, by economic sector 1961, 1966 and 1970

	Agric	Ming. & Quarrg.	Constr.	Manuf.	Services	Total
1961	1.8%	2.6%	7.1%	3.3%	1.1%	2.6%
1966	4.2%	4.5%	12.0%	8.6%	2.3%	6.0%
1970	6.4%	5.4%	16.9%	12.6%	3.3%	8.7%
Index: percent point increase on previous year						
1966	+2.4	+1.9	+4.9	+5.3	+1.2	+3.4
1970	+2.2	+0.9	+4.9	+4.0	+1.0	+2.7

Source: V. Merx (1972), Appendix, table A19
Total labour force data = annual average;   foreign work force
data = at end of September each year.

(b)   The Sociology of Self-Feeding Migration

37.   The economic side of the self-feeding process relates to the employment effects of a foreign work force.   The sociological side relates to the individual and social causes of this development.   Specifically, it relates to the dynamics of the migratory process or what we call the "maturing" of migration streams.   This represents an autonomous factor which is not directly related to the original reasons for importing labour.   Its momentum can uphold the growth of the foreign workforce even when the purposive engagement of foreign workers has been curtailed politically or ended temporarily during a recession.

38.   Migration is in essence a social process.   A migrant decides to leave one social context for another on the basis of a hierarchically ordered set of values.   In the case of economic migrants the socio-economic deprivations at home are generally a sufficient (though not a necessary) condition of his out-migration.   In the case of contemporary target worker migration in Europe, it is typically people from culturally distant backgrounds who set out to participate temporarily in a high wage industrialized economy with the intention of spending as little of their earnings as possible in order to return home and start a new life with sizeable savings.   However, with the industrialized economy goes an urbanized consumer society, and they form a social totality which the migrant cannot escape.   Unknowingly he sets out to undergo what tends to be a complete secondary socialisation at the age of 20 or 30.   Some are unable to cope with the initially overpowering difficulties and return home within a matter of weeks or months.   But most absorb at least super-ficially some of the norms and values of the host society within a year or two, that is, the norms and values of a consumer society.   After about one year's employment most target workers realize that a short-term partici-pation in a high-wage economy does not once and for all eliminate their deprivations back home, however spartan their conduct in the country of employment.   So they decide to extend their stay abroad in the expectation of really amassing the savings they have been hoping for and then returning home.   By this time, however, a polyannual migrant has become subject to new deprivations, namely those of the lower working class in the receiving country.   Some of these deprivations are entirely new in the sense that he has never experienced them before he came in contact with a consumer society (e.g. the wish for such "indispensable" consumer goods as tape recorders, record players, cameras, TV's, etc., conjured up by the news media and advertising).   Others are simply the extension or transference of deprivations he experienced at home to his new environment (as in the case of housing and schooling).

39.   The polyannual migrant, then, is constantly torn between wanting to overcome his new deprivations and returning home to a social context where he must feel the old deprivations even more deeply than when he left.   The result is that again and again he extends his stay abroad, or he re-emigrates repeatedly after returning home for a short while.   Finally this process tends to induce the settlement of a significant proportion of target workers in the receiving country: the migrant becomes an immigrant: the migration stream matures: the difference between target worker migration and settlement migration becomes obscure.

40.   Looking at this process in more detail, one can differentiate analytically between four stages of maturity.   Ideal-typically these stages refer to the development between a receiving country and one send-ing country.   While this is difficult enough to disentangle empirically, it is hopelessly intertwined for the foreign labour force as a whole if

this comprises various nationalities whose immigration has commenced at different points of time.   Fortunately neither the first nor the second stage usually extends over more than one business cycle so that migration streams quickly reach the crucial and much longer third stage.   The sub-sequent tapping of new labour sources then becomes comparatively unimpor-tant relative to the dominance of the third stage in the total foreign work force.   Bilateral situations are possibly reinforced by the so-called "chain migration", i.e. where a father is followed four or five years later by his adult sons or former workmates or friends from the same village and finally whole villages are thus transplanted into the host country.   However, chain migration, though in many aspects resembling the concept of maturity, is basically related to small and tightly knit communities.   In the increasing atomization and anonymity of tradi-tional life styles, particularly in towns and cities, it takes second place to the nation-wide maturing of migration streams.

41.   In the first stage, young single workers, usually male (depending on the social system at origin and the type of labour demand at destination) form the bulk of the initially very small number of migrants.   Young and single workers tend to predominate in the early phases of migration because they are less constrained in deciding whether or not to go abroad and how long to stay there.   These early migrants come from the more developed areas of the sending country, i.e. the bigger towns with their more extensive networks of internal and international communication.   Here the foreign employment opportunities become known first and here the migrants' reports are first relayed.   As the first small batch of migrants originates from the more developed part of the sending country, it tends to comprise a considerably higher level of skills and more industrial skills than the non-migrant population as a whole.   This tendency is reinforced by the receiving country's desire to select only the most suitable workers ("creaming off" effect).   As these first migrants come into a country which has only just started to import labour, their duration of stay is likely to be very short, partly because the migration has not yet matured and partly because the first immigrants are likely to be employed in the most marginal positions. The ratio of (temporarily or permanently) returning workers to the size of the foreign work force is a function of the interrelationship between the state of labour demand in the receiving country and the original short-term time span envisaged by the migrants.   It tends to be very high.

42.   In the second stage the migration stream ages slightly.   Its sex composition remains basically unchanged but its composition in terms of marital status resembles more that of the non-migrant population (except that married workers are not accompanied by spouse and children). Duration of stay increases slightly but perceptibly as both single and married workers tend to extend their stay; the rate of return decreases accordingly.

43.   Looking at the second phase from the viewpoint of the sending country one can discern the following development.   In letters and when the first migrants return home, they talk in glowing terms to friends and neighbours about their experience - to do otherwise would imply that their migration was a failure - then newspapers and radios carry reports, and more and more people in the area where the migration started and in neighbouring areas hear about the apparently easy way of earning unheard of wages.   In the area of original migration it is the hitherto hesitant married worker who now joins the stream: on his own and with the intention of returning home to wife and children as soon as possible.   (Being on average slightly older than single workers this is immediately reflected in the "ageing" of the foreign work force.)   In the new areas to which the message has spread it is again the single worker who predominates in what is for this new catchment area the first phase.

44. In the third stage the receiving country experiences a continuation of the ageing of the migration stream and a change in the sex composition in favour of the originally under-represented sex, as married workers send for their spouses. During this stage the hitherto stable ratio of economically active to inactive immigrants begins to fall: not so much because the wives or husbands of married workers are inactive - they are largely taking up employment themselves - but because younger children join their parents abroad. Duration of stay increases further, especially for families, and the rate of return decreases considerably.

45. During the third stage the married migrant who left the area of original emigration during the second stage begins to realise that he has acquired a new set of deprivations without losing the old one. Savings accumulate at a much slower pace than expected. In the receiving country he finds himself at the bottom of the socio-economic ladder in conditions he would not have wished upon himself but which the circumstances force him to accept. He also has the very human desire to be united again with his family. Back home his wife is using up the money he sends her almost as quickly as it comes in for the basic necessities of life and possibly for paying back some old debt. To return home now after only one year or so would mean that his emigration was unsuccessful - and was seen to be unsuccessful - in terms of his overriding goal of earning a suffi ent amount of money to start his life anew.[42] Thus, he is most likely to come to that typically lower working class conclusion that if he wants to improve his lot, he will have to send his wife and older children out to work, which means sending for them to come and work with him in the receiving country.[43] He might deceive himself and his family that all he needs is more time and more hands to earn the money while cutting down on the living costs of two separate households. Unwittingly, however, he has taken a decisive step towards becoming a long-term settler in the receiving country, especially if his younger children go to school there and are fortunate enough to be able to profit from it. Thus, some years after the migration commenced - and the speed of this development depends of course on the intensity of and the variations in the demand for labour in the receiving country as well as the social and political

---

[42] R. Braun (1970), p.482, found that 80% of the Italians who came to Switzerland because of higher wages were disappointed by their actual earnings.

[43] In Germany, for example, two thirds or more of the foreign wives who are living with their husbands there are themselves economically active at this stage of maturity (which is twice the proportion of the married German women). Cf. W.R. Böhning (1970a), p.18 et seq. E. Zieris (1971), p 30 et seq. Incidentally, however hostile the immigration regulations are towards family reunion, a determined migrant will not be put off by them and will try to satisfy all the provisos : legally if possible, illegally if necessary. Also, in a liberal capitalist society the inhuman regulations hindering family reunion are coming under increasing pressure from enlightened national and international opinion as well as from employers, who find that their foreign workers stay longer and are better workers - that is, more profitable - when they are reunited with their families.

constraints in the sending country - there is a wave of family reunion from the original catchment area. Sooner or later the majority of married migrants will be joined by their families.[44]

46. During this third overall stage the areas from which new migrants were first drawn during the second overall stage now experience their second phase of maturing, i.e. married workers leave from there without spouse, etc.   At the same time the remaining areas of the sending country who had hitherto not participated in this migration stream will be drawn into its ambit as the message spreads into these more backward and less accessible parts of the country.[45,46] For them the development repeats itself by starting with young single workers, and so on.   This new and additional part of the migration stream depresses its skill level further and changes its composition more towards the kind of occupations prevalent in the backward areas.   But it can still be seen that the skill level of the migrant population is on balance higher than that of the non-migrant population.

47. Up to the beginning of the third stage the migratory process is not self-feeding in the sense that the inflow of migrants were not related to the original economic cause of the immigration.   At about this stage, which roughly coincides with the time when the economic side of the self-

---

[44] For empirical evidence on marital status and family reunion see for Germany W.R. Böhning (1972b), table 4-3 p.65, and for Switzerland R. Braun (1970), pp.42-3 and 270-1.   In both countries about two thirds of the Italians were married.   In Germany the latest figures point to a degree of family reunion of over 60% with about half of the remainder desiring future reunion in the host country.   Braun found in the slightly more matured stream in mid-1964 that 85% of the families were together and over two fifths of the remainder desirous of future reunion in Switzerland.   Braun (1970), pp.79 et seq., 473 table x/14, and 488 table x/19, provides figures on the extension of the originally short-term time horizon of Italians.   His questions also discovered that half the Italians had no fixed time horizon when they left their home country.   The increasing duration of stay for Germany is summarised in W.R. Böhning (1972b), table 4-4 p.67, and the same table gives data on "ageing", the changing sex composition, and the rate of return.   For French data see Ministere du Travail, de l'Emploi et de la Population (1971).   There is also a wealth of circumstantial evidence in the reports for the OECD Working Party on Migration, especially in the reports by M. Roux and I. Baucic on Yugoslavia, by S. Reinans on Sweden and by M. Allefresde on Finnish migration to Sweden.

[45] For German data see W.R. Böhning (1972a), table 6 p.194 and table 7 p.195. Whether or not the migration stream from any single country finally comes to be dominated by the flows from the more backward areas depends on the size of those areas relative to the intermediate and more developed areas.

[46] The change in geographical origin is documented for Italians in Switzerland in R. Braun (1970), table II /4 p.39 (although his explanation is somewhat questionable)

feeding process has worked its way through the economy, the swollen number
of immigrants generates a significant consumer demand, especially in terms
of non-durables but increasingly in durables as well. As this is a very
gradual process and the net addition to total consumer demand in any one
year is likely to be relatively small, it should not be equated with a
proportionate widening of consumer goods capacity. In effect, the net
addition to consumer demand may be smaller than the productivity gains
in consumer industries. To take a hypothetical example. If the net
inflow of migrants amounts to 250,000 persons and if 5% of them buy a
car during their first year of immigration (a second hand car probably
but assuming it were a new car or that all second hand cars need to
be **replaced** by new cars), the output of cars would have to be raised by
0.5% if a production level of 2.5 million cars were assumed. Assuming
further that during any subsequent year 10% of this stock of 250,000
migrants buy a car, the additional output required due to this wave of
immigration would be 1% p.a. (or less depending on whether the rate of
growth of car output outstrips the rate of growth of immigrant car demand).
In other words, every given stock of migrants constantly adds a certain
amount of consumer demand to that of the indigenous population. At a
stock of 2.5 million the immigrant-induced car output would be in the
region of 10% p.a. (ceteris paribus). Whether or not the output required
to satisfy immigrant demand is comparatively small and met through capital
deepening or large and met through capital widening, in either case we
have direct or indirect employment effects both in the consumer goods
industries (and therefore in the capital goods industries as well) and in
the distributive services. Over the years, then, a small and possibly
growing proportion of the immigrant labour will have to be employed for
the production of goods and services for the immigrant population itself.

48. Furthermore, during the third stage of maturity the increased
immigrant population exhibits significant infra-structural requirements
in terms of housing, schooling, social care, administration, etc., especially
through the immigration of wives and children and regardless of whether or
not they are themselves economically active. Again the additional demand
is comparatively small in a time perspective when related to the growing
demand of the indigenous population and may be met to some extent by spare
capacity or more intensive use of existing capacity. But directly or
indirectly the provision of immigrant-induced infrastructure will create
additional demand for labour which, in turn, means additional import of
labour. Whether or not the additional labour demand deriving from the
consumer expenditure of immigrants is larger than that deriving from their
social capital requirements is an empirical, not a theoretical question.
It is likely, though, that most of the additional consumer demand is met
out of higher productivity and leads only to a small employment effect
relative to the additional infra-structural demand which mainly involves
capital in the low productivity/labour intensive sector.

49. Finally, in the fourth stage of maturity the increasing length of stay
and the high degree of family reunion lead to an enlargement of the immigrant
population through the appearance of ethnic employers, secular and religious
leaders, etc., either directly (immigration) or indirectly (natural development of the immigrant population). As the psychological comfort afforded
by the company of their fellow countrymen leads immigrant workers and
families to settle in groups and "colonies", there slowly arises a demand
for ethnic shops, schools, churches, etc. Each of these ethnic institutions - even if they are formally integrated into the host society as in
the case of schooling - will subsequently be staffed predominantly by
ethnic workers. This entails additional immigration in terms of both
active and inactive persons, thereby reinforcing the consumer and social
capital effects of the original immigration. The employment/labour import
effect is likely to be smaller than the one deriving from the swelling of

the immigrant population and from the reunion of families, but it is by
no means negligible. This development presupposes a certain number of
ethnic immigrants in a given area. The threshold for the major European
post-industrial societies seems to lie between 100,000 and 200,000 ethnic
immigrants.

50. The fourth stage, however, is subject to social unrest on the part
of the indigenous population and to political intervention by the decision
makers and may therefore be abruptly curtailed. Political intervention
going beyond the customary labour market control is generally absent
during the first two stages because the politicians are secure in their
belief that the issues involved do not arise - until they suddenly come
into the open during the third stage of maturity.

51. It is worthwhile to consider briefly some of the implications for
the return movement of target workers deriving from this four-stage model
of maturity. Sociological theory suggests, and available statistics
support this hypothesis,[47] that migrants with a higher pre-migration
level of education and/or occupation tend to adjust to the host society
more quickly, easily and successfully. Once enmeshed in the demands
and rewards of a consumer society, they tend to prolong their stay more
often and more permanently than their less fortunate colleagues. One
can expect, therefore, a disproportionate number of the more educated and
skilled migrants, especially from the developed parts of the sending
country, to settle in the receiving country, regardless of whether they
were married prior to migration.

52. A second independent variable of equal importance is marital status.
The married migrant who asks his wife and children to join him in the
receiving country tends to become a permanent settler.[48] With his family
he is able to overcome further adjustment problems more easily and may be
able to climb the first rungs of the socio-economic ladder. If his children manage to participate successfully in the receiving country's schools,
the stagnant economic and social climate in his place of origin becomes

---

[47] For Switzerland see R. Braun (1970), pp.482, 491 et passim. and
H.M. Hagmann et al. (1971), p.93 et seq. For Germany, W.R. Böhning
(1972a).

[48] In early 1970 Marplan (1970) surveyed Italians, Greeks, Spaniards,
Jugoslavs and Turks in Germany. Of those who were staying without
their family, 40% had been there for less than one year, 42% for 2-5
years, and 18% for over five years. Of those who had their families
with them, the figures were 15%, 41% and 43% respectively. As regards
the envisaged further length of stay, 10% of those without family
wanted to stay one year or longer, 42% 2-4 years or longer and 37% five
years or longer. On the side of those with families, the figures were
5%, 27% and 50% respectively. In France it was found that of all male
migrant workers who had entered the country during the inter-census
period 1962-68, 41% had returned. A similar proportion (39%) characterised the total group of married migrants, but here practically none
of the married men with wives had left France (0.6%) while 60% of the
married men who had left their wives at home did in fact return
(temporarily perhaps). For Switzerland see R. Braun (1970), p.60.

less and less attractive relative to the growing prospects in his new
environment.   The skilled married migrant, therefore, is the most certain
long-term stayer.   On the other hand, migrants from the least developed
parts of the sending country, especially if they are unmarried, tend to be
the least successful short-term stayers.   Overall, these factors manifest
themselves in the fact that the longer a migrant has stayed in the receiving
country, the more likely he is to stay even longer, and vice versa.[49]

---

[49] Cf. V. Merx's "Verlaufsanalyse", (1972), p.156 et seq.   R. Braun (1970),
p.535 et passim, gives a more detailed and sociologically founded
explanation, which finds the crucial break with the idea of temporary
immigration occuring after six years abroad.   See also B. Kayser (1972),
especially p.21.

III   ECONOMIC EFFECTS: Theory and Practice

53. Having described the structural causes and the dynamic development
of polyannual immigrations in post-industrial societies, we can now enquire
into the specific effects of this development on the macro-economic parameters without unduly restrictive or unreal assumptions.   As the foreign
labour forces in the major receiving countries of Europe are overwhelmingly
in the third stage of maturity, even though not all individual migration
streams have reached that stage, we can concentrate on the effects pertaining to this stage and need only exemplify the effects pertaining to
the first two stages if necessary.

54. A few general remarks are in order here.   Immigrant populations
are commonly characterised by higher activity rates than the native population.   Employment is the reason for immigration and wives and children
exhibit high labour force participation because of their subproletarian
situation.   The fact that a sizeable minority of the married workers have
left their dependants behind also pushes up the activity rate.   This means
that there are more producers relative to consumers than in the native
population.[50]

55. Immigrant workers are young and able-bodied.   Some importing countries
weed out up to 10% of the prospective migrants on medical grounds.   The
existing external turnover helps to maintain this favourable composition
despite the natural ageing of the long-term stayers.

56. In their desire to earn money quickly, immigrants tend to be keen on
overtime, thus permitting employers to cope with erratic demand conditions.
In some cases this prospect may not particularly delight the indigenous
worker whose hands are also required for overtime work (complementarity of
jobs) and who has grown less dependent on the bonus of overtime earnings.

57. These personal factors, however, have as such no beneficial or
detrimental macro-economic effects - in the same sense as illiteracy or
lack of skills have as such no macro-economic effects.   Foreign workers
are put to work not because of their personal properties but because in
in the view of the employer they fill a work place adequately for the
profitable maintenance of a production process.[51]

---

[50] See e.g. Landeshauptstadt München (1972), pp.85-6, and K. Jones and
A. Smith (1970), p.31 et seq.

[51] As the Chairman of the Committee for Foreign Workers of the Netherlands
Employers' Organisation expressed it: we "would be in the red if we
did not have those foreign workers".   J. Barentsz (1972), p.23.
Incidentally, at the micro-economic level it is not necessary that
every work place on which a foreigner is engaged shows a profit as long
as the complex of jobs contributing to a final product (or the balance
sheet) remains profitable.   See also P.B. Doeringer and M.J. Piore
(1971), pp.89-90.

58. In this context it would be false and misleading to argue that the mass-import of low-skilled workers depresses the skill level and/or the productivity potential of a labour force and that this would be detrimental economically. Firstly, the replacement of indigenous low-skilled workers by foreign low-skilled workers does not change the proportion of low-skilled workers itself.[52] Secondly, the argument mistakes cause for effect: it is not the immigration which determines the relative proportions of skill grades, but the latter which determine the volume of the former (at least until a country is well into the fourth stage of maturity). The German-Turkish example is relevant here (see above fn.11) as well as the Swiss experience of the early sixties, when unskilled Southern Italians had to be imported after more highly skilled Northerners had become scarce and when this caused a switch in investment policy towards capital deepening.[53] Besides, employers have generally found that the work performance of foreign workers is as good as that of the indigenous worker.[54] If the micro-economic decisions of an employer as determined by market forces in a capitalist structure are the constitutive element of our economic systems and if he decides to employ a certain number of people in low-skilled jobs, then it is an irrelevant and pious hope to argue that he should employ more workers in skilled positions.

---

[52] Cf. above p.13-4. It is not surprising therefore that the structural decline of unskilled jobs proceeds even with heavy unskilled immigration. For German figures see Materialien . . . (1970)

[53] Cf. E. Tuchtfeldt (1965), p.645/6

[54] See e.g. S. Balke (1966), p.172, and B.G. Cohen and P.J. Jenner (1968), p.52.

(a)   Employment and Unemployment

59.   The import of labour presupposes a demand for it.[55]   Labour import
cannot, therefore, cause unemployment.   But labour import may very well
worsen the competitive situation for some sections of the indigenous work
force.   "Competition" as understood here does not refer to the artifact
of unemployment situations but to the totality of active workers who are,
at least potentially, always jockeying for new positions, even if they
are not currently unemployed.   In other words, competition is given a
substantive rather than a formal meaning.   Were it otherwise, most of
the discussion could be dismissed as irrelevant under conditions of full
employment.

60.   Moreover, the discussion cannot be spared by defining the foreign
and the native work force as non-competing groups with reference to either
socio-economic or legal reasons.   Socio-economically, the replacement of
indigenous by foreign workers in socially undesirable jobs can never be
complete, so that there will always be large sections of the indigenous
work force in a situation of direct competition (substitution).[56]
Legally, the control of the foreign labour force affects only that portion
which due to its recent immigration is still subject to control.   The
long-term stayers are generally free to change jobs.   But even those
subject to control do exhibit a high degree of job mobility[57] which the
authorities are either unable or unwilling to prevent completely - and
in many cases they have sound economic reasons on their side.   That is to
say, while the concept of non-competing groups may be illuminative in various
instances on grounds of either social or institutional discrimination or both,
it is of insufficient explanatory power to be of general use.   We estimate
that the degree of competition between national and foreign blue-collar
workers is somewhere in the middle of that obtaining between national workers
on the one side and national and foreign workers according to the non-
competing notion[58]   Table 3a attempts to give qualitative expression to
these estimates.

61.   The subsequent tables try to quantify what proportion of the indigenous
blue-collar workers may be in a competitive situation relative to foreigners
under hypothetical dispersions of both work forces across the three main
skill grades and hypothetical shares of the foreign in the total work force.
The composition of both the foreign and the native forces approximates those
given for male workers in table 1 (above p.14).   Table 3b shows, for example,
that with a foreign work force comprising 5% of the total, 2% of the total
will consist of unskilled foreigners.   Table 3c indicates that another 9.5%
of the total will consist of unskilled indigenous workers.   Table 3d
expresses the degree of direct competition suggested by the preceding tables

---

[55] See above p.3.

[56] Cf. table 1, above p.14.

[57] Cf. footnote 40 above and footnote 63 below.   The 1968 survey of the
Bundesanstalt für Arbeit (Amtliche Nachrichten supplement of 28 August
1970) found that the great majority of foreigners had already changed
jobs at a time when scarcely anybody was entitled to do so without
special permission.

[58] This is a modified version of Collard's conjectured elasticities of
substitution, see D. Collard (1970), p.78.

Table 3a: Degree of competition between foreign and indigenous blue-collar workers

	(i)	(ii)	(iii)	(IV)	(V)
(i) Immigrant labour unskilled					
(ii) Immigrant labour semi-skilled	Very High				
(iii) Immigrant labour skilled	Very High	Very High			
(iv) Indigenous labour unskilled	Very High	Very High	Very High		
(v) Indigenous labour semi-skilled	Medium	High	Very High	High	
(vi) Indigenous labour skilled	Very Low	Low	Medium	Low	Medium

Table 3b: The relative weight of foreign workers in the three grades of the total blue-collar force.

	Assumed Composition of foreign work force	Weight in grades of blue-collar employment under hypothetical shares in the total			
		total foreign share			
		5%	10%	20%	30%
(i) Immigrant labour unskilled	40%	2	4	8	12
(ii) Immigrant labour semi-skilled	40%	2	4	8	12
(iii) Immigrant labour skilled	20%	1	2	4	6
Overall	100%	5%	10%	20%	30%

72

Table 3c: The relative weight of indigenous workers in the three grades of the total blue-collar force given the share absorbed by foreigners according to table 3b

	Assumed composition of indigenous work force	Weight in grades of blue-collar employment under hypothetical foreign shares in the total			
		total foreign share			
		5%	10%	20%	30%
(iv) Indigenous labour unskilled	10%	9.5	9	8	7
(v) Indigenous labour semi-skilled	30%	28.5	27	24	21
(vi) Indigenous labour skilled	60%	57	54	48	42
Overall	100%	95 (+5% foreign= 100%)	90 (+10% foreign= 100%)	80 (+20% foreign= 100%)	70 (+30% foreign= 100%)

Table 3d: The rate of potential competition between the same grades of foreign and national blue-collar workers given varying degrees of foreign employment

	Total foreign share			
	5%	10%	20%	30%
Unskilled $\frac{nationals}{foreigners}$	$\frac{4.75}{1}$	$\frac{2.25}{1}$	$\frac{1}{1}$	$\frac{1}{1.7}$
Semi-skilled $\frac{nationals}{foreigners}$	$\frac{14.25}{1}$	$\frac{6.75}{1}$	$\frac{3}{1}$	$\frac{1.75}{1}$
Skilled $\frac{nationals}{foreigners}$	$\frac{57}{1}$	$\frac{27}{1}$	$\frac{12}{1}$	$\frac{7}{1}$
Overall	$\frac{20}{1}$	$\frac{10}{1}$	$\frac{5}{1}$	$\frac{3.3}{1}$

as a rate.   Taking the same example: there are almost five nationals to a
single foreigner in a very highly competitive situation ("very high"
according to table 3a).   To this could be added an equally large semi-
skilled foreign force plus a skilled foreign force of half that size which
are in a very highly competitive situation relative to unskilled nationals
(not shown in table 3d, but see table 3a), so that it could be said that
every other national unskilled worker is under very high competitive
pressure from the whole of the foreign work force (1.9 to 1).   The indigenous semi-skilled are in a highly competitive situation with foreign
semi-skilled at the rate of fourteen to one;   indirectly they also face a
medium degree of competition from the sizeable unskilled foreign force.
The indigenous skilled face little more than a medium degree of competition from skilled foreigners at the rate of fifty-seven to one.   And so
on.

62.   When the economic tide turns from full employment to unemployment,
we are likely to find a juxtaposition between macro-economically desirable
effects and undesirable effects for indigenous groups subject to very high
or high competition.   For example, where the institutional enforcement or
the practice of the "last hired - first fired" principle (which would seem
to apply to a disproportionate number of immigrants) are not strong enough,
the employer may well decide to keep a hardworking and able-bodied foreign
worker in preference to a lax or disabled indigenous worker.   The socially
and physically handicapped are therefore the likely losers.   Or the employer
may be able to hire an undemanding foreign worker who is happy to accept a
job at the given wage where an indigenous worker would decline the offer in
the expectation that the economy will soon return to full employment and
that he will again find a job with appropriate status and pay.   Such, it
seems, was the situation during the German recession of 1967.

63.   In general a recession reduces the inflow of foreign workers to a
trickle and increases the usual return movement by a structural component,
by many of the "first fired", and by a number of disappointed target workers [59]
dismayed by loss of overtime, by short time, or fearful of unemployment.
The structural component refers to the fact that unskilled and semi-skilled
jobs are of course hit harder by any recession than skilled or administrative jobs.   Even if the employer's dismissal policy were executed without
regard to nationality (and this seems to hold true in a great number of
cases) and unskilled and semi-skilled foreign and indigenous workers became
redundant in equal numbers, it would still involve a far greater proportion
of foreign than of indigenous workers.   The structural component alone
leads to a smaller degree of unemployment among indigenous workers than
would be the case if labour had not been imported.   On the other hand,
even a severe recession does not put an end to the employment of unskilled
or semi-skilled workers.   A considerable number, certainly the majority of
the jobs in which foreigners are engaged will therefore not be affected
by unemployment.   In effect, a few foreigners may continue to be imported
for less affected sectors or for the replacement of returning foreigners
whose jobs are not sought after by the indigenous population.   In a situation where disproportionate numbers of target workers become redundant, it

---

[59] See also B. Kayser (1972), and V. Merx (1972), p.93 et seq.

can generally be seen that many if not most of them leave the receiving country, at least temporarily ("export of unemployment")[60]. Thus, we have the usual return movement plus the return movement of some of the unemployed plus the return movement of disappointed target workers - together they most certainly turn the migration balance and relieve the competitive situation for indigenous workers. While the unemployment rate of the decreased foreign force tends to be higher than that amongst indigenous workers (and would be much higher if exported unemployment were taken into account), only a relatively small absolute number of unemployed foreigners are now actually competing with the larger number of indigenous unemployed for the available jobs in the host country. The fact that a strong negative migration balance could possibly have re-inforcing effects on the depth of the recession insofar as returning workers take their consumer expenditure with them, in contrast to the remaining unemployed should not be overestimated: this effect can only be very small indeed relative to the other factors influencing the depth of a recession.

64. While in aggregate terms the import of labour neither endangers full employment nor increases unemployment, and while it lowers unemployment for the indigenous population as a whole but possibly worsens the competitive situation for marginal groups at times of unemployment, it is its general labour market effect which reveals the greatest value of labour import. By this we mean the greater elasticity or the introduction of the highly desirable and beneficial element of flexibility during both the upswing and the downswing and in some regions, industries or occupations but not in others.[61] A growing economy requires mobility of

---

[60] This applies of course only to target worker migrations. Settlement migrations are not usually affected by it. In the case of immigrants from the New Commonwealth to Britain the situation is somewhat blurred. On the one hand, this stream too is largely a target worker stream (cf. footnote 20 above), but on the other hand immigrants were in the past admitted for settlement and their behaviour quickly responded to this situation. Moreover, the incidence of temporary and permanent return migration is negatively related to the distance between the sending and the receiving country. A Pakistani pondering return home from Britain faces incomparably more difficulties than, say, an Italian in France.

[61] V. Merx (1972) undertook a detailed examination of four analytically distinct types of flexibility derived from labour import: regional, sectoral (industrial or occupational), conjunctural (i.e. short-term economic), and seasonal flexibility. Regionally, labour import made good the decreasing regional mobility of the German worker (see e.g. p.63-4) and the differential activity rates of the regions. Sectorally, labour import enabled production levels to be maintained if Germans left undesirable jobs, and it enabled growth industries to expand faster than with a closed labour market. /See also S. Bullinger et al. (1972), p.100./ Conjuncturally, the imported labour showed a much higher degree of reaction to changes than the indigenous work force (see e.g. p.77, also the above text). Seasonally, the preceding three types fall together in their special dependency on seasonal patterns (see p.124 et seq.) /See also Th. Keller (1963), p.348./

capital and labour.   Higher living standards, however, induce lower
geographical mobility, especially through the acquisition of owner-occupied
homes.   The continuing ageing of European populations also induces lower
mobility.   Greater job specificity inhibits industrial or occupational
mobility.   And whereas in the past the growth of the working population
represented a considerably mobility potential, the slow growing, stagnating
or even decreasing working populations of contemporary Europe do not fulfil
this function to the same extent.   If, therefore, both the historical
mobility rate deriving from inter-generational change and the actual mobility
rate deriving from the current socio-economic propensity to move decrease,
the economy is faced with mobility deficits or bottlenecks which are unlikely to be made good by capital mobility alone.

65.   The regulated import of labour provides an excellent means of relieving
bottlenecks, which commonly occur when the upswing proceeds under tight
labour market conditions and which restrain the upswing and induce inflationary pressure.[62]   Many regional and sectoral bottlenecks can be eliminated through the engagement of foreigners; and general disequilibria can at
least be delayed, thereby providing the decision-maker with more breathing
space to get a grasp on the economic development.

66.   During the downswing, work places become painlessly vacated by
the usual number of returning emigrants and by the additional return movement of disappointed target workers.   Employers may also
dismiss foreigners where socio-political considerations might have prevented
such a decision if the worker involved had been a national.   In other words,
the import of labour   permits greater variations in employment patterns
during the downswing, too.

67.   Directly and indirectly foreign workers thus contribute disproportionately to the mobility deficit of the economy due to the external turnover of
the foreign work force.[63]   The Appendix attempts to give an indication of
  the size of the potential employment changes that could be obtained from

---

[62]   See also S. Bullinger et al. (1972), p.363, and V. Merx (1972), p.161
et passim.   G.C. Schmid (1971) found a much greater elasticity in the
German labour market due to labour import in his comparison with Britain.
For an analysis of the likely development in the absence of labour immigration see V. Merx (1969), p.104 et seq., and (1972), p.41 et seq.

[63]   D. Collard's regression analysis for male New Commonwealth immigrants in
Britain showed that (exempting the transport sector) "8 per cent of any
occupational expansion or contraction has been met by immigrant labour,
a much higher percentage than the relative size of the immigrant force
would indicate".   D. Collard (1970), p.73.   This is not to say that
immigrants necessarily have a higher degree of inter-firm job mobility
(internal turnover), or change their jobs excessively thereby causing
macro-economic costs.   The determinants of job mobility, such as age,
marital status, socio-economic status, housing, length of employment,
etc., do not lead to different degrees of job changing amongst comparable
groups of foreign and indigenous workers, see. W.R. Böhning (1970a), p.30,
and (1972a), pp.231-2.   On the other hand, as long as immigrants have a
higher propensity to return than the indigenous population to emigrate,
internal and external turnover taken together will characterise the
immigrant population as more mobile.   For Switzerland see R. Braun (1970),
pp.53, 117, 143 et passim.

labour import in comparison with the changes deriving from the inter-
generational replacement of nationals.   It can be seen that at realistic
levels of external turnover (defined as the sum of the rate of entry and
the rate of return) the flexibility potential of labour import is superior
to that of intergenerational change.   It can also be seen that the crucial
variable here is the extent of external turnover, i.e. that the higher it
is (the higher the "rotation" of the foreign work force) the greater are
the potential benefits.[64]

68.   However, "the argument that immigration adds to mobility of the labor
supply can be turned inside out by noting that obtaining high elasticity
with immigrant labor enables a country to escape the necessity of making
its domestic labor more mobile - a task with which it should get on."[65]

69.   Kindleberger's admonition could be related to three aspects: lack
of mobility between occupations (or industries), between activity and
inactivity, or between regions.[66]   The first of these is simply inapplicable if one considers that it is not so much the lack of occupational or
industrial mobility on the part of the indigenous population but the
constraints of a capitalist wage structure in economies with high living
standards and full employment which prevent movements into socially
undesirable and low paid jobs (while inducing movements away from them).

70.   The second aspect refers to the hypothesis that import of labour could
have an inhibiting effect on the employment of indigenous secondary workers,
i.e. on workers who move in and out of the labour force (not merely in and
out of employment) according to the swings of the business cycle.[67]   However,
at our conventional levels of full employment such an effect should per
definitionem not obtain, certainly not during over-full employment.   What
happens in Europe today is that for housewives, older people and other
groups of secondary workers employment has lost its necessity and become an
option.   When a society is assured of a generally high standard of living,
inactivity becomes tolerable and sometimes desirable relative to the low
pecuniary reward and the low non-pecuniary attraction of the jobs in which
secondary workers mainly find employment.   For the most part contemporary
European secondary workers are much further removed from the ideal-type
homo oeconomicus than the bulk of the immigrants.   In a slightly broader
sense one could ask whether more intensive utilization of the indigenous

---

[64]   See also V. Merx (1972), p.142, who comes to the same conclusion.

[65]   C.P. Kindleberger (1967), p.204.

[66]   Kindleberger's criticism could be enlarged by questioning whether
capital mobility is sufficient in the country of employment.   And
since the beginning of the third stage the question can also be posed
to what degree international capital mobility is a valid alternative
for labour import into manufacturing industries.

[67]   This hypothesis has been specified for the United States by M.W. Reder
(1963), p.227, as follows: "Given the growth rate of output, the effect
of increased immigration on labour supply will be partly offset by
reduced labour force participation of native secondary workers.   There
will also be a reduced rate of increase in 'labour force effectiveness'
because of lessened native rural urban migration."

employment potential could not obviate the need to import labour.   One
usually thinks of women in general and married women in particular.   But
quite apart from the question whether indigenous women would be prepared
to take up work in socially undesirable positions, the often forecasted
increase in female activity has not materialized and looks unlikely
despite decreasing family sizes, etc., and despite the slowly changing
image of working women and their low remuneration.   Generally, the
propensity to work declines with increasing living standards!

71.   The third aspect, i.e. the lack of geographical mobility calls in
question the premise on which regional policies in all European countries
rest , that is, the undesirability of depopulating certain areas on socio-
political grounds.   Most European countries are pursuing policies of both
taking the work to the workers in economically weak areas and of taking the
workers to the jobs in strong areas.   The problem is that the former does
not usually work very well and the latter is at times rejected as too
costly on social grounds.[68]   In a more general sense one could say that
the import of labour mitigates the effects of structural change for the
indigenous working population.   Without labour import these changes would
hit indigenous labour harder, faster, and more directly.[69]   This does not
mean that the structural change itself is slowed down.

72.   Obviously it is unreal to evaluate the element of flexibility in the
framework of a model presupposing total industrial and geographical mobility.
The reality of contemporary economic politics leads one to conclude that the
avoidance of the constraints of a tight labour force through import of labour
is highly desirable and beneficial for both the economy and the indigenous
worker.

73.   One further aspect needs to be mentioned, however.   The fact that a
greater or lesser degree of the employment growth generally and in specific
occupations particularly is borne by the import of labour, does of course
create short-term and long-term dependencies on the continued availability
of foreign labour.   With complementary jobs, a few workers in key positions
can upset the flow of work.   Italian crane drivers staying at home between
Christmas and the New Year, with the Swiss people at work, are a case in
point.[70]   When some departments of individual firms or whole branches of
the economy are predominantly or exclusively staffed by foreigners - during
the mid-sixties more than half of Switzerland's employees in textiles,
clothing, and stone quarrying were foreigners - the question arises what
would happen if political developments suddenly made workers return.[71]   It
would be futile to attempt to give a general answer, but it is undeniable

---

[68] D. Stephen (1971), p.130: "British governments had consciously or
unconsciously rejected internal migration (taking the workers to the
jobs) as too costly a way of filling the unfilled vacancies in the
Midlands and the South East.   Commonwealth immigrants could be brought
in at a lower immediate social cost."

[69] Though it may well mean that the tax payers' money is saved in smoothing
the friction of structural adjustment, cf. C. Rosenmöller (1970), p.233.

[70] Bundesamt . . . (1964), p.98.

[71] Cf. E. Tuchtfeldt (1965), p.646;   C. Föhl (1967), p.125; and
H. Salowsky (1971), p.60.

that every receiving country runs the risk of erratic fluctuations
in its foreign labour supply which have to be taken into account in an
overall evaluation of the effects of labour import.   The degree to which
one might trade off short-term flexibility against long-term dependency
is essentially a matter of personal judgement.   Unfortunately one cannot
have the short-term advantages of labour import without the long term
disadvantage of dependency.

(b)   Wage Growth and Income Distribution

74. Economic theory postulates that an increase in the labour supply
relative to demand is followed by a relative if not absolute decrease in
the growth of wages.   For this part of our analysis we have to shift the
focus from occupational status to industrial rank.   Wage differentials
between the three skill grades of labour are almost completely fixed while
inter-industrial wage scales are more flexible although also displaying a
great degree of rigidity.   The occupational status differential, which
assigns wage rates 10% or so higher for semi-skilled than for unskilled
workers and 10% or so higher for skilled than for semi-skilled workers,
accommodates different demand pressures at each level without upsetting
the differential itself.   This does not mean that there are no wage
movements between occupations, especially in countries where the trade
union system still betrays its craft origin and when the dispersion of
occupations over industries is small.   But trade unions generally seek to
maintain intra-occupational differentials while improving their overall
position.   Employers themselves have a much freer hand to award different
pay rises in different industries than for different grades of the same
occupation in any one industry.   Inter-industrial wage spread follows
the differing productivity-profitability situations, although the wage
spread tends to be smaller than the spread of productivity.   High wages
are generally found right across the board of profitable industries,
irrespective of the differing demand conditions for various occupations.
Conversely, the same occupations are rewarded differentially in differing
industries, the more so the greater the dispersion of an occupation over
the whole of the economy (e.g. for storekeepers more so than for miners).

75. In post-industrial societies, industries with high wage levels are
usually characterised by fast growth, high profitability, a tendency to
capital deepening and a below average proportion of undesirable jobs
shunned by the indigenous population.   Opposite criteria pertain to low
wage sectors.   The service sector, itself labour intensive, is more often
than not hampered by its inability to finance wage rises out of productivity
advances.   It tends to induce inflationary pressure because its workers
are unwilling to fall behind the pay rises secured in manufacturing
industries.   As most services, such as health services or public administration, cannot be provided at a profit there is a general tendency to keep
costs low, i.e. to keep wages low.   Moreover, as the government is the
largest employer in this area, one often finds it attempting to induce lower
wage settlements for the economy as a whole through restraining wage rises
in service sectors.   In manufacturing industries themselves it is the fast
growing and profitable branches which set the pace of wage rises and inflation, largely because productivity gains are not passed on in lower prices -
which could compensate for the inflationary pressure from the service sector -
but in higher money wages.   Trade unions in slow growing and low paying
manufacturing industries strive to close the wage differentials opened up
by the wage leaders thereby inducing inflationary pressure on the manufacturing side, especially in industries sheltered from international competition,
such as textiles, clothing, stone quarrying, etc.

76. As regards the import of labour, we must first of all ask ourselves
whether the system of wage bargaining is likely to be influenced by the
import of labour and whether this leads to a general dampening effect on
wages.   If this is not the case, we must enquire whether a disaggregated
analysis indicates any wage-dampening effects in the high wage or low wage
sector of industry.   A direct influence on the service sector is so unlikely
as to be negligible on account of the disproportionately small number of
foreigners entering this sector and because in the short run most service
wage levels are not determined by supply and demand conditions but by the
advances in industry.

77.   Foreign workers are generally fitted into the existing pay scales.
It is well known that discriminatory practices do occur in the form of
outright discrimination, regrading of jobs and also through the very
device which seeks to prevent differential remuneration, namely the
requirement to pay the "same wages for the same jobs". This employers
often interpret as meaning the "same rates for the same jobs" (it is
generally rates which figure in labour contracts) and thereby deprive
newly entering foreigners of the amount of wage drift currently obtaining.   The latter situation, however, is usually corrected when the contract
comes up for renegotiation after one year.   Overall, the impact of discrimination on wage developments is minute and negligible.[72]   This is in strong
contrast to the situation before World War I when trade unions were not
strong enough to repudiate discriminatory claims from their rank and file
or to keep employers to their obligation.[73]

78.   In a situation where foreign labour is continuously flowing into a country
where wage bargaining takes place at set intervals and where these intervals
vary little in relation to demand conditions, the direct influence from a
migration stream could theoretically only be felt after a time lag and even then
the net increase of the labour supply would not dampen the wage growth proportionately because of the downward stickiness of wage movements in post-industrial
societies.During the early phases of an upswing we commonly find that recent major
wage agreements enable employers to accumulate profits quickly due to a favourable wage cost/productivity situation.   When local unemployed workers
become re-employed with a certain time lag, the major trade unions still
tread carefully.   When additional foreign workers appear on the labour
market with an even greater time lag than the unemployed and while the
upswing may already be near or past its highest growth rate, the major
unions begin to seek to redress the social balance between profits and
wages.   Clearly, the relatively small number of net migrants cannot but
play a minor role in this wage round.   (And it is difficult to see it
playing a significant role at all if one bears in mind that the relationship between the increase of the labour supply and the relative/absolute
decrease in its price holds true only if the demand for labour during the
upswing is satisfied.   In most European countries, however, large scale
labour import went hand in hand with excess demand, thus clearly not
satisfying this criterion.)   Before the next wage round new foreigners
will continue to be engaged at the newly fixed wages while the growth of
the economy flattens off.   In the more delicate situation of this round

---

[72] A comparison of foreign with national wages is of course likely to show
lower wages on the side of foreign workers because of the structural
determinants of their employment situation, i.e. as low skilled workers.

[73] The most widespread and serious form of wage discrimination occurs with
illegal immigrants and is particularly widespread in France, although
"regularization" after some months' employment commonly rectifies the
worst excesses.   Illegal immigrants are as much subject to the black-
mail of employers as to that of people who facilitate their entry into
the receiving country.   But even where comparable wages are paid for
comparable work, the employer may still require extra duties without
further pay which he would not do in the case of indigenous workers, see
M. Allefresde (1969), p.69.   On the other hand, foreigners have also
been known to be overpaid - for instance, Britons in Germany - but
this happens only in very rare and untypical cases, see K. Wiborg (1971).

trade unions are under great pressure from the shop floor to secure at
least as high a wage rise as during the upswing and probably a higher one,
for the economy still looks as strong as ever while inflation eats into
earnings. Though one may now expect more frequent references by employers
to the continued availability of comparatively "cheap" foreign labour in a
situation of rising labour costs, the dominant feature of this round of
negotiations is how to share out the spoils of the economic growth between
capital and labour. The following wage round is likely to take place
during the downswing. References to available foreign labour are now an
empty threat in a system where foreigners are supposed to be engaged only
if local workers are not available. The downward stickiness of wages
(like the downward stickiness of prices) depends on the strength and
militancy of the trade unions (and also on the size and the financial
independence of employers) and the degree to which governments are willing
and able to coerce or influence trade unions directly or through keeping
wage settlements in the service sector low. Again, the preceding net
immigration is a completely minor issue in the negotiations.

79. This is not to say that additional labour supply from abroad does
not influence wage levels at all. It is very likely that some of the
bottlenecks developing during an upswing would cause a much greater wage
drift if the option of labour import had not been taken up in the past
and would not be taken up again. At the beginning of the upswing the
economy requires an instant response from the construction industry, for
example. Here local bottlenecks can easily be overcome through the
recruitment of foreigners who need little training for the work. Other,
often smaller bottlenecks in more highly skilled positions can sometimes
be overcome through the employment of indigenous workers who have previously
left undesirable jobs and possibly undergone some form of retraining.
Import of labour from developing countries does not eliminate all bottlenecks in all cases; and while it undoubtedly eliminates some important
bottlenecks in the trend-setting high wage sectors, such as construction
and the car industry, this effect does not lead to a significant lowering
of wage growth in this sector which causes an indirect lowering of the total
industrial wage level. "Earnings-drift is undeniably associated in some
way with 'the general level of demand', but it is a gross oversimplifica-
tion, especially in the more rapidly expanding sectors of the economy with
relatively high earnings, to suggest that it is related directly or exclusively to the inability of employers to obtain suitable labour".[74] On the
other hand, if we look at the slow growing low wage industries such as
textiles, clothing and stone quarrying, we can see that developing bottlenecks would force up wages there if they could not be overcome by labour
import. Foreign workers can be as easily engaged in textile jobs, etc.,
as on the construction site or the conveyor belt of the car industry. In
the absence of foreign workers higher wage rises in the low paying industries
would not necessarily lead to widespread bankruptcies or greater efforts at
capital deepening, because these sectors - like the construction industry -
are largely sheltered from international competition if not actually subsidised.
Their wages, however, bear a much more direct relationship to costs than in
the high wage sector. Labour import obviously is a convenient way out and
does prevent additional wage pressure over and above that which strives for
parity with the high wage branches (which is never a completely successful
enterprise anyway). With some of the steam taken out of the potential wage
pressure in the low wage sector, one would expect them to fall behind the
wage leaders, slowly but inexorably. Since most of these industries are
rather labour intensive, one might also expect that the sum of the small

[74] J. Marquand (1960), p.98 (our italics). See also Statistisches
Bundesamt (1964), and P. Lange (1967), p.109 for Germany.

but noticeable arresting sectoral effects lowers the overall industrial
wage level by a small but significant amount, which in turn opens up the
possibility, though not the certainty, that the wage pressure emanating
from the service sector might be a little less pronounced.

80.   In other words, labour import does not exert a direct general wage
dampening effect through any influence on the wage leaders, despite the
fact that during the third stage of maturity a great proportion of the
newly entering foreigners find work in the high wage sector.   Here, as
in most service sectors, wage rises bear only the most tenuous relationship
to differential demand pressure for various jobs.   In the industrial low
wage sectors the relationship between supply and demand of labour is more
immediate and here it may be assumed that bottlenecks would force up wages
if they could not be relieved through large-scale labour import.   This
sectoral dampening effect is likely to make itself felt as a small
aggregate dampening effect.   It will arrest the wage drift rather than
the growth of wage rates and delay the advent of general disequilibria
and wage pressure rather than prevent them.   The actual situation depends
largely on the state of the labour market.   If the relief of wage pressure
in low wage bottlenecks occurs at constant demand for labour, the dampening
effect is likely to be strong;   if employers are demanding more workers
still, most of this effect is likely to dissipate;   when the economy is in
full swing it is not so much the bottlenecks which induce wage pressure as
the belated efforts of the trade unions to provide their members with a
proper slice of the growing cake.

81.   Finally, it is worthwhile to consider briefly the changing scale of
the short run wage-dampening effect under different stages of maturity of
the migration stream.   The first wave of single worker migration induces
practically no capital expenditure as workers are engaged on existing work
places vacated by the indigenous population. Social capital requirements
are disproportionately low with practically no demand for education and
social welfare and very little additional demand for housing.   If single
workers are not actually housed in communal quarters provided by the employer,
they usually find a gap on the housing market, mostly in places vacated by
the indigenous population.   Their consumer expenditure is low, too, their
remittances are high and the additional supply of goods due to their employment is scarcely affected by the additional demand they create.   In other
words, they satisfy given labour demand, their wage-dampening effect is
not dissipated by induced demand and is therefore large and should be particularly visible in low wage industries.   The following wave of married workers
migrating without dependants is already associated with the spreading of
foreign employment throughout the economy and occasional changes in demand
pattern, i.e. a larger proportion of this stream will be associated with new
capital investment although the greater proportion may still be destined for
existing work places.   The swelling numbers also begin to make an impact on
social capital and consumer goods while remittances stay at their high level.
Overall these repercussions still seem neglible.   The wage-dampening
effect remains and is relatively large and most visible in low wage
manufacturing.   During the third stage of maturity the situation changes
considerably.   The reunion of families will sooner or later induce some
pressure on social capital (how much we shall analyse in a later section).
Also, the completed spread through the economy is likely to lead to the
engagement of an even greater proportion of new entrants in new work places,
possibly of most of them (again we shall seek to answer this question in
more detail later on).   Consumer expenditure soars absolutely and in relation to the number of economically active foreigners.   Remittances begin
to tail off.   Consequently the wage-dampening effect, though analytically
still there, may empirically be compensated by immigrant-induced labour
demand, which may spark off new immigration, which will again entail
further demand, and so on.   At this stage the question arises whether

the sectoral **cum** general wage-dampening effect is progressively outweighed by immigrant-induced demand pressure, i.e. whether after some years of immigrant-induced lower wage growth we now have years of immigrant-induced higher wage growth, possibly more than making good the earlier small loss.[75]

82. The only valid way to establish whether and to what extent a sectoral or general wage-dampening effect obtains would be to compare a hypothetical scenario without immigration with the actual situation. This requires something more than a simple ceteris paribus analysis. It would have to take into account that in the absence of immigration a tight labour market would be characterised by increased economic and social friction ;[76] or conversely that extensive capital deepening would lower the growth rate of wages. Friction, however, would lead to greater wage pressure not only in the low wage bottlenecks but would induce greater inflation all round and possibly lead to hurried governmental attempts at suppression, which in turn might well lead to contractions, rising imports, and falling exports. Workers in rapidly expanding sectors would probably profit from wage rises for a while until the low wage sector and services would induce generalized inflation. In our pressure group democracies marginal employers would seek to secure, and obtain, subsidies. Employers generally might become less willing to bear the increased risks of investment, thereby reducing the demand for labour and finally arresting the wage growth. There are too many unknown factors to be sure, but anything except a static short-term view would seem to indicate that in the end the indigenous workers' wage packet would be smaller compared with the actual situation. One should also bear in mind that the upgrading process of the indigenous work force both in terms of skill grades and in terms of movements from low wage to high wage industries, i.e. the original cause of the immigration, does of course provide them on balance with higher wages than if they had not been mobile.

83. Reverting to the actual situation, in our opinion it is likely that the dynamic effects coming to the fore during the third stage of maturity over-compensate the initial retardation and thus lead to a higher wage growth

---

[75] Various authors have come to different conclusions after using different methods. For instance, A. Kruse (1966), p.429 et seq., and following him U. Mehrländer (1969), p.119, have deduced an initial dampening effect possibly over-compensated by medium term additional pressure and followed by a long-term dampening effect. H. Salowsky (1971), p.30 et seq., sees a negligible general dampening effect as the most likely development though he also notes a possibly pronounced dampening effect for unskilled jobs. K.-H. Hornhues (1970), p.158 et passim, cannot find more than a minute dampening effect because he sees the continuing excess demand for labour related to skilled jobs where immigrants did not exert any marked influence. W.A. Jöhr and R. Huber (1968-69) claim an initial wage pressure effect. Their results, however, follow directly from their assumptions. (For the Swiss and German discussion concerning this problem, see ibid. (1969), pp. 5-22.) See also V. Lutz (1963).

[76] Cf. D. Hiss (1965), p.635 et seq., and D. Petersen (1970), p.4.

than would have obtained if the economy had to develop without immigrants. Figure 1 describes the alternatives in graphic form. It also suggests that even during the third and subsequent stages the import of labour still has a very slight dampening effect, which is much smaller than during the first two stages. If immigration were suddenly to come to a stop, tensions on the labour market would rise, bottlenecks would appear in greater numbers, and before long wage growth would be reduced through friction, etc. As long as the immigration continues and as long as a marked external turnover upholds some of the effects characterising the first two stages of migration, the immigration continues to relieve bottlenecks and permits smooth adaptations in employment patterns. The only difference is that the continuing small dampening effect does not matter during the third stage in absolute terms since the medium-term gain deriving from migration outweighs the short-term loss and wages are now rising faster than they would without immigration at a higher absolute level.

84. Casual empiricism would suggest that the high rate of growth of real wages (and the low level of inflation) in Germany and the Netherlands during the sixties, in Switzerland at the end of the fifties and in Britain in 1961-63[77] are partly attributable to their large scale labour import when the favourable conditions of the first and second stage of maturity prevailed. On the other hand, the interventions by the Swiss authorities since 1963 are probably in part to be blamed for the roaring inflation relative to the growth of the economy. A closer look at the Swiss situation would seem to give some empirical support to our reasoning, although the maturing migrations were of course never allowed to bear out their characteristics when the Swiss decided to curtail immigration. D. Maillat writes:[78]

85. "From 1950 on immigrants have been directed into the less well paid branches of the secondary sector, which entailed a certain stagnation of the wage growth in these branches. During the following years the range of wages widened, i.e. the difference between the high wage and the low wage sector increased. The result was that Swiss workers . . . who wanted to improve their income left the low wage for the high wage sector where employment continued to grow. These departures had no great influence on the rise of wages in the low wage industries for which it was possible to engage foreign workers. But the flexibility of the labour market could only last as long as the mobility of the Swiss wokrers was sufficient to satisfy the demand of the high wage branches. From 1960 on tensions appeared on the labour market; these were re-inforced by the inflation which characterised the Swiss economy at that time. As employment growth continued and because the mobility of the Swiss was insufficient to satisfy the demand, it became necessary to change the immigration policy by making it less selective: foreign workers became employed in all branches while the system of controls over internal movements was maintained. This policy gave the labour market a certain flexibility, but this flexibility was of a quite different nature compared with the previous one. For, in consequence of the progressive decline of the mobility of Swiss workers, new work places in the whole of manufacturing industries could practically be established only in view of the availability of foreign labour. This new situation then became the

---

[77] For Switzerland, see Bundesamt . . . (1964), p.96: for Britain K. Jones and A.D. Smith (1970), p.155.

[78] D. Maillat (1972a). See also D. Maillat (1972b), p.12 et seq.

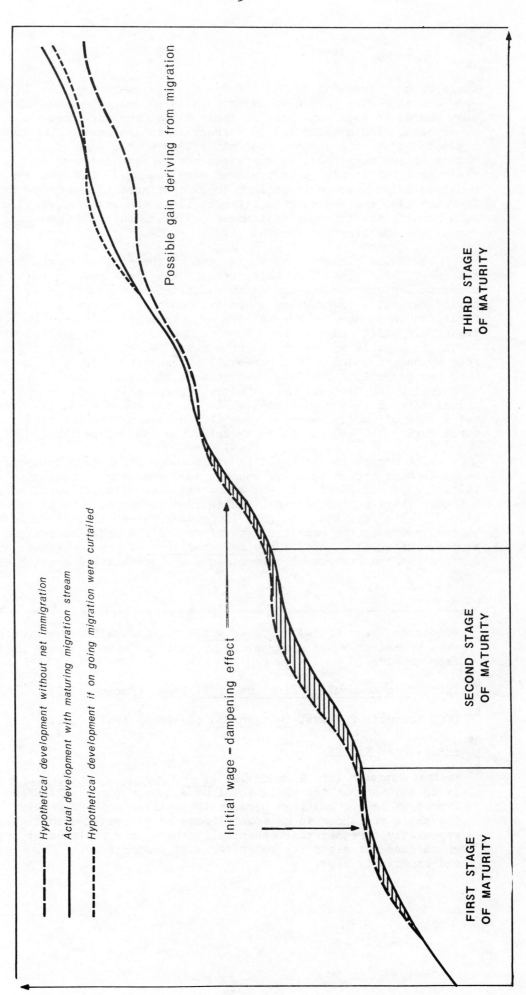

85

Figure 1

ACTUAL AND HYPOTHETICAL GROWTH OF PER CAPITA WAGES IN OPEN AND CLOSED POST-INDUSTRIAL LABOUR MARKETS

Hypothetical development without net immigration

Actual development with maturing migration stream

Hypothetical development if on going migration were curtailed

Possible gain deriving from migration

Initial wage-dampening effect

FIRST STAGE OF MATURITY

SECOND STAGE OF MATURITY

THIRD STAGE OF MATURITY

cause of the narrowing of the inter-industrial wage range.   In effect, low
wage branches were forced to improve their salaries because, on the one hand,
they wanted to keep some part of their indigenous work force and, on the
other hand, remain sufficiently attractive to immigrants for whom they had
a great need.   One notices that since 1959-60 the wage rises in the greater
number of low wage branches surpassed the average and that at the same time
the wage rises in high wage branches were weaker.   The branches where rises
remained below average (clothing, food) continued to lose more Swiss workers.
In March 1963 the Federal Council restricted the entry of foreign workers.
As a result, the labour market became tight to such a degree that the wages
spread was smaller than in 1949 . . .".

86.   The Swiss situation up to the end of the fifties is characterised by
the first two stages of maturity (though the large proportion of seasonal
and frontier workers introduces some distorting elements here).   For this
period Maillat's description shows a pronounced sectoral effect without
saying anything about the existence of a sectorally induced general dampening effect, which other authors have suggested.[79]   The general wage effect
should be visible in the growth of wages.   Hourly rates in Swiss industries
rose by only 6 index points between 1957 and 1960, but by 15 index points
over the years 1960 to 1963,[80] which were the first years of the third stage
of maturity for Switzerland.   Hourly average earnings even climbed at an
annual rate of 7.4% during 1961-63.[81]   On the other hand, the average annual
net inflow of foreign workers amounted to 1.1% of the total civilian labour
force during 1950-60 and to 3.2% during the 1960-63 period.[82]

87.   With regard to the question of income distribution the preceding
analysis must not be taken to suggest that the over-compensation of the
initial wage retardation in the third stage of maturity would bring labour
a higher share of the national wealth than in the absence of labour immigration.[83]   The fact that the cake is growing faster than it would otherwise is
basically due to the profitability of production under conditions of labour
import - after all, this is the raison d'etre of the employment of foreigners.
But because the structural determinants of capitalist societies effect an

---

[79] Bundesamt . . . (1964), p.94 et seq.   Incidentally, a narrowing of the
wage spread does not necessarily prevent the absolute wage differential
from growing.

[80] OECD, Main Economic Indicators, 1957-1966, (Paris, 1968).

[81] OECD Economic Surveys, Switzerland (De-ember 1967), p.12.

[82] Ibid., p.10 et seq.

[83] Another approach (cf. S. Bullinger et al. (1972), p. 255 et seq.)
is to assume that the skill level of a labour force is lowered through the
import of labour and that because low skilled workers receive lower wages
the share of labour in national income is depressed accordingly.   We have
repeatedly stressed that essentially there is a replacement process at work
which does not alter the relative skill proportions.   Cf. above Part II
and especially p.27.

unequal distribution of wealth, the employer profits more from the import of labour than the employee.[84]

88.   This does not mean, however, that the indigenous labour force does not reap a certain profit from the employment of foreigners in absolute terms.   First of all, the smooth growth of the economy under labour import compared with friction in a closed labour market ensures a higher real growth of wages in per capita terms with the beginning of the third stage of maturity.   Secondly, the social upgrading of many indigenous workers ensures that they earn relatively more than if they had remained in their old work places.   Thirdly, while immigrants contribute approximately in the same proportion to tax and social security as the indigenous population,[85] they certainly receive much less than the average per capita expenditure.[86]   Consequently, taxes on wages and profits and/or on consumer goods need not be raised in proportion to the increase of the working population or total population.

The most glaring example of this is the fact that the receiving country imports labour which has been schooled and possibly trained at no cost to

---

[84] As is well recognised by the Dutch study referred to earlier, Centraal Planbureau (1972), p.38.   See also G. Kade and G. Schiller (1972), p.27: "Additional profits . . . are retained by employers (where they may, eventually, be subject to taxes) whilst additional burdens have to be borne by society as a whole.   This is also the reason why increased social burdens do not react upon the growth in demand."

[85] As far as direct taxes are concerned, the over-representation of foreign workers in low wage positions leads to a lower per capita tax contribution relative to the national worker.   This deficit tends to be compensated by extensive overtime earnings.   In relation to the population as a whole this deficit is more than over-compensated by (a) the fact that immigrants tend to derive a higher share of their income from (high tax-bearing) employment than the indigenous population (where low tax-bearing unearned income is more significant, cf. K. Jones and A.D. Smith (1970), p.92), and (b) by their higher degree of economic activity.   In Munich it was calculated that for direct taxes the foreign contribution was 10% below the German per capita employee level, but that in relation to the population as a whole the foreign per capita level was 18% higher.   See Landeshauptstadt München (1972), pp.86-8.   As far as indirect taxes, which usually make up about half of a nation's receipts, are concerned, the relatively low paid foreigner probably contributes a smaller per capita amount than his national counterpart.   But this is by no means a negligible contribution to a state's finances, see S. Bullinger et al. (1972), pp.188 et seq. and p.390.   In addition to the directly relevant social capital outlays there is also "a large part of public expenditure . . . of an 'overhead' variety which does not vary appreciably with population; for example, expenditure for foreign aid, national defense, agricultural assistance, servicing of public debts, etc.   Therefore, tax contributions from immigrants would reduce the tax burden of natives on account of these very important items of public expenditure". M.W. Reder (1963), p.224.

[86] Cf. Chapter IIIe below.

itself - these infrastructural costs have been borne by the sending country.[87]
And fourthly, in countries where current social security benefits such as
old age pensions are paid for by the present working population (as opposed
to the insurance-type accumulation systems), the proportionate receipts
from foreigners are not matched by out-payments because immigrant populations are young and healthy.   This permits higher national out-payments[88]
and/or lower deductions than in the absence of immigration - an effect
from which both employers and employees profit according to their differential liabilities (though in the final analysis it is probably the employee
who profits most because employers tend to consider social security contributions as part of the "real" wages they pay because these contributions
are part of their total labour costs).

89.   In evaluating these various effects one cannot but draw the conclusion
that the net inequitable effect must be very small indeed.[89]   Even authors
who have used most unrealistic assumptions in this context have come to
the conclusion that "the effects on per capita real income and distribution
are less immediate and certain . . .   These longer run changes are likely
to be small compared with the changes wrought by managerial and technological

---

[87] Insofar as this enables the receiving country to keep taxes on wages
and profits low relative to the sending countries, it strengthens its
competitive situation vis-a-vis those countries.   The higher the
external turnover, the more pronounced this effect.

[88] H. Salowsky (1972), pp.16 and 22, calculated that in 1970 in Germany
foreign workers contributed 16% of the in-payments for old age pensions
and received 0.5% of the out-payments.   Moreover, about one third of
the out-payments was compensated by pensions paid to Germans formerly
employed abroad, see ibid, n.21 p.18.   Another German calculation
reports that "the pension system paid out no more than 11% of the amount
to foreigners which they had contributed to it in 1965.   During this
year the system would have been in the red had it not been for the
contributions from foreign workers . . .   Due to this additional
income of the pension system from foreigners it was not necessary to
raise the rate of contributions from 14% to 15% before the year 1968.
Otherwise this measure would have been necessary much earlier".
U. Mehrländer (1969), p.76.   The draw-back to this momentary relief
is of course that it incurs long-term liabilities, that is, the pensions
or part of them accruing to foreigners formerly employed in the receiving
country will have to be financed by the future working population.   See
ibid., p.77 et seq., especially p.83, and Steinjan (1966), p.14 et seq.

[89] E.J. Mishan and L. Needleman (1966a), (1966b) and (1968), and E.J. Mishan
(1970).   Their model measures the impact of large scale net migration
(446,000 workers p.a. or 632,000 people including dependents over a 30
year period) associated with corresponding new capital investment in a
situation of given excess demand - a model which necessarily results in
additional inflation, higher imports and lower exports.

innovation over time."[90]   We suggest that, ceteris paribus, the wage growth
determinant of variations of the share of labour in national income comes
near to have compensated in the third stage of maturity the initial losses
relative to capital and is likely to have overcompensated them in absolute
terms.   That is, while the beneficial dynamics of labour import are not[91]
likely to restore completely the original situation, ceteris paribus,
because of the distributive norms of our societies, the open labour market
brings forth a higher real per capita growth than would be possible without
immigration.   (In a closed labour market the initial increase in employee
compensation would be shortlived if, given increasing internal and external
demand for goods and services, employers were able to pass on their losses
in increased prices, thereby recovering profits; and in modern conditions
of "stagflation" this would seem to be possible even without an increase
in final demand.   If employers reacted to a decrease in their share of the
national wealth with reduced investment, this would quickly depress the
compensation of employees and a new balance might be found at a lower level,
possibly with a lasting "brake" effect.)   Figure 2 expresses our reasoning
in graphic form.

90. Furthermore, even though in an aggregate model increasing returns to
capital outstrip increasing returns to labour, a consideration of the national
labour force relative to capital would suggest that it has not been negatively
affected at all because considerable sections have moved into more highly
paid positions.   Per capita the national worker is as well off in respect
of equity as without immigration (for his move into better paid jobs is
analytically independent of the availability of foreign labour, i.e. it
affects labour import but labour import does not affect his upgrading).
In terms of the absolute growth of per capita wages and the share of labour,
the national worker   is likely to receive markedly more due to the
beneficial dynamics of labour import than without immigration.   For once,
he can have his cake and eat it.

---

[90] E.J. Mishan and L. Needleman (1968), p.282.   Their quantitative results
are as follows: "For the standard case of constant returns to scale
(and) for an elasticity of factor substitution, σ, of 0.5 this differential loss in real per capita income (in an open as opposed to a closed
labour market) runs at the rate of £19 per annum in the 30th year -
taking no account . . . of the terms of trade effect . . .   For
the increasing returns to scale case given by V equals 1.2 (and) for
a σ of unity, however, the per capita income loss increases until the
20th year after which it starts to decline, while for a σ of 0.5 the
loss grows to the 6th year, then declines steadily until the 15th year,
after which there appears a positive per capita income gain that reaches
close to £19 in the 30th year." Ibid., p.294.   Adverse movement in the
terms of trade (built into the model) increase the differential loss
appreciably, while smaller net immigration reduces it proportionately.
See also E.J. Mishan (1970), p.105 et seq.

[91] Ceteris paribus need not obtain, of course.   With increasing wealth
governments are less constrained to adjust the tax system in favour
of labour than otherwise.

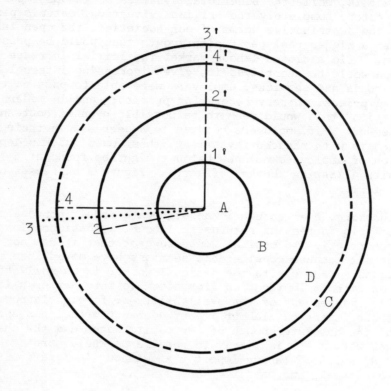

Figure 2

SHARE OF CAPITAL AND LABOUR
IN GROWING NATIONAL INCOME UNDER IMMIGRATION

1 - 1' = Share of capital
A = Share of labour   when immigration commences

2 - 2' = Share of capital
B = Share of labour   during first two stages of migration

3 - 3' = Share of capital
C = Share of labour   during third stage of migration

— ■ — · — = Size of national income if there had been no **migration**

4 - 4' = Share of capital
D = Share of labour   if there had been no migration or when migration stops

(c)   Goods Price Inflation and the Balance of Payments

91.   The preceding section suggests that, while the initial wage-dampening
effect has a noticeable anti-inflationary influence, it is uncertain whether
the net effect of continuing slight dampening of wage growth in relation to
immigrant-induced wage pressure during the third stage of maturity is
positive or negative in terms of factor price inflation.[92]   The net result
can only be very small either way and will depend primarily on the degree
of external turnover.   For argument's sake the net effect of the third
stage of maturity on factor price inflation may be assumed to be zero.
However, this does not mean that other anti-inflationary effects associated
with polyannual migrations have lost their force during this stage.   These
relate to the deflationary impact of immigrants on internal consumer goods
prices directly and through the balance of payments.

92.   Polyannual migrants are **originally** motivated by the desire to earn
and save as much money as possible.   The first wave of single migrants
does just that and large sums are remitted to their families.   The
subsequent wave of married migrants, who initially leave their families behind
may remit an even higher portion of their total savings while living at near
subsistence levels in the receiving country.   When dependants rejoin the
breadwinner the most pressing reason for a large part of the remittances
disappears and more consumer expenditure will now be effected in the
receiving country.[93]   When the individual family time and again extends
its stay and while it increasingly becomes adjusted to and enmeshed in
the receiving country's society, its consumer behaviour becomes progressively indistinguishable from that of the indigenous population.   Still,
the external turnover which feeds unadjusted single and married migrants
into the system and releases those who cannot or will not stay longer
assures that even after the first two stages of migration the immigrant
population as a whole has a markedly higher savings ratio than the
indigenous population.   In Switzerland, for instance, the savings ratio
stood at 60% in 1950 and 50% in 1955.   Since that time it has decreased
to 30%.[94]   External transfers amounted to 35% of the total income of
foreigners in 1950, to 25% in 1966 and to 18% in 1970.[95]   In Germany in
1970 external transfers in the region of 25% indicated at least double the
savings ratio of the indigenous population, 12.5%.[96]

---

[92] M. Peston (1971), p.83, emphasizes the distinction between immigration
as a possible cause of inflation and immigration as an effect of inflation.   Besides, immigrant-induced wage pressure is not simply the difference
between satisfied and generated demand.   At the higher rate of wage
growth during maturity one is likely to have a relatively higher rate of
inflation than at the lower rate of growth which would occur in the
absence of immigration.

[93] R. Braun (1970), p.260, found that 57% of the single but only 19% of the
married Italians in a matured stream sent money to their parents in Italy.
See also ibid., p.255 et seq.

[94] E. Tuchtfeldt (1965), p.645.

[95] H. Salowsky (1971), p.43 n.99.

[96] Ibid., p.50.   For Germany, see also R. Hentschel et al. (1968), p.10/11,
and U. Mehrländer (1969), p.135.   For Britain, K. Jones and A.D. Smith
(1970), p.93.

93. Not only does the statistical average of single plus unaccompanied plus foreign workers with dependants show a lower consumer expenditure relative to the national average, but the lower dependency ratio of the foreign population means that it produces more and consumes less than the indigenous population.[97] The average propensity to save and the dependency ratio effect combine to exert a strong deflationary impact on consumer goods prices and indirectly on capital goods prices as well. Food and clothing, which form the bulk of the expenditure of the unadjusted and supposedly temporary migrant, possibly experience the smallest deflationary effect; waves of demand for certain consumer durables from adjusted migrants can lead to minute changes in the structure of imports and production and some accelerator effects may even send ripples through the capital goods industry; but overall the net effect can only be a marked reduction of pressure in final demand.[98] This is highly desirable in a generally inflationary situation. During a recession the net deflationary effect pales into insignificance relative to the main determinants of a recession.

94. It could now be argued that a higher savings ratio on the side of foreigners provides a proportionately greater amount of investment resources (assuming no hoarding) and could thereby fuel the fires of inflation. But the relationship between current account holdings and investment spending is very tenuous indeed and whether greater investment is desirable or not in a given situation is not a question that can be answered by reference to the availability of capital.

95. Remittances have the advantage of withholding money from the consumer market as well as from the banking system and putting it at the disposal of the central bank. Whether or not the loss of foreign currency itself is desirable depends again on the given situation. When the trade balance leaves the current account in sizeable surplus even after a reduction by invisibles, countries are usually happy to see their balance of payments brought nearer to equilibrium by remittances. Conversely, when a trade deficit is just about rectified by net invisible earnings, the gross outflow of foreign currency in terms of remittances is not welcome.[99]

96. However, "in evaluating the remittances of foreign workers one should always bear in mind their close connection with other items of the balance of payments. Without additional foreign workers . . . production would doubtless be smaller than is the case now, exports would be smaller and imports larger."[100] Looking at the import side first, the consequence of the high savings ratio of immigrants is that the import content of their current expenditure is likely to be below that of the indigenous population; and as immigrants satisfy more demand than they create on consumer markets, the import content of immigrant-induced capital expenditure in this sector

[97] In 1969 foreign workers formed about 7% of the total German labour force. The consumer demand during that year amounted to 3% of total private demand. See. H. Salowsky (1971), p.47.

[98] If, as we assumed in our introductory example (p.23), the net addition to total private consumer demand in a single year is absorbed by productivity advances, the net inflow of foreign workers in consumer goods industries has a corresponding deflationary impact on consumer goods markets.

[99] M. Allefresde (1969), p.32, pointed out a simple remedy to this currency drain, namely to encourage family migration and the reunion of separated families.

[100] Monatsberichte der Deutschen Bundesbank, No.6/1971, quoted in H. Salowsky (1971), p.46.

is also likely to be below average.[101]   The postulated extra production through labour import may of course serve to some degree as a substitute for imports where imports are caused by supply shortages.

97.   As far as exports are concerned, the mere fact that foreigners contribute to the growth of production means, ceteris paribus, that they contribute to the growth of exports - either directly through employment in the export sector or indirectly through the replacement-upgrading process. More importantly, the import of labour causes a strong positive movement in the terms of trade during the first two stages of maturity through its dampening effect on both factor price and goods price inflation.   This does of course strengthen the competitive situation of the receiving country.   While the effect on factor price inflation may be assumed to be neutral in the third stage of maturity, the deflationary effect on goods price inflation remains significant, thus maintaining some of the positive development in the terms of trade.

98.   Furthermore, in a disaggregated model one must accord most of the dampening and deflationary effects to the secondary sector and most of the immigrant-induced wage pressure to their infrastructural requirements. Manufacturing exports, therefore, continue to draw a disproportionate benefit from the employment of foreigners in terms of export prices.   The greater adaptability of the receiving country's labour force - achieved through bottleneck relief, better capacity utilization, overtime, and shorter delivery times - in conjunction with the general deflationary impact on goods prices, enables the receiving country to respond more effectively to changes in comparative advantage.[102]   From the viewpoint of the labour sending country this means that it suffers under a permanent disadvantage which derives from its own emigration.   In other words, the beneficial effects of labour import under conditions of external turnover widen the competitive gap between the sending country and the receiving country.[103]   While the latter is dependent on the former for its prosperity, the former becomes ever more dependent on the latter for the export of its

---

[101] E.J. Mishan and L. Needleman (1966b), p.36, and K. Jones and A.D. Smith (1970), p.156, assume average per capita proportions.   It is interesting to note that even for countries associated with the traditional type of family immigration such as Australia, there is no negative influence on imports, cf. J. Kmenta (1966), and the critique in J.H. Duloy (1967), p.232.

[102] In a closed labour market export prices would soon come under pressure with negative repercussions for the balance of trade and the balance of payments and possibly depressing effects on the economic development as a whole.

[103] These results contrast sharply with those of Mishan and Needleman who presuppose a one-way relationship between domestic output and exports: ". . . there is no evidence that any of the increase in output (deriving from immigrants) would be exported." (1966b), p.37.   They then go on to say: ". . . we have assumed that the whole of the immigrants' output is available for the home market.   Should any proportion be exported, the larger this is, the less adverse the immigrants' effect on the balance of payments.   But at the same time, the longer will it take for their domestic supply to offset the domestic demand they generate". Ibid., p.43/4.   On the other hand, even Swiss authors not known for their favourable disposition towards foreign workers have maintained that the desirable export effects, which they admitted, outweigh any undesirable currency losses.   See e.g. W. Wittmann (1962), p.279, and Th. Keller (1963), pp. 348-9.   See also fn. 87 above.

labour surplus.   Obviously the only way to alter this situation is to
bring the work to the worker.

99.   In effect, remittances can be seen to be a vehicle of this feedback
effect.   "It is an old rule that currency which flows abroad has the
tendency to return in the form of increased demand for goods and services."[104]
Recent research has shown a negative relationship between the rate of growth
of remittances from Germany to Greece and the rate of growth of the trade
deficit between the two countries, i.e. increasing remittances paid for a
decreasing part of the growing trade deficit.   "Here the function of
remittances becomes clear.   They not only satisfy the needs of the population which stayed at home, they also satisfy the demand for higher consumer
goods which have to be imported from abroad.   Empirical surveys show that
in the beginning remittances serve to feed the families and to provide them
with the most necessary household goods.   Afterwards they are used for
buying consumer durables, such as refrigerators, washing machines, radios,
furniture, etc., and only then for the acquisition of land, a house (and so
on) . . .   The picture of a foreign worker who drives home during his
holiday in his own car is not a rarity any more. . . .   Foreign workers
help to cover the existing trade deficit of their country of origin towards
their country of employment but they also contribute to the widening or at
best the maintenance of this deficit through their steadily growing demand
and that of their families."[105]

---

[104] S. Balke (1966), p.173/4.   See also C. Rosenmöller (1970), pp.234-4.
K. Jones and A.D. Smith (1970) regarded their own estimate that half
the remittances would return as export demand as on the high side, see
p.157.

[105] M. Nikolinakos (1971b), p.787-8.

(d)   Capital Deepening and Capital Widening - Productive Capital

100. Target workers are not in the possession of a significant amount of
personal capital at the moment of immigration that could be used to finance
additional productive assets.   Indirectly, however, contemporary polyannual
migrations in Europe seem to have attracted overseas investors.   But assuming that this was of no significance, how true is the traditional deduction
that labour import retards capital deepening and thereby inhibits the long
run determinant of real economic growth?[106]   "This raises a question in
which our ignorance is profound.   The steady level of wages did not inhibit
rapid technological change in Britain in the period from 1815 to 1873, nor
did rising wages after the latter date prevent the slowing down of technological progress up to World War I.   More currently . . . Britain has had
a relatively slow rate of increase in productivity with a limited labor
force and rising wages, whereas Germany has been able to shift smoothly
from capital-widening to capital-deepening as called for by the classic
mechanism.   In France, technical changes seem to have been relatively
independent of the labor position.   In Switzerland it may be true that the
availability of large numbers of foreign workers prior to 1964 slowed down
the movement toward automation and more capital intensive methods, but the
evidence is far from complete."[107]   The validity and reliability of the
traditional deductive reasoning could also be questioned by reference to
the empirical fact that in post-war Europe the growth of the labour force
has effected productivity increases in the receiving countries[108] and by
reference to the situation in the sending countries where a superabundance
of labour has not hindered the setting up of the most modern capital-intensive
equipment.[109]   What accounts for this gap between theory and practice?

---

[106] See e.g. U. Harms (1966), p.280: "The changes in the structure of
industries and firms which are necessary for the long term growth of the
economy, especially the continuous substitution of labour by capital
which provides productivity advances, are economically not enforced to
the same degree with easy availability of foreign labour as with a closed
labour market. The elimination of marginal firms and unprofitable production processes is delayed. These delaying effects in the structural
change of the economy must doubtlessly be regarded as negative because
they hinder growth." In effect, "an influx of additional labour does not
itself prevent the adoption of a labour-saving device: the influx must
be such as to cause a sufficient rise in the price of capital. Conversely,
no shortage of labour in such an economy will of itself encourage the
adoption of known cost reducing labour-saving devices." E.J. Mishan
and L. Needleman (1968), p.516 note 2. Ibid.: "No casual observer of
the U.K. economy would find it hard to believe that some cost-reducing
labour-saving innovations are fairly readily available but which, either
for institutional reasons (peaceful labour-management relations) or
because of the force of inertia, are just not adopted."

[107] C.P. Kindleberger (1967), p.203-4.   For the Swiss situation see also
Bundesamt . . . (1964), p.101 et seq.

[108] The U.N. Economic Commission for Europe (1964), ch.II, n.18 p.13, found
that "each 1 per cent increase in labour force is associated with an
additional 0.39% increase in labour productivity."   H. Giersch came to
a similar result for the 1950-1965 period in Germany, see V. Merx (1969),
p.34 et seq., and (1972), p.4.

[109] Cf. G. Schiller (1971), p.182 et seq.

101. In the first place it is often not appreciated that capital widening, too, leads to productivity advances in the form of rationalisation of the production process. Capital widening through the expansion of existing capacity or the setting up of new firms implies that the most up-to-date machinery, etc., is installed.[110] "Employers, if they invest, always effect the most economical solution for the production process, regardless of whether additional labour is available or not."[111]

102. Secondly, labour import helps to realize economies of scale, at least in the short run.

103. Thirdly, the additional labour market flexibility deriving from the external turnover of the foreign workforce makes itself felt in significant productivity advances, especially in periods of slack employment.[112]

104. Increased capital deepening in a closed labour market, on the other hand, would demand a higher mobility from the indigenous work force and a faster disappearance of marginal firms - when, as we have shown, it is the socio-economically determined lack of geographic mobility of indigenous workers and in particular their movement out of socially undesirable jobs which causes the immigration in the first instance and when it is well known that competitive problems are likely to be "solved" by subsidies. Marginal producers, incidentally, are by no means confined to the low productivity sector, and any wage pressure relief they obtain through labour import is only momentary and does not change their structural situation.[113] Increased capital deepening would presumably also entail greater imports of capital goods.[114] If the demand for capital goods could not be satisfied quickly enough, this might well cause prices to rise and production to stagnate. And lastly, since the third stage of maturity, i.e. when foreigners are concentrated in manufacturing in general and therefore in capital goods industries as well,[115] the receiving country could quite literally not produce the required capital goods without immigrants.[116]

---

[110] Cf. A. Nydegger (1963), p.326. A.N.E. Jolley (1971), p.56, also emphasises that embodied technological progress tends to be under-measured.

[111] C. Föhl (1967), p.126. See also the instructive chapter 6 in P.B. Doeringer and Michael J. Piore (1971), where it is shown how manufacturing industries introduce labour saving techniques without bothering about the labour market situation except when manning new machinery appears as a major hurdle.

[112] V. Merx (1969), p.126, also attributed the flexibility element with productivity gains. For empirical evidence see G.C. Schmid (1971).

[113] Cf. K.-H. Hornhues (1970), pp.86-8.

[114] Bundesamt . . . (1964), p.105-6.

[115] In Germany foreign workers are over-represented in capital goods industries compared with total manufacturing, see V. Merx (1972), Appendix table 29.

[116] One could "even speak of a desirable effect of the employment of foreigners on the trend towards capital deepening. The relatively strong employment . . . in the capital goods industry has surely contributed decisively to the fact that this industry was able to satisfy almost completely the strong demand for new machinery during the last years." S. Balke (1966), p.173. See also M. Nikolinakos (1971a).

105. What influence is immigration likely to have on the investment decisions of employers? Private employers are basically guided by trends in market developments. Markets are largely influenced by per capita income changes and by the growth of the population itself. Matured immigrations raise real per capita wages faster than in the absence of immigration and net immigration of course increases the population. Therefore, labour immigration tends to increase the propensity to invest.[117]

106. Increased general propensity to invest does not necessarily lead to a differential propensity to capital widening or deepening, especially if one bears in mind that macro-economically the net addition to the labour force amounts at most to 1-2% of the labour force and to a slightly lower proportion in relation to the total population (and to an even lower proportion in relation to final demand). What is nationally a small and gradual addition to a highly fluctuating quantity may, however, be more pronounced in various regions and sectors of the economy.

107. Yet to condemn any capital widening as being a priori detrimental, is to clamour for an abstract notion of profitability which has no counterpart in the varied realities of economic life where industrialists always choose the most cost reducing type of investment relevant to their circumstances irrespective of the labour market situation.[118]

108. Moreover, the pure models of economic theory abstract from a reality where "the innovations might not have been made which enable one to make the most desirable investment . . . the supply of the necessary investment goods and services is liable to be slow due to the conditions of persistent heavy demand and hence bottlenecks . . . even if the innovations have been made and the finance is available, a considerable time lag inevitably occurs between the realization that a project is feasible and its being brought into operation. This time lag cannot just be discounted, for the system has to keep going in the meantime. In the long run clearly the answer is to be found in new techniques, but we live in the perpetual short-term."[119]

109. Much of the theoretical reasoning seems to be guided by the picture of corporate giants like IBM or General Motors which can afford to trade off short-term against long-term profitability. But the vast majority of private employers does not fall into this category,[120] and smaller employers

[117] Cf. K. Jones and A.D. Smith (1970), p.125, and V. Merx (1969), p.24.

[118] Cf. above p.52.

[119] P. Jenner (1966), p.114/5. See also the similar reasoning based on extensive interviews in Bundesamt . . . (1964), p.104 (where the intriguing idea was put forward that temporary abstention from immediate introduction of new technology might enable one to skip intermediary steps of the technological development, i.e. to save capital). D. Maillat (1972b), p.21, also stresses the inhibiting effects of time lags.

[120] D. Maillat (1972b), p.21, emphasizes the small size and family ownership of many Swiss businesses.

and their financiers are reluctant to incur delays arising from the introduction of capital intensive processes, especially under conditions of
rising demand.[121]

110. Lastly, the traditional deductive approach does not even consider that
new capital investment may be induced by the availability of immigrant labour.
New equipment is often too expensive to be worked only a standard working
week and it must be employed as intensively as possible thus necessitating
shift work.[122] While indigenous labour's reluctance to take up shift work
could in many cases only be overcome at a cost which would make the undertaking uneconomic, this does not hold true for target workers.[123] Therefore,
"a rise in wage rates, especially for shift work, would have had an inhibiting effect on the rate of new capital investment and it would have been
cheaper to use older machinery."[124]

111. In summary it could be said that if in the short-term situation the
most economical type of investment is effected regardless of labour market
pressure, if economies of scale are realized, if productivity advances are
gained through increased labour market flexibility, if there is a greater
propensity to invest but not necessarily a differential propensity to
widen or deepen, and if the short-run constraints of the situation inhibit
the introduction of labour-saving techniques - then it is presumptuous to
translate this into a permanent retardation of real growth. The continuous
short-term productivity gains, which increase national wealth all the time,
outstrip the gains obtainable from a hypothetical switch towards greater
capital deepening in a closed labour market.[125] Even though one may find
instances where availability of foreign labour and a tendency to capital
widening are linked, such as in quarrying and construction for example
(and whether or not this matters in terms of international competitiveness),
the questions which have to be answered are whether the benefits derived
from labour import outweigh the disadvantages,[126] and secondly, whether
the competitive process is blunted by the availability of labour or by some
other factor such as the rapid expansion of final demand which enables firms
to shelter from the winds of economic change.

---

121 A leader of Dutch employers reiterated that "the replacement of manual
labour by more sophisticated machinery, because of the relatively lower
wages during that time did, in many cases, not show a reasonable pay-out
time." J. Barentsz (1972), p.22. American manufacturing industries
seem to be characterised by a pay-out period of 2-3 years, see P.B.
Doeringer and M.J. Piore (1971), n.12 p.125.

122 B.G. Cohen and P.J. Jenner (1968), p.54. See also above p.11.

123 Ibid. See also M. Peston (1969), p.644.

124 B.G. Cohen and P.J. Jenner (1968), p.55.

125 V. Merx (1969), p.70, also suggests that the gains outweigh the
productivity losses.

126 For the construction industry both the Swiss commission (Bundesamt . . .
(1964), p.102-3), and W. Steinjan (1966), p.13, answer the question in
the affirmative.

112. Given this overall evaluation what are the specific effects of labour import on capital deepening/widening with respect to the self-feeding migration stream in a disaggregated model?   At the beginning we find that foreigners are solely engaged on work places vacated by the indigenous population.   This is usually of little importance to manufacturing industries because the initial demand for foreign labour generally origi- nates in the agricultural or service sector or in construction.   The re- placement of indigenous workers in vacated work places means that immigrants do not cause new investment expenditure in terms of productive capital, whether or not there is general excess demand for labour.   (One could arrive at a different conclusion only by mistaking cause for effect.) Also, the amount of resources set aside for the renewal of equipment (i.e. apart from deepening or widening) will not differ simply because the nationality of the worker has changed.   These work places, moreover,   have a generally low capital endowment (i.e. cleaners, auxiliary workers, etc.).   The fact that indigenous workers tend to move out of low paid/low productivity jobs into high wage/high productivity jobs does in itself constitute a gain of productivity.

113. Sooner or later the manufacturing sector will be drawn into this process.[127]   Here, too, indigenous workers begin to leave socially undesir- able jobs and move either into high wage sectors or out of manufacturing altogether.   The same happens with school-leavers who begin to shun even high wage and/or expanding industries in preference for the social status of service employment.   Consequently, the existing (highly productive!) capital stock could not be used fully and growth potential of the economy would have to be wasted if foreign workers could not be engaged instead. Initially this process may hit the low wage manufacturing branches hardest - and it may well lead to the first instances of immigrant-induced new invest- ment on the pattern Cohen and Jenner described.   Gradually it will affect all branches, whether high wage or low wage, growing or declining in employ- ment.   Natural wastage, net out-movements to the service sector and dis- proportionately low numbers of indigenous new entrants cannot be recovered by productivity under conditions of high demand and therefore require the immigration of foreigners.   While the bulk of the immigration may still be of the vacation-replacement type which does not entail new capital expenditure, the rest becomes increasingly involved with the ongoing expenditure of capital in manufacturing - not necessarily with capital widening, but with a capital stock which is fast developing and which would be underutilized if it failed to attract enough workers.

114. In the final stages of the self-feeding process the employment of foreigners in vacated work places is accompanied by the employment of foreigners in work places necessary for the satisfaction of immigrant- induced demand.   The latter certainly causes new capital expenditure, though there is no a priori way of knowing the incidence of capital widening vs. capital deepening.   But what is equally certain is that if immigration were curtailed, the given highly productive capital stock could not be worked economically, which would mean a corresponding loss of wealth. Surely, it is putting the cart before the horse under these conditions

---

[127] Cf. above p. 11 et seq.

to speak of the capital requirements of immigrants.[128] Rather one should
speak of the labour requirements of capital.

115. In looking for empirical evidence one is first attracted by the
example of Switzerland where the problem has been most hotly disputed.
The OECD Economic Survey of 1967 states: "The years of a sharply accelerated rise in employment (1961 to 1963) saw a significant fall of productivity
advances, and, conversely, the period of virtual stable labour input (1964-
1966) an even more pronounced upturn . . .   The repercussions of the less
ample labour supply on productivity have been particularly important in the
industrial sector, which had most heavily drawn on foreign labour during
the early sixties . . .   Given the virtually unchanged wage trend,
the accelerated rise in labour productivity has been associated with an
improvement of the cost position of the Swiss economy . . .   While the
favourable repercussions of the new foreign labour regulations on labour
productivity and costs can hardly be disputed, it is by no means certain
whether the overall domestic output/demand balance has also been favourably
influenced . . .   On the production side there is, however, little doubt
that, despite increased labour saving investments and the more economical
use of available manpower resources, the growth potential of the Swiss
economy has been reduced, notably after the initial benefits from the
adaptation period had been passed.   On the demand side, the expansion of
total private consumption has been curbed because of the stabilization of
employment and the weaker growth of total population which should also
have produced a dampening effect on housing demand and certain types of
infra-structural and productive investments . . . It would be difficult
to explain the sharp weakening of the propensity to invest without
relating it somehow to the changed labour supply situation."   Whether
this allows one to reason a contrario that it was the labour import which
led to an uneconomical use of labour resources is, in our opinion, a
different question.   Manufacturing has from time to time undergone a
"shake-out" of labour in situations where availability of labour, foreign
or otherwise, played no role.   And in Switzerland the unchanged wage
growth after the curtailment of immigration would seem to indicate that
the mismanagement of labour resources was not primarily related to the
easy availability of foreign labour.[129]   What is indisputable, however,
is the fact that Switzerland's growth of wealth received a severe and
more than temporary setback, in absolute if not per capita terms.[130]

---

128 Cf. E.J. Mishan and L. Needleman (1966a),(1966b), and H.-J. Rüstow (1965),
     (1966), who assume that all immigrants require capital expenditure and
     that all of this will be new investment.   The calculations by Mishan
     and Needleman lead them to conclude, "if there is so much spare capacity
     in the economy that less than one-tenth of immigrant capital needs has
     to be met from new investment, then from the first year of the inflow
     there is primary excess supply."   (1966b) p.43.   Our estimate would
     put the cushion of spare capacity at about 50%.   Shift work, for
     example, is a form of spare capacity embodied in existing capital.
     The correspondence between the regional distribution of spare capacity
     and immigration is assured by the entry procedure and well reflected in
     the concentration of immigrants in the industrial conurbations.

129 D. Maillat (1972b), p.22, reports that labour costs had not decreased
     relative to capital during the period of unrestricted immigration,
     1950-1963.   In other words, labour import did not lessen the incentive
     to substitute capital for labour.

130 Cf. ibid., p.3.

116.   In the case of France[131] the indigenous employees increased by 5.5%
in the secondary sector and by 21.0% in the service sector during the inter-
census period 1962-1968 (foreign employees = 28.8% and 23.2%, respectively).
During this period 468,000 new work places in the still expanding secondary
sector were filled by Frenchmen and 1,400,000 in the growing tertiary sector
(foreign workers = 195,000 and 61,000 respectively).   Of the total of
256,000 additional work places filled with foreigners, 9,000 relate to
textiles and clothing, two sectors where overall employment declined while
foreign employment still increased - the sort of situation which would
suggest that in France, too, foreign immigration may well have induced new
capital investments here.[132]   Another 13,000 of the additional jobs were
in domestic services, where the total employment figure for foreign and
French workers declined in absolute terms.   Immigrants for those 256,000
new jobs could have been imported from abroad or have left the declining
branches of the secondary and tertiary sector (extractive industries,
metal production, public administration and domestic services).   The net
increase of foreigners in the secondary and tertiary sector amounted to
231,000.   9,000 of these are attributable to the out-movement from the
primary sector, leaving 222,000 to derive from immigration and a maximum
of 34,000 from intra-sectoral shifts (256,000-222,000), always assuming
that the natural increase of the immigrant population, changes in labour
force participation and changes from seasonal or frontier status to
permanent status are negligible.   During the period 1962-1967/8[133] France
admitted 693,000 foreigners for the secondary and tertiary sector.   As
figures on net migration are not available, we assume that half of these,
i.e. 347,000 were net immigrants.[134]   The other 347,000 entrants were
therefore engaged to replace returning foreigners on existing work places.
(If the average length of stay is 3 years, almost one fifth of the foreign
work force will have to be replaced every year assuming their work places
are not abolished or filled by indigenous labour.)   Relating the flow
figures of 222,000 new jobs to the net inflow of 347,000 net immigrants
indicates that 64% of the net immigrants were placed on new work places
(36% on existing work places).   Subtracting the domestic service jobs
(13,000) and new entrants (79,000), respectively, raises the proportion
slightly to 68% (assuming that no intra-sectoral movements from declining
industries into the additional domestic service jobs have taken place).
Conversely, if one takes into account the total immigration stream, i.e.
including foreigners newly entering the primary sector and the net out-
movement there of 9,000 workers, the percentage falls to 57%.   Eliminating
domestic services here raises it again to 60%.   Thus, in the French situation of still expanding industrial employment, at most two in three of the
net immigrants (or one in three of the gross migrants) are associated with
new capital expenditure - though there is no way of knowing whether this is
related to capital deepening or capital widening.   The other third of the
net immigration is of the vacation-replacement type (while half the gross
inflow fills the gap left by returning foreigners).   If the share of net
immigration in total immigration had been greater, the proportion of net

---

131
The following calculations are based on the "Dossier sur l'Immigration"
prepared by M. Vidal and M. Sallois for the 6th French Economic and
Social Plan, and on Annuaire Statistique de la France.

132
Cf. footnote 33 above.

133
The census date and immigration periods are not completely congruent
but the bias is the same in 1962 and 1968 and should not result in
significant distortions.

134
A. de la Presle (1971), p.17, suggests that half of all immigrants to
France settle there.

immigrants associated with capital expenditure would have been lower.
For instance, if all 693,000 new entrants had been net entrants[135], the ratio
of new jobs to new immigrants would have been one in three.   These
quantities would need to be examined further with reference to such questions as how many of the new work places were in bottleneck situations and
how many have been associated with new machinery in order to evaluate fully
the contribution of immigrant labour to France's growth.

117. In the case of Germany, table 4 suggests that there is no consistent
relationship between net immigration and capital widening/deepening except
perhaps for the end of the sixties when speculative money deluged Germany.
The earlier peaks in demand for goods around 1959/60 and 1964/65 had also
induced a slightly greater tendency towards capital widening.[136]   Generally[137],
however, the whole period was characterised by increased capital intensity
and a high and slightly increasing level of productivity growth,[138]   which
fully supports our reasoning.

Table 4:   Investment intentions of German employers and net immigration of
foreign workers, 1956-1970.

	Net immigr. of foreign workers	Foreign share of increase in employees	Manufacturing (excl. constr.)			Capital goods industry			Consumer goods (excl. food).		
			Deepen	Widen	Replace	Deepen	Widen	Replace	Deepen	Widen	Replace
	'000	%	%			%			%		
1956	11	4	44	35	21	42	38	20	52	22	26
1957	19	3	50	33	17	56	31	13	64	21	15
1958	28	10	54	28	18	56	31	11	66	14	20
1959	71	9	54	32	14	44	45	9	64	23	13
1960	148	39	49	39	12	41	49	10	66	23	11
1961	149	67	50	40	10	42	49	9	65	25	10
1962	165	82	55	36	9	52	39	9	65	25	10
1963	106	53	54	35	11	58	31	11	66	22	12
1964	182	13	53	36	11	55	35	10	58	27	15
1965	190	83	47	40	13	41	40	19	60	33	7
1966	-15	(100)	51	37	12	47	41	12	56	31	13
1967	-198	(-29)	57	27	16	68	16	16	62	23	15
1968	201	134	49	25	16	50	34	16	50	33	17
1969	434	74	37	53	10	25	63	12	50	41	9
1970	400	78	34	55	11	22	66	12	37	53	10

Source: Ifo-Institut für Wirtschaftsforschung, and own computations.

---

[135] The French experience of 38,500 net immigrants p.a. associated with capital
expenditure points towards an absorption of 0.1% of capacity, whereas
E.J. Mishan and L. Needleman (1966b), pp.40 and 43, assume the equivalent
of 1% of the existing capital stock.

[136] See also K.-H. Hornhues (1970), p.138-9.   His results for the 1960-65
period point to the prevalence of a vacation-replacement process, see ibid.
p.135.   In aggregate terms this can also be deduced from the fact that
the total labour force worked as many working hours at the beginning of the
migration as after maturation, see H. Salowsky (1971), p.29.

[137] Cf. K.-H. Hornhues (1970), p.137.

[138] Cf. OECD "The Growth of Output" (1970), p. 35 e t seq.

(e)   Social Capital Requirements

118. Net immigrants entail demands on social capital - housing, health
and social welfare services, education and training, water and energy
supply, waste disposal, communications, leisure facilities, administrative
services, and so on.   This is not to say, however, that net immigrants
"cause" demands on social resources - for they also contribute to their
financing, and polyannual immigrant populations actually tend to contribute more than the average indigenous person.[139]   Moreover, because of
the personal characteristics of target workers they are likely to place
a proportionately lower demand on social capital.   The net result is
that the receiving country's fiscal strength is enhanced enormously.
This can best be exemplified by reference to the various stages of
maturity.

119. In the first stage of a polyannual immigration stream, young, healthy
and predominantly single workers make scarcely any demands on social capital
except perhaps in the field of housing.   Where employers have traditionally
looked after their workers, as in agriculture or domestic service, there
will be no immigrant-induced demand for housing whatsoever, and the same
holds true when employers generally are obliged to provide housing for
target workers (as is the case for officially recruited workers in France,
Germany, and the Netherlands).

120. In the second stage of maturity the swelling numbers of immigrants
are beginning to make themselves felt on the private housing market,[140]
even in countries where employer-provided-accommodation is the norm.
Here, more and more immigrants, especially those who want their families[141]
to join them, leave employer-provided-accommodation for personal reasons
or after changing jobs.   Immigrants who are not subject to the official
procedure land of course straight on the private housing market.   The
fact that unaccompanied married workers have joined the migration stream
does not alter the almost unnoticeable effects associated with single
worker migration.   Both kinds of target workers are originally inclined
to live at near subsistence level in order to save money and neither
causes any significant repercussions in welfare services, etc.   On the
housing market they filter through into areas where (a) there is a
certain amount of spare capacity and (b) where they perceive relatively
low monetary and social costs, which generally means that they filter
through to the decaying inner areas of cities and towns or to the out-
lying bidonvilles.

121. With the onset of the third stage of maturity the picture changes
noticeably.   The foreign work force is still growing and wives and
children and sometimes other dependants join the breadwinner. The impact
on the housing market is immediate, although in many cases the strain on
resources is more apparent than real and softened by the high absorptive
capacity of the existing stock.   The impact is more apparent than real
because one finds on the housing market the same type of vacation-
replacement process as on the labour market.   With the increasing
standard of living the native population tends to move out of the decaying

---

[139] See footnote 85 above.

[140] They are usually barred from public housing on account of either
institutional discrimination or because waiting lists extend over a
longer period than their duration of immigration.   As the latter
lengthens, more immigrants become eligible for public housing if
they are not discriminated against on grounds of nationality.

[141] Cf. W.R. Böhning (1970a), p.32, for Germany.

inner cities into the suburbs, leaving behind the old and the infirm and the spare capacity of which immigrants are only too glad to avail themselves.[142]

122. Since the third stage all the consequential services - water, leisure, waste disposal, communications and administration - come under additional strain and often require additional labour input. But most important, health and social welfare services as well as child care and educational facilities are now affected and need to make room for immigrants. A few sentences may exemplify the size of the problem.

123. Health and social welfare services first. The favourable age structure of polyannual migration streams assures that few immigrants need to be cared for in costly geriatric hospitals or other institutions for old people. The other side of the coin is that a comparatively strong demand on maternity services develops, although even here the immigrant-induced demand may be below that of the indigenous work force because of the large portion of married immigrants who leave their spouses behind. Adjustment problems of (both internal and international) migrants are sometimes said to raise the incidence of mental illnesses, but the evidence is far from clear. Illnesses occuring in certain sending

---

[142] K. Jones and A.D. Smith (1970) write in their detailed study of the British situation : "The most relevant development in the housing market was the settlement of New Commonwealth immigrants in the older housing stock, near urban centres, vacated by indigenous residents or earlier immigrant groups as they moved to more modern housing in the suburbs. If no New Commonwealth immigrants had appeared to occupy this old housing stock, one of two things would have happened : either the indigenous population would have remained in these old houses, or it could have behaved as it did and left. In the former case, movement to the suburbs and the demand for new housing would have been substantially lower, consequently indigenous residents would not have enjoyed such a large improvement in their housing standards, but there would have been less, potentially inflationary, investment in housing. In the latter, the old housing stock would have been scrapped, and an additional demand created for new houses. Doubtless, in the absence of immigration, the actual reaction of the indigenous population would have taken a middle course, implying rather less new housing demand than in fact appeared - and, paradoxically, a smaller all round improvement in housing conditions than that which actually occurred - but a higher rate of slum clearance. There are reasons, however, for supposing that the second of the two alternatives would have been the more important, and that most of the movement from slums to suburbs would have occurred in any case". (p.115) "Government housing policy has been directed towards slum clearance partly to improve housing standards by means of resettlement in better accommodation and partly to liberate space which, being near town centres, it is thought could be made to serve the economy more fruitfully. This policy has been substantially retarded by the arrival of new immigrants . . . The capital cost of the new arrivals in terms of old, unwanted, bricks and mortar may well have been minimal; but in terms of land usage, an opportunity-cost which seems to have been generally overlooked, it may well have been substantial." (p.117) And: "There is no evidence, however, that in setting their (housing) targets the governments of the day were particularly influenced by the number of new households expected to be formed, with or without account being taken of immigration . . . In the past, therefore, the level of immigration and its effect on the size of the population and new household formation can have had little influence on the size of the housing programme, which has been largely determined by political considerations or by limited resources". (p.116)

countries may not always be detected by medical checks upon entry, but individual illnesses rarely acquire group proportions. In the receiving country the initial unfamiliarity with industrial work affects the average accident rates, but with increasing experience and given the favourable age structure of immigrant workers the average incidence of accidents is not likely to be higher than among indigenous workers.[143] In toto, then, the preponderance of young and able-bodied immigrants assures that "in spite of special factors, immigrants' demands on health and welfare services have been lower than the national average. It seems likely that this effect will be a fairly long-lasting one."[144] The same holds true for social security benefits in the narrow sense. For example, greater family size may entail relatively greater family allowances where there is no institutional discrimination,[145] but the fact that there are always large numbers of married immigrants who leave their children behind more than compensates for this in average per capita terms. And even though comparatively greater numbers of immigrant workers may receive unemployment benefits during times of recession, provided there is no institutional discrimination and assuming export of unemployment to be negligible, the net contributions to retirement, widow and health pensions more than redress the balance. "Benefits are some ten times as great for the old as for the rest of the population . . . So for the whole immigrant population the average benefit per head in 1961 was only some 60 per cent of that for the total population, falling to 56 per cent in 1966. In 1981 it would be some 62 per cent on the assumption of no further net immigration; but, assuming immigration continues, the average benefit would then still be only 56 per cent of that for the total population."[146]

124. With regard to child care and educational facilities the balance is more even - though only if one disregards the enormous savings accruing to the receiving country through the immigration of people it did not have to school. First generation immigrants from different ethnic backgrounds and particularly their children require special teaching in the language of the host country. Here greater family size magnifies the problems. Similarly, the high degree of economic activity among target workers means that foreign women may induce relatively more demand for child care facilities than indigenous women. On the other hand, the subproletarian existence excludes immigrants from a proportionate participation in the highly expensive sector of higher education.[147] So, when K. Jones and A.D. Smith conclude that outside the sector of higher education the overall cost of education per head of the population was 7% higher for immigrant families in 1961 and 37% in 1966 than for indigenous British families,[148] the figures need to be scaled down drastically in order to arrive at a true overall evaluation.

---

[143] See U. Mehrländer (1969), p.54 et seq., and H. Salowsky (1972), p.30 et seq., also generally S. Bullinger et al. (1972), p.209 et seq.

[144] K. Jones and A.D. Smith (1970), p.101; see also ibid., p.118 for hospital usage in Britain.

[145] Cf. U. Mehrländer (1969), p.85, and H. Salowsky (1972), p.45 et seq., for Germany.

[146] K. Jones and A.D. Smith (1970), pp.104-5.

[147] Cf. W.R. Böhning (1972c), pp.23-4.

[148] K. Jones and A.D. Smith (1970), p.103; but see also ibid., p.120.

125. The exact weight of the various factors does of course depend on the composition of the immigration stream.   As a rule of thumb we would suggest that in the third stage of maturity **two thirds of newly entering target workers** consist of married workers, at least half of whom will sooner or later be joined by their spouses and children.[149]   About nine out of ten of these will finally turn into permanent settlers.[150]   Estimating further that about one in ten of both single workers and unaccompanied workers are likely to settle in the receiving country, gives a total permanent immigration in the region of **two fifths of the inflow.** While the external turnover certainly adds undemanding new migrants to the foreign work force, the replacement of old migrants by new migrants ("rotation") effectively by passes the united families.   Rotation principally affects single and unaccompanied workers!

126. Governments are well aware of the extremely favourable effects associated with the first two stages of maturity.   These are represented during the third stage by the two groups of single and unaccompanied foreign workers.   Normal external turnover gives these two groups a combined weight of up to two thirds of the foreign work force.   Governments are apt to understate the extent of the permanent settlement and of the immediate capital needs of immigrants because, on the one hand, they are unwilling to admit that "rotation" tends to be confined to single and unaccompanied workers and, on the other hand, because they are loath to take measures to improve the lot of the "foreigner" for fear of arousing political hostility in the electorate.   In their desire not to forfeit the economic advantages of polyannual immigration, governments also tend to rely tacitly on the high elasticity of the absorptive capacity of infrastructure.   (Infrastructure is generally designed or able to accommodate future needs.   You can, for instance, squeeze more people in a house or school or hospital than originally designed - whereas you cannot squeeze more people into a given work place.)   The combination of objectively lower requirements by immigrants in a situation of high absorptive capacity of the existing infrastructure and disinclination to incur the wrath of the electorate means that governments are likely to spend very little of their additional income on the people from whom they obtained it in disproportionate amounts.[151] Moreover, any spending which is undertaken is likely to be spread over a number of years.[152]   The receiving country's finances are, therefore, greatly strengthened by contemporary target worker migration.   The more a country is willing and able to enforce its original Konjunkturpuffer approach, the stronger this favourable effect.   Conversely, the more a country is inclined to

---

149
    Cf. above p.21-2, and W.R. Böhning (1972), table 4-3 p.65.

150 Cf. above **footnote 48.**

151 See **footnote 85 above for immigrant-derived income.**

152 See also P.H. Karmel (1953), p.89, K. Jones and A.D. Smith (1970), p.107-8, and D. Collard (1970), p.75.   Mishan and Needleman, Rüstow and others generally proceed from the assumption that indigenous and foreign social capital needs are the same and will all have to be met by new investment within a year or two of arrival.   In German political circles it has long been maintained that the infrastructural demands of foreigners are below those of the indigenous population; see e.g. Deutscher Bundestag (1967), p.4; W. Steinjan (1966), p.12; also U. Mehrländer (1969), p.126; C. Rosenmöller (1970), p.233; and S. Bullinger et al. (1972), p.168.

integrate its immigrant population[153] and to guide rather than follow electoral opinion, the more of the favourable effect will dissipate in the field of social capital.

127. The alternative scenario, however, of a closed labour market where indigenous migrants have to satisfy the mobility requirements of the economy is unlikely to appeal to the receiving country. This would tend to induce much greater social capital outlays without a commensurate increase in receipts. The indigenous worker is "likely to expect a far better standard of social capital and this is likely to be met much more swiftly than with the immigrant."[154]

128. Albeit that the effective requirements of the total immigrant population are markedly lower in average per capita terms than those of the indigenous population - even in the case of united families as long as their low dependency ratio, their relative youth and health distinguishes them favourably - the repercussions are still extensive in terms of the absolute amount of induced demand for labour. This is particularly noticeable because the areas affected - housing, education, administration, etc. - are highly labour intensive.[155] The Dutch study referred to earlier suggested that infrastructural services to immigrant families commensurate with those expended for an average Dutch family would turn the desired satisfaction of labour demand into an additional demand in the region of one quarter of the original demand.[156] The fact that Western European governments do not measure up to such exacting standards should not blind one to the fact that the immigrant-induced infrastructural repercussions make the satisfaction of labour demand with family immigration a vain goal.

---

[153] The problem poses itself more dramatically in certain local situations than on a macro-economic scale because of the tendency of immigrant populations to be concentrated in the decaying inner cities or outer bidonvilles of the great conurbations.

[154] P. Jenner (1966), p.166.

[155] Cf. the study on immigrant-induced/satisfied demand of Swiss housing by W. Schultheiss (1966).

[156] Cf. Centraal Planbureau (1972), pp.23-5.

IV   CONCLUSION

129. On balance the receiving country draws a considerable benefit from the employment of target workers.   Only the most marginal groups of indigenous workers would be negatively affected in the somewhat unlikely case of a prolonged recession.   Potentially, however, the dependence upon the continued availability of foreign labour constitutes an important disadvantage.

130. Essentially the benefits of labour import derive from its external turnover.   As far as the labour market and production are concerned this imparts an element of flexibility which permits smoother adaptations to the vagaries of the economic development.   As far as social capital is concerned, this assures that the effective requirements of immigrants remain below those of comparable indigenous populations with consequential beneficial effects on the state's finances.   The higher the degree of external turnover and the lower the degree of settlement, the more pronounced are the beneficial effects.[157]

131. Target worker migrations do, however, mature into settlement immigrations. In matured migrations the human and social needs of immigrants tend to be correlated inversely with their economic profitability, although this need not be the case for each single measure.

132. Reviewing the issues discussed under narrowly economic criteria it can be summarised, firstly, that while full employment or unemployment are not subject to a beneficial or detrimental effect as such, the indigenous work force undergoes an upgrading process which in average terms leads to higher pay and lower unemployment, although the competitive situation of marginal indigenous workers may be worsened during times of recession.

133. Secondly, matured migrations play a small role relative to other determinants of wage growth and income distribution.   Basically this role takes some of the steam out of the wage pressure and cost-push inflation.   The aggregate effect is probably compensated in absolute terms by feedback effects in the third stage of maturity, but effectively it is still at work because an end of immigration would immediately send up wages and prices.   This situation permits a less inhibited and therefore faster growth of the economy and wages.   Before long real per capita wages will rise faster than they would in the absence of immigration.   On the other hand, labour import is regressive in relative terms even under maturity, although this effect can only be infinitesimal relative to other determinants of income distribution.   As in the case of wages, this does not matter in absolute terms because the wealth to be distributed has grown faster than it would without immigration.

134. Thirdly, the spreading of the foreign work force into consumer goods industries in particular and manufacturing in general significantly counters demand-push inflation, even where consumer goods employment does not fully reach average levels.   This derives from the immigrants' low dependency ratio and high savings ratio.   In terms of international competitiveness it induces a positive movement in the terms of trade.   But here, too, there are feedback effects through remittances returning as consumer demand.   The net deflationary

---

[157] See also Appendix below.

impact on the balance of payments by remittances is certainly
smaller than the gross outflow of currency and probably much
smaller than generally assumed.   In the private sector, the
receiving country's export industries probably derive the greatest benefit from labour import.   For not only do they enjoy a
continuous comparative advantage but they are also provided
with greater markets.   It would not be too far from the truth
to say that parts of the export sector import both raw material
and labour, export the finished product to the countries of
origin and keep the profits to themselves.   It is here that   :
the export of capital as an alternative to labour import - in
effect, as an alternative to widening the gap between the "haves"
and the "have-nots" - appears intuitively imperative.

135. Fourthly, the preceding conclusion is reinforced by an examination of
labour productivity under conditions of labour import compared
with the likely development in its absence.   In short, labour
import enables greater productivity gains to be made than an
unrealistic switch to even more capital deepening.   Equally
important is the fact that the structural causes of the immigration in the receiving country would entail an underutilization
of the highly productive capital in the industrial sector were
it not for the availability of target workers.

136. Fifthly, in average per capita terms the social capital requirements
of matured immigration streams tend to be markedly lower than
those of a corresponding indigenous population while the income
derived from immigrants tends to be higher.   Seen in conjunction
with the fact that immigrant needs are likely to be scaled down
by xenophobia and spread over a number of years in situations
of high elasticity of absorption in the existing capacity, this
enables the receiving country to amass greater means for the
distribution of wealth and the erection of new infrastructure
than would otherwise be the case.

137. In summary it could be said that polyannual migration streams with external
turnover permit a smooth running of the economy at high growth rates and
that they contribute more to the supply of goods and services than to their
demand.   Consequently they bring about a greater growth of wealth in real
per capita terms.

138. A look into the future suggests that the potential for employment of
target workers is far from exhausted in contemporary post-industrial societies.
The secondary sector, which is still growing in some countries due to overall
population growth albeit that in relative terms it has reached its peak, is
unlikely to loose its unfavourable image relative to white-collar employment.
Thus, the whole of the manual work force in the whole of the secondary sector
is potentially an area of employment for foreigners and the absolute numbers
of foreign workers may grow there for many years to come.   While the service
sector may approach a threshold of immigrant absorption in some countries
due to language problems and other social factors, the absolute number of
foreigners there will grow as long as white-collar employment itself grows.
Furthermore, second generation immigrants coming from settled foreign families
are not subject to the same limitations as their parents and are therefore
likely to attempt to push into a wider area of service employment.   Even
discounting this, it is clear that the economics of polyannual immigration
streams do not put an end to the further increase of foreign workers in the
foreseeable future.

V   APPENDIX

139. The additional flexibility imparted to the labour market and production process by labour import can be assessed in a generalised way by comparing the potential inter-generational flexibility of the national labour force with the potential flexibility deriving from a foreign labour force under varying degrees of external turnover, whereby external turnover is defined as the sum of the rate of entry and the rate of return.

140. For simplicity's sake a stationary national labour force is envisaged with a constant degree of intra-generational mobility (i.e. occupational/ industrial/regional mobility and movements in and out of the labour force). A working life is counted as 40 years on average.

141. During one year this labour force could enjoy a maximum additional mobility ("flexibility") of 5% if all the jobs which are vacated by nationals leaving the labour market ($\frac{1}{40}$ = 2.5%) were abolished and if all newly entering nationals ($\frac{1}{40}$ = 2.5%) were employed on new work places.   This 5% flexibility potential would decrease to 2.5% if only half of the vacated jobs were abolished (and half of the new entrants were employed on the remaining vacancies) or to 0.5% if only 10% of the vacated jobs were abolished (and 90% of the new entrants were employed on the remaining vacancies).   In other words, the maximum inter-generational flexibility potential of the native labour force amounts to 5% p.a. and decreases proportionately with the extent of flexibility which is not realised.

142. This can be compared with the potential and the actual flexibility effect deriving from a foreign work force of a given proportion of the total work force under varying rates of external turnover.   For example, if the share of the foreign in the total work force were 5% and if with a return rate of 50% and a rate of new entrants of 50% exactly half of the foreign force were exchanged, the maximum flexibility potential accruing to the labour force as a whole would amount to 5% p.a. if all the jobs which are vacated by foreigners leaving the country of employment (50%, or 2.5% of the total work force) were abolished and if all newly entering foreigners (50%, or 2.5% of the total work force) were employed on new work places, i.e. newly erected work places or work places previously filled by indigenous workers who are undergoing some form of intra-generational mobility other than withdrawal.   The following tables (case a, b and c) illustrate this potential effect for different sizes of the foreign work force and for differing situations.   Case a refers to a situation of complete exchange under hypothetical rates of external turnover (as in the foregoing example). Case b shows the situation under a constant rate of return which might be assumed to obtain in the third and fourth stage of maturity under normal demand conditions.   Case c refers to a situation of net immigration in the region of 50% of gross immigration.   With the foreign work force standing at 10% of the total and a return rate of just over one fifth, the maximum flexibility potential due to the import of labour is considerably higher (6.5%) than the one deriving from inter-generational mobility of the indigenous population (5%).

143. For net immigration we can also introduce some more realistic assumptions on the degree to which vacated work places are abolished.   Case d is comparable to the above second alternative of actual inter-generational flexibility in that only 10% of the vacated work places are abolished.   The table for case d shows that the realized flexibility decreases strongly compared with cases a, b and c (the results for a, b and c are the same in each column as only the composition of the external turnover has been varied but not its extent).   Finally, because of the specific structural determinants of the employment of foreign workers we cannot attribute to the whole of inflow which is not used for filling the gaps left by returning foreigners a flexibility effect.   Some part of it will be directed to work places

vacated by the indigenous population.   Case e assumes that one third of
the gross inflow or two thirds of the net inflow (given a rate of net
immigration of 50%) may be attributed with a flexibility effect.[158]   One
third of the net inflow therefore goes to filling places vacated by
indigenous workers (its flexibility effect being nil if vacation is due
to withdrawal from the labour market).   Under these assumptions and given
a foreign work force of 10% of the total, an external turnover of 35%
would effect exactly twice the flexibility of inter-generational mobility
under similar assumptions.   Given the socio-demographic situation in
Europe's highly industrialised countries the real situation would seem
to lie somewhere between the cases d and e with perhaps a slightly lower
degree of net immigration (approx. 40%) and a rate of external turnover
in the region of 50%.   While at a given rate of return a rising degree
of net immigration increases the extent of external turnover correspon-
dingly, the additional flexibility is reduced by the extent to which
returning foreigners have to be replaced.

---

[158] Cf. the French example above p. 58-9.

Case a: Potential additional flexibility of total work force deriving from stationary foreign work force at varying rates of external turnover related to varying weights of the foreign work force

Share of foreigners in total employees	Category	External turnover					
		10%	20%	35%	50%	65%	80%
	enter	+5	+10	+17.5	+25	+32.5	+40
	return	-5	-10	-17.5	-25	-32.5	-40
5%	new	+0.25	+0.5	+0.88	+1.25	+1.63	+2.0
	old	-0.25	-0.5	-0.88	-1.25	-1.63	-2.0
	total	0.5%	1.0%	1.75%	2.5%	3.25%	4.0%
10%	new	+0.5	+1.0	+1.75	+2.5	+3.25	+4.0
	old	-0.5	-1.0	-1.75	-2.5	-3.25	-4.0
	total	1.0%	2.0%	3.5%	5.0%	6.5%	8.0%
15%	new	+0.75	+1.5	+2.63	+3.75	+4.89	+6.0
	old	-0.75	-1.5	-2.63	-3.75	-4.89	-6.0
	total	1.5%	3.0%	5.25%	7.5%	9.75%	12.0%
30%	new	+1.5	+3.0	+5.25	+7.5	+9.75	+12.0
	old	-1.5	-3.0	-5.25	-7.5	-9.75	-12.0
	total	3.0%	6.0%	10.5%	15.0%	19.5%	24.0%

"External turnover"	= rate of entry plus rate of return, disregarding sign
Rate of entry ("enter")	= new entrants as % of average size of foreign work force
Rate of return ("return")	= returnees as % of average size of foreign work force
"New"	= Work places not previously filled by foreigners (possibly newly formed work places)
Case a	assumes that all foreign new entrants will be employed on "new" work places
"Old"	= Work places vacated by returning foreigners
Case a	assumes that none of the work places vacated by foreigners will be filled by new immigrants
"Total"	= Maximum flexibility potential, i.e. "new" plus "old", disregarding sign
Single underlying	= Flexibility potential greater than that deriving from maximum intergenerational mobility.

Case b: Potential additional flexibility of total work force ~~deriving from changing foreign~~ work force with a constant rate of return of 20% at varying rates of external turnover related to varying weights of the foreign work force

Share of foreigners in total employees	Category	External turnover					
		10%	20%	35%	50%	65%	80%
	enter	–	–	+15	+30	+45	+60
	return	–	–20	–20	–20	–20	–20
5%	new	–	–	+0.75	+1.5	+2.25	+3.0
	old	–	–1.0	–1.0	–1.0	–1.0	–1.0
	total	–	1.0%	1.75%	2.5%	3.25%	4.0%
10%	new	–	–	+1.5	+3.0	+4.5	+6.0
	old	–	–2.0	–2.0	–2.0	–2.0	–2.0
	total	–	2.0%	3.5%	5.0%	6.5%	8.0%
15%	new	–	–	+2.25	+4.5	+6.75	+9.0
	old	–	–3.0	–3.0	–3.0	–3.0	–3.0
	total	–	3.0%	5.25%	7.5%	9.75%	12.0%
30%	new	–	–	+4.5	+9.0	+13.5	+18.0
	old	–	–6.0	–6.0	–6.0	–6.0	–6.0
	total	–	6.0%	10.5%	15.0%	19.5%	24.0%

For explanation of categories, see case a

Case b differs from case a only insofar as the rate of return has been fixed arbitrarily but plausibly at 20%. The rate of entry would have to be at least as high as the rate of return before a complete exchange (to the degree indicated by the fixed return rate) could take place. If the rate of entry is below 20%, the migration balance is negative. If the rate of entry is larger than 20%, net immigration occurs.

Case c: Potential additional flexibility of total work force deriving from constant net immigration of 50% of gross immigration at varying rates of external turnover related to varying weights of the foreign work force

Share of foreigners in total employees	Category	External turnover					
		10%	20%	35%	50%	65%	80%
	enter	+6.67	+13.33	+23.33	+33.33	+43.33	+53.33
	return	−3.33	−6.67	−11.67	−16.67	−21.67	−26.67
5%	new	+0.33	+0.67	+1.17	+1.67	+2.17	+2.67
	old	−0.17	−0.33	−0.58	−0.83	−1.08	−1.33
	total	0.5%	1.0%	1.75%	2.5%	3.25%	4.0%
10%	new	+0.67	+1.33	+2.33	+3.33	+4.33	+5.33
	old	−0.33	−0.67	−1.17	−1.67	−2.17	−2.67
	total	1.0%	2.0%	3.5%	5.0%	6.5%	8.0%
15%	new	+1.0	+2.0	+3.50	+5.0	+6.5	+8.0
	old	−0.5	−1.0	−1.75	−2.5	−3.25	−4.0
	total	1.5%	3.0%	5.25%	7.5%	9.75%	12.0%
30%	new	+2.0	+4.0	+7.0	+10.0	+13.0	+16.0
	old	−1.0	−2.0	−3.5	−5.0	−6.5	−8.0
	total	3.0%	6.0%	10.5%	15.0%	19.5%	24.0%

For explanation of categories, see case a

Case c differs from the preceding ones insofar as there are always twice as many new
        entrants as returnants, i.e. a rate of net immigration is fixed at 50% of the
        gross inflow. The rate of external turnover is, therefore, three times as large
        as the rate of return.

Case d: Potential additional flexibility of total work force deriving from constant net immigration of 50%, where 90% of the work places vacated by returning foreigners have to be filled from the gross inflow, at varying rates of external turnover related to varying weights of the foreign work force

Share of foreigners in total employees	Category	External turnover					
		10%	20%	35%	50%	65%	80%
	enter	+6.67	+13.33	+23.33	+33.33	+43.33	+53.33
	return	-3.33	-6.67	-11.67	-16.67	-21.67	-26.67
5%	new	+0.18	+0.37	+0.64	+0.92	+1.2	+1.47
	old	-0.02	-0.03	-0.06	-0.08	-0.11	-0.13
	total	0.2%	0.4%	0.7%	1.0%	1.3%	1.6%
10%	new	+0.37	+0.73	+1.28	+1.83	+2.38	+2.93
	old	-0.03	-0.06	-0.12	-0.17	-0.22	-0.27
	total	0.4%	0.8%	1.4%	2.0%	2.6%	3.2%
15%	new	+0.55	+1.1	+1.93	+2.75	+3.58	+4.4
	old	-0.05	-0.1	-0.18	-0.25	-0.33	-0.4
	total	0.6%	1.2%	2.1%	3.0%	3.9%	4.8%
30%	new	+1.1	+2.2	+3.85	+5.5	+7.15	+8.8
	old	-0.1	-0.2	-0.35	-0.5	-0.65	-0.8
	total	1.2%	2.4%	4.2%	6.0%	7.8%	9.6%

"External turnover"/"enter"/"return" = see case a

"Old" = A flexibility effect is attributed only to 10% of the work places vacated by returning foreigners, i.e. these are not filled by foreigners.

"New" = A flexibility effect is attributed to 55% of the gross inflow, which is available for employment on "new" work places. (For "new" cf. case a).

"Total" = The actual overall flexibility effect is in the region of -60% of the one calculated for cases a, b and c. (Cf. case a).

Single underlying = Flexibility effect greater than for 10% actual inter-generational mobility.

Double underlying = Flexibility potential greater than for 50% actual inter-generational mobility.

Case e: Potential additional flexibility of total work force deriving from constant net immigration of 50%,
where 90% of the work places vacated by returning foreigners have to be filled from the gross inflow
and where two thirds of the net inflow are directed to new work places, at varying rates of external
turnover related to varying weights of the foreign work force

Share of foreigners in total employees	Category	External turnover					
		10%	20%	35%	50%	65%	80%
	enter	+6.67	+13.33	+23.33	+33.33	+43.33	+53.33
	return	-3.33	-6.67	-11.67	-16.67	-21.67	-26.67
5%	new	+0.12	+0.25	+0.43	+0.61	+0.8	+0.98
	old	-0.02	-0.03	-0.06	-0.08	-0.11	-0.13
	total	0.1%	0.3%	0.5%	0.7%	0.9%	1.1%
10%	new	+0.25	+0.49	+0.85	+1.22	+1.59	+1.95
	old	-0.03	-0.06	-0.12	-0.17	-0.22	-0.27
	total	0.3%	0.6%	1.0%	1.4%	1.8%	2.2%
15%	new	+0.37	+0.73	+1.29	+1.83	+2.39	+2.93
	old	-0.05	-0.1	-0.18	-0.25	-0.33	-0.4
	total	0.4%	0.8%	1.5%	2.1%	2.7%	3.3%
30%	new	+0.73	+1.47	+2.57	+3.67	+4.77	+5.87
	old	-0.1	-0.2	-0.35	-0.5	-0.65	-0.8
	total	0.8%	1.7%	2.9%	4.2%	5.4%	6.7%

"External turnover"/"enter"/"return" = see case a

"Old" = see case d

"New" = A flexibility effect is attributed to 66% of the net inflow which is available for employment on newly established work places

"Total" = At the given rate of net immigration, the actual overall flexibility effect is in the region of 28% of the one calculated for cases a, b and c

Single underlining = Flexibility effect greater than for 10% actual inter-generational mobility

Double underlining = Flexibility effect greater than for 50% actual inter-generational mobility

VI BIBLIOGRAPHY

(References marked with an asterisk are not quoted in text)

AMTLICHE NACHRICHTEN   (various), ed. by Bundesanstalt für Arbeit (Nuremberg)

M. ALLEFRESDE (1969)   "Forms and Effects of Foreign Immigration in the Lyons Region", Report to the Manpower and Social Affairs Directorate (OECD: Paris, 21 July 1969)

S. BALKE (1966)   "Die Ausländerbeschäftigung aus der Sicht der Wirtschaft", in Magnet Bundesrepublik, Heft 42 Schriftenreihe der Bundesvereinigung der Deutschen Arbeitgeberverbände (Bonn: Köllen Verlag), pp.168- 82.

J. BARENTSZ (1972)   "Migration labour and employers", in H. van Houte and W. Melgert, eds., Foreigners in our Community (Amsterdam and Antwerp: Keesing, n.d. /1972/), pp.21-5.

S. BARKIN (1968)   "The economic costs and benefits and human gains and disadvantages of international migration", The Journal of Human Resources, Vol. 2, pp.495-516.

P. van BERKEL (1968)   "Structural Shifts and Job Preferences on an Overstrained Labour Market", Sociologia Neerlandica, Vol. 4, No.2, pp.119-36.

*R.A. BERRY and R. SOLIGO (1969)   "Some Welfare Aspects of International Migration", Journal of Political Economy, Vol.77 (September-October), pp.778-94.

W.R. BÖHNING (1970a)   "Foreign Workers in Post-war Germany", The New Atlantis, Vol. 2, No. 1, pp.12-38.

W.R. BÖHNING (1970b)   "The Differential Strength of Demand and Wage Factors in Intra-European Labour Mobility: With Special Reference to West Germany, 1957-1968", International Migration, Vol. VIII, No. 4, pp.193-202.

W.R. BÖHNING (1972a)   "The Social and Occupational Apprenticeship of Mediterranean Migrant Workers in West Germany", in M. Livi Bacci, ed., The Demographic and Social Pattern of Emigration from the Southern European Countries (Firenze: Dipartimento Statistico Matematico dell' Universita di Firenze and Comitato Italiano per lo Studio dei Problemi della Populazione), pp.175-259.

W.R. BÖHNING (1972b)   The Migration of Workers in the United Kingdom and the European Community (London: Oxford University Press for Institute of Race Relations).

W.R. BÖHNING (1972c)   "Problems of immigrant workers in West Germany", in N. Deakin, ed., Immigrants in Europe, Fabian research series, 306 (London: Fabian Society), pp.18-24.

R. BRAUN (1970),   Sozio-kulturelle Probleme der Eingliederung italienischer Arbeitskräfte in der Schweiz (Erlenbach-Zürich: Rentsch).

S. BULLINGER et al. (1972)   Die volkswirtschaftliche Bedeutung der Beschäftigung ausländischer Arbeitnehmer in Baden-Württemberg, Gutachten im Auftrag des Arbeits- und Sozialministeriums Baden-Württemberg (Tübingen: mimeographed).

BUNDESAMT . . . (1964)   Das Problem der ausländischen Arbeitskräfte, Bericht der Studien- kommission für das Problem der ausländischen Arbeitskräfte, ed. Bundesamt für Industrie, Gewerbe und Arbeit (Bern).

G. and S. CASTLES (1970)   "Immigrant Workers and Class Structure in France", Race, Vol. XII, No.3, pp.329-35.

*S. CASTLE (1972)   "Some general features of migration to Western Europe",
                                     New Community, Vol. 1, No. 3, pp.183-8.

Centraal Planbureau (1972)   Economische effecten voor Nederland van de werving van buitenlandse
                                     werknemers (s'Gravenhage: mimeographed) /used thanks to the
                                     unofficial translation by the OECD/

B.G. COHEN and P.J. JENNER (1968)   "The Employment of Immigrants: A Case Study within the Wool
                                     Industry", Race, Vol. X, No. 1, pp.41-56

D. COLLARD (1970)   "Immigration and Discrimination: Some Economic Aspects", in
                                     Economic Issues in Immigration, ed. by the Institute of Economic
                                     Affairs (London), pp.67-87.

*COMMISSION OF THE EUROPEAN   Preliminary guidelines for a social policy program in the Community,
COMMUNITIES (1971)   Supplement 2/71-Annex to the Bulletin of the European Communities
                                     4/1971 (Brussels).

*D.C. CORBETT (1958)   "Immigrants and Canada's Economic Expansion", International
                                     Labour Review, Vol. 77, pp.19-37.

*W.M. CORDEN (1955)   "The Economic Limits to Population Increase", Economic Record,
                                     No. 61, pp.242-60.

L.E. DAVIS (1971)   "Readying the Unready: Post-industrial Jobs", California Management
                                     Review, Vol. 13, No. 4, pp.27-36.

DEUTSCHER BUNDESTAG (1967)   "Einsatz von Gastarbeitern und Stabilität der Wirtschaft", Der
                                     Bundesminister für Wirtschaft, Drucksache V/1700 (Bonn, 2.Mai 1967)

P.B. DOERINGER and M.J. PIORE (1971) Internal Labor Markets and Manpower Analysis (Lexington, Mass.: Heath)

J.H. DULOY (1967)   "Structural Changes Due to Immigration: An Econometric Study",
                                     Australian Economic Papers, Vol.6 (December), pp.223-33.

*H. ERNST (1971)   "Hilfe für die deutsche Wirtschaft: Unser Arbeitsmarkt reicht nicht
                                     aus", Das Parlament, Vol. 21, No. 34-35, p.2.

EWG, SOZIALSTATISTIK (1969)   Struktur und Verteilung der Löhne 1966 - Deutschland (BR) (Luxemburg)

C. FÖHL (1967)   "Stabilisierung und Wachstum bei Einsatz von Gastarbeitern",
                                     Kyklos, Vol XX, pp.119-46.

A.H. GNEHM (1966)   Ausländische Arbeitskräfte: Vor- und Nachteile für die Volkswirtschaft
                                     (Bern und Stuttgart: Verlag Paul Haupt).

H.-M. HAGMANN (1971)   "Les pays d'immigration", in M. Livi-Bacci and H.-M. Hagmann, eds.,
                                     Report on the demographic and social pattern of migrants in Europe,
                                     especially with regard to international migrations (Strasbourg:
                                     Council of Europe, CDE(71)T.IV).

U. HARMS (1966)   "Wirtschaftliche Aspekte des Gastarbeiterproblems", Hamburger Jahrbuch
                                     für Wirtschafts- und Gesellschafts-politik, Vol. 11, pp.277-83.

R. HENTSCHEL et al. (1968)   "Die Integration der ausländischen Arbeitnehmer in Köln,
                                     Tabellenband", (Cologne: mimeographed).

D. HISS (1965)   "Hereinnahme von ausländischen Arbeitskräften - eine vernünftige
                                     Massnahme", Wirtschaftsdienst, Vol. 45, No. 12, pp.635-8.

P.J.A. ter HOEVEN (1964)   "Changing Patterns of Labour Market Behaviour", Sociologia Neerlandica,
                                     Vol. II, No. 1, pp.20-40.

119

K.-H. HORNHUES (1970)   "Die volkswirtschaftlichen Auswirkungen der Beschäftigung
ausländischer Arbeitskräfte vor allem hinsichtlich der Lohn-
und Preisentwicklung und des wirschaftlichen Wachstums unter
besonderer Berücksichtigung der Entwicklung in der Bundesrepublik Deutschland von 1955 bis 1966" (Münster: Dissertation)

P. JENNER (1966)   "Some Speculations on the Economics of Immigration" in
Immigration: Medical and Social Aspects, ed. by G.E.W. Wolstenholme
and M.O'Connor (London: Churchill), pp.112-8.

W.A. JÖHR and R. HUBER (1968-69)   "Die konjunkturellen Auswirkungen der Beanspruchung ausländischer
Arbeitskräfte: Untersuchungen mit Hilfe eines Simulationsmodelles
der schweizerischen Volkswirtschaft", Schweizerische Zeitschrift
für Volkswirtschaft und Statistik, Vol. 104, No. 4, pp. 365-610,
Vol. 105, No. 1, pp.3-92.

A.N.E. JOLLEY (1971)   "Immigration and Australia's Post-War Economic Growth", The Economic
Record, Vol.47, No. 117, pp.47-59.

K. JONES and A. SMITH (1970)   The Economic Impact of Commonwealth Immigration, (London: Cambridge
University Press for the National Institute of Economic and Social
Research).

G. KADE and G. SCHILLER (1972)   "Foreign Workers - Development Aid by LDCs?", Intereconomics, No. 1, pp.24-7.

K. KAISER (1971)   "Volkswirtschaftliche Aspekte der Beschäftigung ausländischer Arbeitnehmer",
in Gastarbeiter-Mitbürger, ed. by R. Leudesdorff and H. Zillessen
(Gelnhausen: Burckhardthaus-Verlag), pp.98-112.

P.H. KARMEL (1953)   "The Economic Effects of Immigration", in Australia and the Migrant,
ed. by H.E. Holt et al. (Sydney: Angus and Robertson), pp.82-103.

*B. KAYSER (1971)   Manpower Movements and Labour Markets, (Paris: OECD).

B. KAYSER (1972)   "Cyclically-determined homeward flows of migrant workers and the effects
of emigration", OECD, 1972.

TH. KELLER (1963)   "Volkswirtschaftliche Aspekte des Fremdarbeiterproblems", Aussenwirtschaft,
Vol. 18, No. 4, pp.341-57.

*C.P. KINDLEBERGER (1965)   "Emigration and Economic Growth", Banca Nazionale del Lavoro Quarterly
Review, Vol. XVIII, No. 74, pp.235-54.

C.P. Kindleberger (1967)   Europe's Postwar Growth: The Role of Labour Supply, (Cambridge, Mass.:
Harvard University Press).

J. KMENTA (1966)   "An Econometric Model of Australia, 1948-61", Australian Economic Papers,
Vol. 5 (December), pp.131-64.

F. KNESCHAUREK (1961)   "Entwicklungstendenzen auf dem europäischen Arbeitsmarkt", Aussenwirtschaft,
Vol. 16, pp.61-81.

A. KRUSE (1966)   "Der deutsche Arbeitsmarkt und die Gastarbeiter", Schmollers Jahrbuch,
Vol. 86, No. 4, pp.423-34.

LANDESHAUPTSTADT MÜNCHEN (1972)   Kommunalpolitische Aspekte des wachsenden ausländischen Bevölkerungsanteils
in München - Problemstudie, Arbeitsberichte zur Fortschreibung des
Stadtentwicklungsplans, No. 4 (n.p. /Munich/: mimeographed).

P. LANGE (1967)   "Die Förderung der freien Beweglichkeit der Arbeitskräfte durch
wirtschaftspolitische Massnahmen in der Europäischen Wirtschaftsgemeinschaft",
(Bochum: Dissertation).

V. LUTZ (1963) "Foreign Workers and Domestic Wage Levels, With an Illustration from the Swiss Case", Banca Nazionale del Lavoro Quarterly Review, Vol. XVI, No. 64, pp.3-68.

D. MAILLAT (1972a) "La structure des salaires et la representation des relations qui existent entre les differents salaires", private communication to OECD Working Party on Migration (31 January 1972).

D. MAILLAT (1972b) "The Case of Switzerland", Report to the Manpower and Social Affairs Directorate (Paris: OECD, 22 April 1972).

*D. Maillat (1972c) "Le cas de la Suisse", Report to the Manpower and Social Affairs Directorate (Paris: OECD, 21 March 1972).

MARPLAN (1970) Gastarbeiter in Deutschland - Ergebnisse zu Fragen der sozialen Situation (Frankfurt a.M.).

J. MARQUAND (1960) "Earnings-drift in the United Kingdom, 1948-1957", Oxford Economic Papers, Vol. 12, pp.77-104.

*A. MARSHALL (1972) "Labour Force Immigration in the Netherlands" (Rotterdam: Nederlandse Economische Hogeschool /mimeographed/) (Summary made available to OECD Manpower and Social Affairs Directorate).

MATERIALIEN AUS DER ARBEITSMARKT UND BERUFSFORSCHUNG (1970) "Die männlichen Hilfsarbeiter in der Bundesrepublik Deutschland", No. 15.

G. MATERNE (1970) "Vierzig Nationen polieren am weiss-blauen Image", Frankfurter Zeitung - Blick durch die Wirtschaft, 23.1.1970.

J.R. MCDONALD (1969) "Labor Immigration in France, 1946-1965", Annals of the Association of American Geographers, Vol. 59, No. 1, pp.116-34.

U. MEHRLÄNDER (1969) Beschäftigung ausländischer Arbeitnehmer in der Bundesrepublik Deutschland unter spezieller Berücksichtigung von Nordrhein-Westfalen (Cologne and Opladen: Westdeutscher Verlag).

V. MERX (1969) Der Beitrag ausländischer Arbeitskräfte zum Sozialprodukt, Gutachten erstellt im Auftrage des Ministers für Wirtschaft, Mittelstand und Verkehr des Landes Nordrhein-Westfalen (Institut für Wirtschaftspolitik an der Universität Köln: mimeographed).

V. MERX (1972) Struktur und Flexibilität des Arbeitsmarktes der Bundesrepublik Deutschland unter dem Einfluss der Beschäftigung ausländischer Arbeitnehmer, Gutachten erstellt im Auftrage des Bundesministeriums für Wirtschaft und Finanzen (Institut für Wirtschaftspolitik an der Universität Köln: mimeographed).

MINISTERE DU TRAVAIL, DE L'EMPLOI ET DE LA POPULATION (1971) M.P.1/332: Dossier sur l'immigration familiale pendant les annees 1960-1970

M.P.1/334: La situation matrimoniale et la structure familiale de la population etrangere recensee en mars 1968

M.P.1/335: Etude sur les sorties d'etrangers maries entre 1962 et 1968 en fonction du regroupement familial.

*M.P. MIRACLE and S.S. BERRY (1970) "Migrant Labour and Economic Development", Oxford Economic Papers, Vol. 22, No. 1, pp.86-108.

E.J. MISHAN and L. NEEDLEMAN (1966a) "Immigration, Excess Aggregate Demand and the Balance of Payments", Economica, Vol. 46, pp.129-47.

E.J. MISHAN and L. NEEDLEMAN (1966b) "Immigration: Some Economic Effects", Lloyds Bank Review, Vol. 81, pp.33-46

E.J. MISHAN and L. NEEDLEMAN (1968) "Immigration: Some Long Term Economic Consequences", Economia Internazionale, Vol. XXI, Nos. 2 and 3, pp.281-300 and 515-24.

E.J. MISHAN (1970) "Does Immigration Confer Economic Benefits on the Host Country ? in Economic Issues in Immigration, ed. by the Institute of Economic Affairs (London), pp.91-122.

M. NIKOLINAKOS (1971a) "Warum kommen die Gastarbeiter? Zur Sozialökonomie der Ausländerbeschäftigung", Frankfurter Zeitung - Blick durch die Wirtschaft, 21.1.1971.

M. NIKOLINAKOS (1971b) "Zur Frage der Auswanderungseffekte in den Emigrationsländern", Das Argument, Vol. 13, No. 9/10, pp.782-99.

A. NYDEGGER (1963) "Das Problem der ausländischen Arbeitskräfte im Rahmen der schweizerischen Konjunkturpolitik", Zeitschrift für Volkswirtschaft und Statistik, Vol. 99, No. 3, pp.321-32.

OECD (1970) The growth of output, 1960-1980: retrospect, prospect and problems of policy (Paris).

OECD Economic Surveys Switzerland, (Paris, December 1967)

C. PEACH (1965) "West Indian Migration to Britain: The Economic Factors", Race, Vol. 7, No. 1, pp.31-46.

*C. PEACH (1967) "West Indians as a Replacement Population in England and Wales", Social and Economic Studies, Vol. 16, No. 3, pp.289-94.

M. PESTON (1969) "Effects on the Economy", in Colour and Citizenship, ed. by E.J.B. Rose et al., (London: Oxford University Press for the Institute of Race Relations), pp.639-56.

M. PESTON (1971) "The Economics of Immigration", Race Today, Vol. 3, No. 3, pp.82-3.

D. PETERSEN (1970) "Welche Vorteile bringen uns die Gastarbeiter?", Frankfurter Zeitung - Blick durch die Wirtschaft, 17.12.1970.

P. van PRAAG (1971) "Aspects economiques a long terme des migrations internationales dans les pays de la C.E.E.", International Migration, Vol. IX, No. 3/4, pp.126-38.

A. de la PRESLE (1971) "Immigrant and minority groups in France", New Community, Vol. 1, No. 1, pp. 16-20.

M.W. REDER (1963) "The Economic Consequences of Increased Immigration", The Review of Economics and Statistics, Vol. XLV, No. 3, pp.221-30.

*C. RICHTER (1968) "Umfang, Grenzen und Auswirkungen der Beschäftigung ausländischer Arbeitskräfte in der Bundesrepublick Deutschland: Zur Frage der internationalen geographischen Mobilität des Produktionsfaktors Arbeit" (Mannheim: Dissertation).

C. ROSENMÖLLER (1970) "Volkswirtschaftliche Aspekte der Ausländerbeschäftigung", Bundesarbeitsblatt, Vol. 21, No. 4, pp.231-35.

H.-J. RÜSTOW (1965) "Gastarbeiter-Gewinn oder Belastung für unsere Volkswirtschaft?", Wirtschaftsdienst, Vol. 45, No. 12, pp.631-5.

H.-J. RÜSTOW (1966) "Gastarbeiter-Gewinn oder Belastung für unsere Volkswirtschaft?", in Probleme der ausländischen Arbeitskräfte in der Bundesrepublik, Beihefte zur Konjunkturpolitik, Heft 11 (Berlin: Duncker & Humblot), pp.35-48 (plus discussion).

*A. SABEL (1966) "Die arbeitsmarktpolitische Bedeutung der Beschäftigung ausländischer Arbeitnehmer", in Magnet Bundesrepublik, Heft 42, Schriftenreihe der Bundesvereinigung der Deutschen Arbeitgeberverbände (Bonn: Köllen Verlag), pp.159-67.

H. SALOWSKY (1971)   "Gesamtwirtschaftliche Aspekte der Ausländerbeschäftigung", Beiträge des Deutschen Industrieinstituts, Vol. 9, No. 10/11.

H. SALOWSKY (1972)   "Sozialpolitische Aspekte der Ausländerbeschäftigung", Berichte des Deutschen Industrie Instituts zur Sozialpolitik, Vol. 6, No. 2.

* F. SCHÄLLER (1972)   "Le role de la main-d'oeuvre etrangere dans l'economie suisse", Revue syndicale suisse, Vol. 64, No. 5, pp.145-61.

G. SCHILLER (1971)   Europäische Arbeitskräftemobilität und wirtschaftliche Entwicklung der Mittelmeerländer: Eine empirische Untersuchung über die Wirkungen der Gastarbeiterwanderungen auf die Abgabeländer (Darmstadt: J.G. Bläschke Verlag, n.d. /1971/).

G.C. SCHMID (1971)   "Foreign Workers and Labor Market Flexibility", Journal of Common Market Studies, Vol. IX, No. 3, pp.246-53.

*W. SCHOLTEN (1969)   "Die sektorale Beschäftigungsstruktur der ausländischen Arbeitnehmer verschiedener Herkunftsländer", in J. Chr. Papalekas, ed., Strukturfragen der Ausländerbeschäftigung (Herford: Maximilian-Verlag), pp.77-92.

W. SCHULTHEISS (1966)   "Die Beeinflussung des schweizerischen Wohnungsmarkts durch ausländische Arbeitnehmer", Schweizerische Zeitschrift für Volkswirtschaft und Statistik, Vol. 102, No. 1, pp.189-94.

*A. SCOTT (1971)   "Transatlantic and North American International Migration", in C.P. Kindleberger and A. Shonfield, eds., North American and Western European Economic Policies (London and Basingstoke: Macmillan), pp.425-51 .

*N. SCOTT (1967)   "Towards a framework for analysing the costs and benefits of Labour Migration", Bulletin of the International Institute for Labour Studies, No. 2, pp.48-63.

*J.J. SPENGLER (1958)   "Effects produced in receiving countries by pre-1939 immigration", in B. Thomas, ed., Economics of International Migration, Proceedings of a Conference held by the International Economic Association (London: Macmillan), pp.17-51.

W. STEINJAN (1966)   "Ausländische Arbeitnehmer in der Bundesrepublik", Beiträge des Deutschen Industrieinstituts, Vol. 4, No. 3.

*W. STEINJAN (1970)   "Beschäftigungskurve sollte allmählich abflachen – Ausländische Arbeitnehmer in Deutschland: Wirtschaftliche Bedeutung", Auslands-kurier, Vol. 11, No. 5, pp.6-7.

D. STEPHEN (1971)   "The social consequences", in D. Evans, ed., Destiny or Delusion: Britain and the Common Market (London: Gollancz), pp.122-38.

*I. SVENNILSON (1966)   "Swedish Long-term Planning – The Fifth Round", Skandinaviska Banken Quarterly Review, No. 2.

B. THOMAS (1968)   "Migration II: Economic Aspects", in International Encyclopaedia of the Social Sciences, Vol. 10, ed. by D.L. Shils (London & Glencoe) pp.292-300.

E. TUCHTFELDT (1965)   "Das Problem der ausländischen Arbeitskräfte in der Schweiz", Wirtschaftsdienst, Vol. 45, No. 12, pp.643-47.

U.N. Economic Commission for Europe (1964)   Some Factors in Economic Growth in Europe during the 1950s (Geneva).

*U.N. Economic Commission for Europe (1966)   The European Economy in 1965 (New York), Chapter II.

VOLKS- UND BERUFSZÄHLUNG VOM   ed. by Statistisches Bundesamt, Heft 7, <u>Ausländer</u> (Stuttgart and Mainz:
6. JUNI 1961   Kohlhammer).

H. WANDER (1971)   <u>Der Geburtenrückgang in Westeuropa wirtschaftlich gesehen</u>, Kieler
                                      Diskussionsbeiträge zu aktuellen wirtschaftspolitischen Fragen, No. 9
                                      (Kiel: Institut für Weltwirtschaft).

K. WIBORG (1971)   "VFW- Fokker würde nächstes Mal vieles anders machen", <u>Frankfurter
                                      Zeitung - Blick durch die Wirtschaft</u>, 11.2.1971.

W. WITTMANN (1962)   "Wachstums- und Konjunkturaspekte des Fremdarbeiterproblems", <u>Wirtschaft
                                      und Recht</u>, Vol. 14, pp.276-86.

E. ZIERIS (1971)   <u>Wohnverhältnisse von Familien ausländischer Arbeitnehmer in Nordrhein-
                                      Westfalen: Auswertung einer Erhebung des Ministeriums für Arbeit,
                                      Gesundheit und Soziales des Landes Nordrhein-Westfalen</u> (Düsseldorf:
                                      Kurt Dehl, n.d. /1971/).

THE ECONOMIC EFFECTS OF THE EMPLOYMENT

OF FOREIGN WORKERS: THE CASE OF SWITZERLAND

by

Denis Maillat,

Professor at the University of Neuchâtel

Preliminary remarks

There are many assumptions concerning the effects of immigration in host countries. Analysis usually covers the advantages and disadvantages of immigration(1). We did not wish to make an analysis of this type since we felt it would be more interesting to try and fit the phenomenon of immigration in with the process of the economic system's operation. This highlights the structural effects and enables the migratory phenomenon to be set in the context of economic growth(2). We shall lay particular emphasis during this study on the operation of the Swiss labour market and on the trend of the employment structure and the productive apparatus. Rather than endeavouring to define precise stages of development(3), we

---

(1) A list of the various advantages and disadvantages from the short-term economic standpoint may be found in the article by W.A. Jöhr and R. Huber, "Die konjunkturellen Auswirkungen der Beanspruchung ausländischer Arbeitskräft", "Revue suisse d'économie politique et de statistique", No. 4, 1968, pages 375 et seq.; see also the mimeographed study by the Central Planning Office, "Economic effects of the recruitment of foreign workers in the Netherlands", The Hague, March 1972.

(2) In most analyses, the structural effects have been overlooked in favour of the short-term economic effects. But from the point of view of economic policy, it is the former which we regard as being more important. See J.L. Reiffers, "Le rôle de l'immigration des travailleurs dans la croissance de la République Fédérale d'Allemagne de 1958 à 1968", Aix-en-Provence, 1970. W.A. Jöhr and Huber, op.cit., have also analysed for Switzerland the effect of immigration on secondary investment, which is a way of setting the migratory phenomenon into the context of economic growth phenomena.

(3) However, our study will be found to contain the various stages described by W.R. Böhning, "The economic effects of the employment of foreign workers, with special reference to the labour markets of Western Europe's post-industrial countries", Centre for Research in the Social Sciences, University of Kent at Canterbury, Sept., 1972.

have preferred using as reference points the various stages in the short-term economic trend, considering that long-term growth underlies the short-term trend(1).

This approach seems realistic since it has often been argued that its immigration policy had enabled Switzerland to economise in the use of the normal instruments of counter-cyclical and growth policies, but also because it was quite soon observed that immigration was becoming increasingly structural (permanent immigration)(2). In point of fact, immigration policy (which is implicitly a labour market and wages policy) has been practically the only instrument available to the Government for direct intervention in economic life. Switzerland had thus had a rather unique instrument of counter-cyclical policy at its disposal up to 1970, when immigration was stopped. It has moreover been increasingly felt since then that the Government ought to be given other means of intervention to regulate growth.

---

(1) "Without disregarding the interest for the economic policy authorities to have estimates of certain costs and benefits of immigration (expenditure on housing, cost of vocational training, repatriation of capital, consumer savings, etc.), the economist should more especially consider the forms taken by the growth of an economy which imports labour. Thus, it is by no means absurd to feel that even if it were proved that immigration considerably increased the fixed costs of the host economy, it might still be considered desirable because of its effects on the development of the other components of economic growth. When at the time of the New Deal public works were carried out which were of no great intrinsic value for reviving the American economy, there was no cost-benefit study which would have undoubtedly dissuaded the authorities from undertaking such operations. But we feel that immigration raises a similar problem when the economy concerned is approaching the barrier of full employment. By easing the labour market, it can pave the way for economies in a too deflationary monetary policy, a restrictive budgetary policy and even, as C.P. Kindleberger points out, an incomes policy." J.L. Reiffers, "Le rôle de l'immigration des travailleurs dans la croissance de la République Fédérale d'Allemagne de 1958 à 1968", Aix-en-Provence, 1970, p.51.

(2) The concept of permanent immigration should not only be understood on an individual level. As regards infrastructure, for example, the permanence of the migratory flow is just as important as the shorter or longer stay of the immigrant in the host country.

In spite of the interventionist nature of this Swiss labour market policy, it has never been seriously challenged, at least as long as it remained a general policy. As its main advantage was that it could act as a wages policy, it was quite logically accepted without too much reticence by the private sector, since it did not have the compulsive character of so many other direct interventionist measures which offend the principle of freedom to engage in trade and industry. Besides, it is usually agreed that official intervention on the labour market is justified in difficult situations, for example when cost inflation has to be stopped, so that this attitude is not peculiar to Switzerland.

The changes in immigration policy, like the rate of immigration, were determined by short-term economic trends and little attention was paid to their long-term consequences, although the latter are what matter in the end. Given the way in which the Swiss economy functions, this was only to be expected, since it is mainly the private sector which decides the priority of requirements. Meanwhile, with the arrival and permanent settlement of ever growing numbers of immigrants in Switzerland, the cost of immigration to the community gradually began to make itself felt, although its full extent was not realised or recognised until after 1965(1). Once aware of the fact, the authorities had of course to change their attitude towards immigration since they were responsible for meeting community needs. In addition to this, the Swiss economy was becoming too dependent on this immigrant labour. Thus, up to 1965, but more probably up to 1970, Switzerland aided its economic growth by ensuring that manpower was always in plentiful supply(2). There were several reasons for this policy:

(1) The inflow of foreign workers took place in a micro-economic context and was accordingly regarded as a factor of production. Moreover, this factor of production was for long considered to be merely a standby reserve. It may be claimed that foreign labour produced its main effect at the level of supply, at least until 1960, insofar as it

(1) General considerations on this phenomenon will be found in W.R. Böhning, op.cit., pages 20 and 21.

(2) C.P. Kindleberger, Europe's Postwar Growth, The Role of Labour Supply, Harvard University Press, 1967.

prevented the formation of bottlenecks(1). This state of
affairs might have continued if the structural effects resulting
from the permanence and continual rise in the migratory flow
had not produced their consequences, especially on demand. Thus,
as soon as foreign labour became a significant factor in total
demand (especially for investment in social services and infrastructure), what held good at micro-economic level no longer
did so at macro-economic level. The unforeseen or unacknow-
ledged effects of immigration made their appearance: the
interests of the micro-units were therefore no longer in harmony
with a balanced national economy, either from the economic or
the sociological standpoint(2). In these circumstances, it
became imperative for the Government to intervene on the basis
of a different logic from that which had prevailed hitherto,
since it was other interests and even other pressures which had
now to be considered. This led the Swiss to revise their
immigration policy and hence their labour market policy and to
abandon their traditional immigration policy(3). The latter
has been practically stopped, although the regulations governing
the internal movement of aliens (geographical and occupational
mobility) have been considerably relaxed. However, the controls
on the use of foreign labour have been strengthened by the
establishment of "labour distribution boards" (in some cases,
a timid attempt at a structural policy).

---

(1) J.L. Reiffers, op.cit., page 182, concludes his analysis
    as follows: "Short-term study has shown the essential
    role played by foreign worker immigration in the adjustment
    of labour supply to desired employment, defined:

    - overall, by behaviour on the markets for products and
      on the currency market;

    - at micro-economic level, by a certain ideal structure
      of employment where entrepreneurs can reduce their cost
      function to a minimum."

    See also A. Rossi and K. Schiltknecht, "Uebernachfrage
    und Lohnentwicklung in der Schweiz - Eine neue Hypothèse",
    Kyklos, Vol. XXV, 1972.

(2) This situation might have been avoided if a balance had
    constantly been maintained between the satisfaction of
    private needs and the satisfaction of community needs
    (including housing). But this would have necessitated
    instruments of economic policy which were not feasible
    at that time.

(3) See V. Lutz, "Manodopera straniera e livelli salariali
    interni con particolare riferimento alla situazione
    svizzera", Moneta e Credito, 1963, and D. Maillat,
    "Structure des salaires et immigration", 1968.

(2) It should not be forgotten that Swiss immigration policy was only made possible because of the unequal levels of development in the various European economies. This entailed the displacement of labour towards the centres of capital accumulation. In short, the polarisation effect has operated, leaving very little scope for more evenly balanced development. Furthermore, manpower movements have made very little contribution towards the improved integration of the various labour markets, which have each remained subject to their own particular regulations.

(3) The target of maintaining full employment at national level only and achieving the highest growth rate as compared with other countries has made such an immigration policy possible.

Being incapable of seriously considering methods of achieving a more balanced economic growth, the European Governments were reduced (or else submitted) to practising a "free" market policy which favours certain growth points and exaggerates asymmetrical development.

(4) Another factor is also important in order to understand Swiss immigration policy. This was the attitude entertained towards economic growth at the beginning of the '50s. At the end of the war, it was realised that reconstruction would keep the productive apparatus busy for some time, but opinions were very divided and very sceptical as to the prospect of prolonged and permanent growth, and people therefore continued to think in terms of business cycles. Immigration policy was of course geared to this opinion and did not admit any idea of a prolonged stay by immigrants in Switzerland.

People were inclined to think that the same attitude was appropriate as in the second decade of the century. The foreign worker could not acquire permanent status and must be always ready to go back to his home country as soon as the economy showed the least signs of slowing down(1). In these conditions, his presence in the country could not harm Swiss workers, nor would it make any lasting change in the infrastructure.

---

(1) The idea was therefore that the immigrant acted as a "cyclical shock absorber". See Böhning, op.cit., page 9 (Konjunkturpuffer approach).

1. <u>Growth trends and short-term economic fluctuations</u>
    <u>since 1950</u>

    Like all Western countries, Switzerland's economic growth
was remarkable after the War, and especially after 1950(1). On
the basis of real GNP percentage annual variations, it will be
observed that economic activity fell appreciably in 1949
(- 3.5 per cent) and then resumed its expansion in 1950 and 1951
(7.2 per cent and 8.1 per cent) owing in particular to the
Korean War. The end of that war entailed a sharp decline in 1952
since real GNP rose by a mere 0.8 per cent. In 1953, a fairly
steady period of growth began which only stopped in 1958. In
that year, real GNP fell (- 1.8 per cent). Then, in 1959, there
was a new phase of growth which up to 1961 was faster than before
and then average up to 1966. After a pause in 1967 (+ 1.8 per
cent), expansion resumed in 1968. But 1969 (+ 5.9 per cent) was
a culminating point since the growth rate then began to decline
(4.4 per cent in 1970, 4.0 per cent in 1971, 4.0 per cent in
1972).

    Apart from the situation on the employment market,
which is of more particular interest for the present research,
the most striking features in this trend should be noted:

    (1) During the 'fifties, and more especially in 1960,
the Swiss economy was marked by a "pronounced growth in breadth
due to the rapid quantitative expansion in the labour and
capital factors, while the productivity of their employment
and the influence of technical progress were relatively
small"(2).

    (2) Although the trend of industrial production (the
index has only existed since 1958) has developed on the whole
in the same way as real GNP, a substantial difference began
to be observed in the 'sixties. Thus, "the rate of variation
in industrial production rose from 8.0 to 10.2 per cent,
whereas GNP fell from 7.2 per cent to 5.8 per cent. This
demonstrates both the considerable weight of industry in
Switzerland and the cyclical influence of other branches

_____

(1) Jacot, "La surchauffe économique" (Economic overheating),
    Lyons University thesis, 1970; F. Kneschaurek, "Perspec-
    tives de l'évolution de l'économie suisse jusqu'en l'an
    2000" (Swiss economic prospects up to the year 2000),
    Volume 2, St. Gallen, 1970.

(2) See Weber, "Etude pour une politique conjoncturelle en
    Suisse", Lausanne thesis, 1971, page 119; A.A. Rossi
    and R.L. Thomas, "Inflation in the Post-war Swiss Economy -
    an Econometric Study of the Interaction between Immigration
    and the Labour Market", Revue suisse d'économie politique
    et de statistique, 4, 1971, p. 763; O.E.C.D., Switzerland,
    Economic Surveys, 1967, page 11; J.C. Ardenti and
    J.P. Reichenbach, "Estimation de la fonction de production
    CES pour la Suisse", Revue suisse d'économie politique et
    de statistique, No. 4, 1972.

such as building, where activity proceeds at a specific pace, and to a smaller extent agriculture and tourism, which are subject to the hazards of climate"(1).

(3) As regards prices, "the long-term trend was rising but moderate for the period 1948-1960. The annual geometrical mean increase in GNP prices between 1948 and 1968 was about 2.5 per cent. However, the price rise became much sharper at the turn of the 'sixties; during the period 1948-1960, the geometrical average rate was 1.2 per cent; for the period 1960-1968, it increased almost fourfold and amounted to 4.5 per cent"(2). This rise became even steeper subsequently.

Up to 1960, "the annual variation in prices was constantly lower in Switzerland than the average in the other European countries, except in 1953, when it was in the same region; moreover, the extremes in Switzerland were as a general rule one year later than those noted in O.E.C.D. Europe as a whole, which seems to indicate that the rising prices in Switzerland were essentially 'imported'. After 1960, on the contrary, the annual price variation was always higher in Switzerland than that observed on average in the other European countries, except in 1965, and had its own development without any apparent connection with the latter. From being imported before 1960, the price rise appears thus to become peculiarly Swiss after that date"(3). The situation was therefore deflationary up to about 1960.

(4) Economic development in the 'fifties, but more especially in the 'sixties, was marked by the increased importance of exports and investment.

This reminder of the salient points in the economic trend between 1950 and 1970 must not let it be forgotten that a too general analysis does not give the details of the various cyclical phases. This was noted by Jacot when he wrote: "We have already observed several times that there was a sharp change at the turn of the 'sixties in the trend of the main representative variables in the short-term economic situation in Switzerland when taken separately. This change during the course of the economic cycle comes out still more clearly when we consider the combined positions of these different variables".

Up to 1958, economic growth was spread fairly evenly over the time scale, thanks to recurring cyclical swings, but after 1958/59 it was no longer so. "The kinds of business cycle experienced in Switzerland after 1958/59 were unlike those which had recurred fairly regularly before then: during the decade from 1959 to 1968, the economy suffered from latent

---

(1) Jacot, op.cit., p. 180.

(2) Jacot, op.cit., p. 184.

(3) Jacot, op.cit., p. 186.

overheating up to 1961 and after 1964, and from blatant overheating from 1961 to 1964. The new feature after 1960 was that
price rises in Switzerland were distinctly steeper than the
average rises in O.E.C.D. countries, which meant that the Swiss
economy was exhibiting relative inflation for the first time
since the Second World War and perhaps for the first time in
its history"(1).

Thus, the pressure of demand was with few exceptions a
dominant feature of the period 1950-1970. It was also mainly
after 1960 that it was strongest and most constant(2). Owing
to the phenomena of recurrence and the flexibility of the labour
market, the surplus demand which made its appearance before 1960
did not entail any substantial inflationary difference, but the
situation changed radically in the 'sixties. Up to 1960, the
elasticity of total domestic supply was relatively great. When
we look for the cause of this elasticity, we note that the
supply of foreign labour is an important factor(3).

---

(1) Jacot, op.cit., page 198.

(2) See Rossi and R.L. Thomas, op.cit., pages 763 et seq.

(3) This has been observed by several authors. The best known
    is of course C.P. Kindleberger in "Europe's Postwar Growth,
    the role of Labour Supply". J.L. Reiffers, op.cit., page 35,
    mentions that for Kindleberger immigration has two bene-
    ficial effects:

    - it enables the rate of wage increase to be lower than
      productivity and also meets the conditions for the simul-
      taneous achievement of both external and internal
      equilibrium;

    - it is responsible for an increase in (or at the very
      least for preserving) the proportion of profits in
      national income which entails a greater propensity to
      save and thereby facilitates the growth of investment
      unaccompanied by any unbalancing tensions on the market
      for products.

    On this latter point, the O.E.C.D. (Economic Surveys,
    Switzerland, 1972) observes that "between 1950 and 1969,
    the share of income from capital in Swiss GNP rose steadily
    and fairly rapidly at a rate well above that of most other
    O.E.C.D. countries for which a similar calculation can be
    made" (page 49). And again: "the shift in factor availa-
    bilities can also be expected to have an impact on factor
    remunerations. Growing labour scarcity and rising capital-
    labour ratios are likely to increase returns to labour
    relative to those of capital. Despite literally full-
    employment conditions over the last 20 years, this does not
    seem to have happened in Switzerland" (page 48).

Footnote continued:

Reference should also be made here to F. Schaller's arguments ("Le rôle de la main-d'oeuvre étranger dans l'économie suisse" - The role of foreign labour in the Swiss economy - Revue syndicale suisse, 5, 1972, pages 145 et seq.) when he writes: "having been untouched by any military action, our country was in a position as early as the 'fifties to take advantage of the new technology to which the war had given birth and which was further developed in the prosperous period immediately following the war. The unemployment expected when our army was completely demobilised did not occur. Although no one was fully aware of it, we were faced with a twofold trend with each branch moving at a very different pace. On the one side, technology was changing at a rate which exceeded anything imaginable during the preceding period. On the other side, the population increase which is essential for adopting advances in technical processes was by the vary nature of things much slower than would have been desirable. We were therefore threatened by a profound disequilibrium between the possibility of using modern technology and the population figure which, having suddenly become too small, prevented the adoption of modern methods of production.

"This left us a choice between two paths. The first consisted in sacrificing the use of postwar technology and thus renouncing high growth for our economy and a fast rate of increase in our national income; this meant risking the rapid elimination of international markets and laying ourselves open to relative underdevelopment. The second path obliged us to make up for the inadequate numbers of our population by calling on foreign manpower." Thus, "as the adoption of innovation is very expensive nowadays, it is only economically justified by much more considerable production than previously. A larger population is necessary for this production and the corresponding consumption."

2.   Operation of the labour market

2.1   Level of employment up to 1960

       From 1959-60 onwards serious strains began to be felt on
the labour market, as the various indices show(1), but these
indices are only significant when related to the process of
geographical and occupational mobility, as we shall see later.
The fluidity which was a feature of the labour market between
1949-1958/59 was generally due to the geographical and occupational mobility of Swiss manpower. But this mobility was often
only possible thanks to the immigration of foreign workers.

       The consequence of this abundant undifferentiated supply of
labour was that Switzerland found itself in the '50s in a state
of virtual underemployment (unlimited labour supply). This is
important as the existence of margins of underemployment enables
any greater demand for goods and services to be reflected in
increased production and employment rather than rising prices.

       This period warrants study as immigration was then much
smaller than after 1960 and it was at that time that the machinery
was introduced which was to govern the '60s and to give rise to
new problems.

       Therefore it is not so much the general level of wages
which should be stressed but the fact that this supply of labour
prevented bottlenecks from forming and frequently enabled the
actual level of production to be brought nearer to the desired
level without too much delay(2), largely thanks to the mechanism
of geographical and occupational mobility. The influence of this
abundant labour supply was therefore mainly important for the
differential trend of wages as between industries, since it is
the latter which largely determines geographical and occupational
mobility.

---

(1) D. Maillat, "Structure des salaires et immigration" (Wage
    structure and immigration), page 83, Rossi and Thomas,
    op. cit., page 775.

(2) "A comparison of the variations in the surplus demand for
    labour with the variations in the migratory balance of
    foreign workers gives an idea of the short-term consequences
    of such immigration. Should the immigration of foreign
    workers rise with the surplus demand for labour, we would
    then deduce that the effect of immigration has been partly
    to make up the difference between the product desired and the
    potential product with the available national labour supply.
    In these circumstances, the immigration of foreign workers
    has avoided any restrictive action on behaviour, which action
    usually takes the form of a restrictive financial policy and
    a deflationary monetary policy. In other words, instead of
    having to achieve equilibrium by action at behavioural level,
    this action is taken at input level." Reiffers, op. cit.
    page 104.

One can of course presume that average wages have increased less with immigration than without immigration, but it
is also probable, on the other hand, that inflation has been
less(1) (at least up to the '60s). Two other aspects deriving
from this abundant undifferentiated supply of labour are also
worthy of attention. These are the effects on the capital/
labour mix and the increased demand due to the rise in incomes
and the number of permanent immigrants. However, we shall first
analyse the mechanism of geographical and occupational mobility.

2.2 Formation of "non-competing" groups

The trend followed by the dynamic of geographical and
occupational mobility (especially of Swiss workers) was set
mainly by the policy followed in allocating jobs to new immigrants. As opposed to practice in the second decade of the
century and to the logical dictates of a free labour market,
foreign workers were not given jobs indiscriminately in just any
industry. They were given jobs in accordance with various
policy criteria aimed (so runs the argument usually put forward)
largely at protecting the interests of Swiss workers (i.e. at
eliminating the risk of competition). It may be noted in
passing that legal practice has perhaps only covered a de facto
situation, but this is difficult to prove(2).

(a) The premises of this policy

Up to the First World War, foreigners in Switzerland were
quite free to follow any trade they wished. They were free to
settle in the country and to work there as self-employed persons
or in the employ of others. But, as everywhere else, the First
World War saw the end of this liberal policy of freedom of
establishment and Switzerland gradually evolved regulations for
controlling the entry and residence of foreigners, one of the
objects being to avoid congestion on the labour market.

---

(1) "Despite the exceptional pressure in the Swiss labour market,
   the average annual percentage increases in the level of money
   wage-earnings and the cost of living were considerably below
   those experienced by other Western European countries.
   Large injections of foreign manpower into the Swiss labour
   supply appear to have caused a damping down of the rate of
   price and wage inflation. Consequently, the average rate of
   inflation is considerably below that which might be expected,
   given the situation in the labour market." Rossi and Thomas,
   op. cit., page 761.

(2) If Böhning's arguments concerning the various stages were
   confirmed, they would constitute the beginnings of proof,
   however. He says that the legal regulations governing the
   employment and geographical and occupational mobility of
   immigrants are in fact merely a protective fence to prevent
   too much competition with national labour. But this fence
   is of little effect under the pressure of events.

(b) <u>Trend of types of permit granted</u>

(1) <u>Policy followed up to 1965</u>

The bulk of permits between 1924 and 1931 were granted to seasonal workers, as well as to farm labour and domestic staff.

During the critical years, i.e. between 1931 and 1939, account had to be taken of the reduction in employment capacity caused by the non-renewal of expiring residence permits so as to reserve the maximum number of jobs for Swiss workers. Since 1945, "the cantons are invited only to accept capable workers and to subject the issue of a permit to the express condition that the employment, as well as the working conditions and remuneration, of Swiss workers are in no way compromised by the recruitment of foreign labour"(1).

With the rise in economic growth, foreigners flocked into Switzerland so that it was necessary to tighten up the controls, in particular by making it more difficult to change jobs, the idea always being that an orderly labour market must be maintained.

During the years immediately following the last war, "the employment of foreign labour was distinctly temporary in nature. This concept facilitated application of the employment policy pursued by Switzerland, which could not be based on continuing economic growth and an exceptionally high level of employment. It was always necessary to ensure that the number of foreign workers settling did not exceed the foreseeable requirements of business returning to a normal level"(2).

It was for this reason that the OFIAMT asked the cantons in in 1954 to keep the number of foreigners settling in Switzerland at as low a figure as possible.

However, it became gradually necessary to bow to the facts; although the foreign labour force was subject to continual renewal, an increasing number of foreigners had been working in Switzerland for many years. The view that immigration was merely temporary was very much given the lie, especially as the immigrant was beginning to be allowed to settle his family in Switzerland, a movement which was also gradually to grow.

In 1960, the OFIAMT presented "new directives on the admission of the members of foreign workers' families". Now "the family's entry is authorised at the same time as its head or, as appropriate, after a short probationary period where the foreigner takes up an executive position or a highly specialised job which is of particular importance for a firm's economic or

(1) OFIAMT, "Le Problème de la main-d'oeuvre étrangère", Bern, 1964, page 78.

(2) OFIAMT, op. cit., page 80.

technical activity. For all other workers, it is generally
possible to consider that after three years' continuous residence
in Switzerland their situation has been so consolidated that the
preliminary conditions on which authorisation of the family's
entry depends are fulfilled. In the case of skilled workers,
entry of the family may even be authorised before three years
have elapsed"(1).

However, 1960 and the following years were marked by
vigorous economic growth and a very tight employment market,
which encouraged more and more foreign workers to immigrate. In
order to reduce the danger of inflation, it was considered
necessary to keep their numbers down. As a first step, employers
were advised not to increase their total payroll (Swiss and
foreign) unduly. Then, in 1963, the Government took steps to
regulate the arrival of new immigrants. It was sensitive to the
political problems and the first steps taken were apparently
non-selective in that manpower restrictions were to affect all-
firms. This non-selective feature soon proved impracticable. In
the meantime, the measures taken did not improve mobility on the
labour market; moreover, they made no allowance whatever for
changes in the structure of employment.

Then, in March 1963, the Federal Council passed its first
Decree "in the light of the unduly large alien population and
excessive economic growth", which included the decision not to
grant or renew residence permits or permits to change jobs so
long as the firm's total payroll (Swiss and foreign) exceeded
by 2 per cent its maximum level in December 1962.

These measures to restrict the right of foreigners to
change their jobs further increased the strain on the labour
market since they impeded geographical and occupational mobility.

In 1964, the measures were still further tightened up.
"The new regulations stipulated that permits for foreign workers
to reside in Switzerland or change their jobs might only be
issued or renewed if the employer undertook in writing not to
increase his firm's total payroll (Swiss and foreign) beyond its
total size as at 1st March, 1964 or its average size for the year
1963. The Decree also aimed at reducing firms' payrolls by
stipulating that residence permits could only be issued to new
foreign workers taken on to replace outgoing workers if this did
not raise the total payroll to above 97 per cent of the reference
figure. But this regulation only applied to firms employing over
25 persons. Like the earlier Decree, the Federal Council Decree
of 21st February, 1964 did not apply to agricultural and forestry
undertakings, private households, hospitals, asylums and other
institutions. But all public enterprises were covered by these

(1) OFIAMT, op. cit., p. 83.

measures, whereas in the previous year the Federal Railways, the Swiss Post, Telephone and Telegraph administration and the concessionary transport enterprises were exempt"(1).

Under the Order of 9th October, 1964, the total payroll was brought down from 97 per cent to 95 per cent, of the reference figure. In addition, spontaneous immigration (pseudo-tourist) was ended by making employment conditional on the guarantee of a residence permit. This meant that workers could no longer enter Switzerland by showing a promise of a job or an employment contract.

(2) The 1965-1967 twin-ceiling system

In 1965, it was realised that the arrangements for limiting a firm's total payroll (Swiss and foreign) were ineffective in keeping down the number of foreigners and a system was therefore introduced for reducing the number of foreigners (required to report to the police) employed per firm.

The regulations in force until then had limited each firm's total payroll irrespective of the workers' nationality, so that Swiss workers leaving a firm could be replaced by foreigners provided the firm's total payroll did not exceed 95 per cent of the reference figure. In order to remedy this weakness, the new Decreee of 1st March, 1965 set up a twin-ceiling system under which:

1. the ban was maintained on increasing the payroll per firm;

2. a ceiling was imposed on the number of foreign staff per firm.

Firms were obliged to reduce the number of foreign workers by 5 per cent (with reference to 1st March, 1963). In the building and construction industry, the number of seasonal workers was limited to 145,000.

On 1st March, 1966, a new Federal Council Decree was published maintaining the twin-ceiling system, but modified as follows:

1. employers were obliged to reduce the number of foreign workers employed by 8 per cent of the base figure (1st March, 1965) by 31st July, 1966, and again by 2 per cent by 31st January, 1967, i.e. by a total of 10 per cent;

2. the maximum number of workers allowed per firm was fixed at the maximum number of workers per firm as at 1st March, 1964, plus 4 per cent;

---

(1) OFIAMT, op. cit., p.84.

3. frontier workers ceased to be counted as
   foreign workers.

In 1967, further reductions were made and employers were
given up to the end of July 1967 to bring down the number of
foreigners employed in their firms by 12 per cent of the base
figure as at March 1965 (Federal Decree of 10th February, 1967).

The required reduction in seasonal workers was only
10 per cent of the base figure (5 per cent in hotels and catering). This concession was justified by the fact that seasonal
labour has a less noticeable effect on the degree of alien
penetration.

The permitted total payroll per firm was limited to the
number fixed in 1964 plus 10 per cent.

The quota for seasonal workers in building and construction was now put at 125,000.

(3) Towards a global manpower ceiling system

The twin-ceiling system proved an increasing drag on the
economy and was replaced by a global ceiling system for the
whole of Switzerland and by arrangements for improving the geographical and occupational mobility of foreign workers.

In 1968, it was decided that employers must reduce the
number of foreigners employed in their firms by 5 per cent, over
and above the cuts made in 1965, 1966 and 1967, so bringing the
total reduction to 17 per cent over the whole period from 1965
to 1968. But it should be noted that seasonal and frontier
workers were not counted as foreigners, nor were foreigners who
had lived continuously in Switzerland for at least seven years
(in 1969, five years).

The maximum figures for seasonal workers were fixed
separately for building and construction (115,000), hotels and
catering (21,000) and other industries (16,000).

Then in 1970(1) came the global ceiling system. Under
this system, the authorities were to determine the number of new
foreigners to be allowed into Switzerland (40,000), after which
this number would be divided up between the cantons, who would
themselves distribute the workers among the various firms (in
most cases, the cantons were to set up labour allocation com-
mittees).

---

(1) The aim was to stabilize the number of foreigners engaging
    in paid employment who had no annual residence or permanent
    settlement permit at 600,000, i.e. the figure obtaining at
    the end of December 1969. Frontier workers were not subject
    to this restriction.

As regards seasonal workers, the numbers allowed in were kept at the 1968 level (112,000).

The regulations on changing jobs, occupations and cantons were also amended so as to improve geographical and occupational mobility among foreigners. This problem will be discussed in the following chapters.

In 1971, the total number of new immigrants was reduced to 20,000.

The results of these various measures in terms of size of the foreign population are given in Table 1, which shows that their numbers in 1972 were the same as in the years 1966-68, with one important difference: the drop in the number of workers engaged by the year and the rise in the number of seasonal and frontier workers. Side by side with the drop in the number of workers engaged by the year, the number of permanently settled immigrants (those with over ten years' continuous residence in Switzerland) increased. These two categories accounted in 1972 for some 600,000 people.

It should also be noted that every time an administrative measure was taken, the problem was which classes of foreigner to treat as alien. As a rule, seasonal and frontier workers and permanently settled immigrants were left out when calculating the number of foreign workers covered by the above Decrees. All these difficulties are connected with the fact that the phenomenon of alien penetration cannot be tackled simply by controlling the entry of foreigners. This explains the growing tendency to adopt a policy of assimilating long-term foreign residents in Switzerland, so that the problem becomes how to reduce the threat of too large a foreign population by according aliens Swiss national status in one way or another.

All in all, the principles governing the admission of foreign labour have evolved in the absence of any real analysis of the trend of the employment structure and the aims defended during the '50s. Yet it was already apparent since 1958/1959 that immigration was becoming increasingly permanent, or in other words, structural(1). Various trade associations have of course warned private industry and the Government from time to time of the dangers inherent in such a policy; the attitude of these associations has not been very systematic since it was usually a matter of safeguarding micro-economic interests quite independently of macro-economic considerations. This would probably not have been the case if the target had been manpower planning and certain growth targets, but our system did not in fact permit the determination of priorities or orders of urgency. The contribution of the various industries to GDP has never been seriously considered. Yet a forward-looking attitude would have

(1) See Böhning, op. cit., pages 22/23.

TABLE 1

Number of controlled foreign workers according to category of permit

Category of permit	1962	1963	1964	1965	1966	1967	1968	1969	1970	1971	1972
	Total figures										
Workers engaged by the year	405,713	441,765	465,366	446,493	435,979	435,931	440,912	442,687	429,956	391,814	355,150
Seasonal workers	194,110	201,348	206,305	184,235	164,569	153,514	144,081	149,201	154,732	180,828	196,632
Frontier workers	44,883	46,900	49,230	45,600	48,000	58,637	63,062	67,341	74,797	87,838	97,203
Total	644,706	690,013	720,901	676,328	648,548	648,082	648,055	659,229	659,485	660,480	648,985
	Per thousand										
Workers engaged by the year	629	640	646	660	672	673	681	672	652	593	547
Seasonal workers	301	292	286	273	254	237	222	226	235	273	303
Frontier workers	70	68	68	67	74	90	97	102	113	134	150
Total	1,000	1,000	1,000	1,000	1,000	1,000	1,000	1,000	1,000	1,000	1,000

Source: La Vie Economique, August survey.

been conducive to a better policy for the allocation of foreign manpower. It was only later that the necessity for this was felt. Mr. Schaffner, an ex-Federal Counsellor, stated in 1970(1): "The economy will certainly be obliged to change its structures and it is these indispensable changes - Swiss farming has already been confronted by this process for some time - which will be the main features of our time and the decades to come. As for our large industries and businesses with their international interests, they will be still more obliged than in the past to take on the risk of standing up beyond our frontiers against the dangerous competition making its appearance on the world front. As has in any event been the case so far, our production programmes will have to be carefully examined and worked out. In order to economise on staff, new forms of collaboration will have to be found - and they will certainly be found, as is already proved by many examples - which do not nonetheless bring the independence of each firm to an end. In addition to the necessary concentrations - which are not in any case the only possible solution - it will be necessary to consider certain forms of disengagement by dropping lines of production where output is not as might be desired and by giving up certain kinds of business. For instance, it is not especially advisable to continue producing large quantities of certain day-to-day products. What we should do, on the contrary, is to concentrate on the production of goods whose high quality we can really guarantee. Our motto should be 'multum non multa'. What is in fact important for the future of businesses is neither their size nor their turnover but the higher quality of their products which should be produced as efficiently as possible. We should not therefore let ourselves be dazzled by the slogan of increased production."

In short, this immigration policy conforming to purely micro-economic aims has led to an impasse from which it is difficult to return as it is no easy matter to set priorities in the absence of investment policy instruments in an economy where requirements are always determined by the private sector.

In conclusion, the important factor is the structural character assumed by immigration(2). This aspect emerges clearly from the statistics on the average length of stay (Table 2) and the rise in the number of immigrants not in gainful employment(3).

---

(1) SDES, Revue des faits de la semaine, No. 48/1970.

(2) It is from this phenomenon of the permanence of immigration and its impact on the structure of employment and production that the necessity for overall action derives. See also Böhning, op. cit., pages 23/24.

(3) cf. "Evolution et effectif de la population étrangère résidant en Suisse en 1971". La Vie Economique, April 1972, pages 192-206.

TABLE 2

Length of stay of workers engaged by the year

Date of survey	Total No. of workers	Of whom resident in Switzerland for					
		Less than 3 years	%	3 years or more	%	5 years or more	%
1st October, 1955	150,000	113,000	75	37,000	25	16,000	11
End February 1959	199,000	150,000	75	49,000	25	22,000	11
End December 1968	440,000	192,000	44	248,000	56	169,000	38
End December 1969	444,000	195,000	44	249,000	56	186,000	42
End December 1970	410,000	164,000	40	246,000	60	180,000	41
End December 1971	370,000	126,000	34	244,000	66	170,000	46

Source: La Vie Economique, April 1972.

146

    (c) <u>Non-competing groups</u>(1)

    The general principle governing the policy on admitting foreign workers is full equality of treatment for foreign and native workers with regard to pay and working conditions. It is generally agreed that this principle "does not go counter to the interests of local manpower and therefore preserves industrial peace", besides preventing discrimination against foreign workers.

    However, another principle also governs immigration policy, namely that order must be maintained on the employment market. This means that "in examining each application for a residence permit, enquiries are usually made as to whether there is not a Swiss worker on the employment market or a foreign worker holding a permanent settlement permit who could do the job applied for". For this reason, "the gainful employment which the foreigner is allowed to take up is specified in the residence permit"(2).

    A distinction should therefore be made between two major categories in the undifferentiated supply of manpower:

1. the supply of Swiss manpower, including foreign workers who have been granted a permanent settlement permit(3);

2. the supply of foreign manpower.

---

(1) Some caution should be exercised in interpreting this concept. See Böhning, page 28: "Labour import may very well worsen the competitive situation for some sections of the indigenous work force. Moreover, the discussion cannot be spared by defining the foreign and the native work force as non-competing groups with reference to either socio-economic or legal reasons. Socio-economically, the replacement of indigenous by foreign workers in socially undesirable jobs can never be complete, so that there will always be large sections of the indigenous work force in a situation of direct competition (substitution). Legally, the control of the foreign labour force affects only that portion which due to its recent immigration is still subject to control. The long-term stayers are generally free to change jobs."

(2) OFIAMT, op. cit., p.42.

(3) A permanent settlement permit puts the foreigner on the same footing as Swiss citizens with regard to the exercise of paid employment; it also enables him to work on his own account, except in a few trades which are exclusively reserved for Swiss nationals. It is granted for an unlimited period and is unconditional.

These two categories of labour do not have the same status on the employment market. Although nationality as such does not entail any discrimination as regards pay, this is not the case as regards geographical and occupational mobility, since foreign workers may not freely switch from one industry, firm or occupation to another.

The residence permit indicates the gainful employment which the foreigner may take up and is always for a limited period; it rarely exceeds one year the first time it is granted. In practice, the duration of the residence permit is determined according to the purpose of residence and the situation on the labour market.

The validity of the residence permit may be restricted to the season or to nine months.

Within the limits of the residence permit he holds, the foreign worker needs a special permit if he:

- wishes to take another job in the same trade (change of job);

- wishes to follow a trade other than the one he is authorised to engage in (change of occupation);

- wishes to take an additional job on a fairly regular basis for the same employer or another employer;

- wishes to work as a self-employed person.

The restrictions on changing jobs or occupations are reinforced by territorial restrictions, since residence permits are only valid for the canton which issued them. Changes of occupation are "strictly controlled in view of the danger that foreigners in occupations which are short of manpower may switch to other occupations and the labour shortage may keep increasing in the least sought after occupations"(1). This policy has often prevented foreigners from improving their occupational situation even though job changes have in practice been authorised. It should be noted that change of occupation frequently involves a change of industry and this is of particular concern to us in the present study.

In addition to these legal restrictions, which in some cases have not operated, there has been a practical restriction which often proved more severe in that some industries have preferred to employ Swiss workers rather than foreigners (at least until 1959/60).

_____

(1) OFIAMT, op. cit., p.89.

It was eventually realised that, since immigration had come to stay, the policy adopted was not only helping to immobilise foreign workers in certain industries but was also enabling some inefficient and even marginal firms to survive by continually supplying them with new workers who were employed at the minimum prevailing wage rates. "That was why the authorities began to think of allowing foreigners to circulate freely although they were well aware of the consequences. With the free circulation of manpower, a heavy exodus from the least sought after occupations would have to be counted on towards those which workers find much more attractive. When considered as a final aim, such labour movements are desirable since they will oblige inefficient industries and firms to adjust themselves to economic development, to make the essential conversion or to withdraw from business. But such structural changes cannot be caused by the sudden complete abolition of the ban on changing occupations without a permit. A certain lapse of time is necessary for adjusting to the new conditions. It will therefore only be possible to authorise the free change of occupation gradually and to begin with after, say, two or three years' residence in Switzerland.

"With a system where changes of job and occupation are freely allowed, foreigners will in time succeed in the same way as Swiss workers in finding the jobs in which they can give of their best. They will leave jobs where wages are low and working conditions bad. Efficient firms will have more labour at their disposal and will be able to develop. In the case of inefficient firms, the process of elimination will be speeded up by the free circulation of foreign manpower. The structural improvements will enable the Swiss economy to increase its productivity and this will at the same time raise the national income."(1)

As from 1966/67, the principles governing the geographical and occupational mobility of foreigners were gradually relaxed. Accordingly, in 1970, changes of job, occupation and canton were made subject to the following regulations:

- workers engaged by the year are not allowed to change their job during their first year of residence (or during the season in the case of seasonal workers) (no change);

- it is normally possible to change one's occupation after three years' residence or after a season in the case of seasonal workers (formerly eight years);

- changing one's canton together with a change of job is not normally allowed before completing three years' residence, and the same applies to seasonal workers during the season.

(1) OFIAMT, op. cit., p.133.

This means that, despite the brake on immigration, there has been a real improvement in the geographical and occupational mobility of foreign workers.

But these principles will probably be still further relaxed, as stated by Mr. Gruebel: "Our long-term policy with regard to workers engaged by the year is to give them the possibility of changing their job, occupation and canton after one year's residence. It is already agreed today in many circles that we must come to such a solution in time, both for economic reasons and bearing humanitarian and political considerations in mind. We are convinced that there can be no question of jeopardising the free choice of job by Swiss workers. What is right for Swiss workers cannot be wrong for foreigners, on the sole condition, however, that such mobility will only be allowed when a certain stability has been proved, i.e. after one year's residence. This liberal solution is also necessary for economic reasons so as to avoid distortions on the labour market. The system of general stabilisation has as a corollary the greater mobility of foreign manpower in Switzerland. We cannot and should not base our structural and regional policy on the shortage of labour. Other means should be used to this end where they are judged necessary."(1).

(1) Statement made at Lausanne on 15th September, 1971.

3.   The dynamics of manpower movements

The immediate post-war years and the early fifties saw the emergence of the factors which were to steer the trend of migration and its consequences for the Swiss economy, especially its productive apparatus.

TABLE 3

Resident population according to origin

	Total population	Swiss	Foreign	Foreign population as a % of the total
1960	5,360,200	4,846,200	514,000	9.6
1961	5,508,400	4,889,800	618,600	11.2
1962	5,639,200	4,930,000	709,200	12.6
1963	5,749,200	4,969,500	779,700	13.6
1964	5,829,700	5,010,800	818,300	14.0
1965	5,883,700	5,046,600	837,100	14.2
1966	5,952,300	5,080,600	871,700	14.6
1967	6,031,400	5,112,300	919,100	15.2
1968	6,104,100	5,140,700	963,400	15.8
1969	6,168,700	5,165,900	1,002,800	16.3
1970	6,204,800	5,191,100	1,013,700	16.3

Source: BFS, Selected population data 1960-1970, Working document 72.02, Bern, 1972.

3.1   Distribution of foreign manpower by industry and occupation

The foreign population resident in Switzerland has increased steadily since 1945 and now accounts for some 15 per cent of the total population (Table 3).

The overall figures are intersting but it is also important to analyse the trend of the distribution by skill and by industry. The information available on skills is scanty. However, the OFIAMT has published a survey on occupational trends among workers newly arriving in Switzerland since 1959 (Table 4).

151

TABLE 4

Initial residence permits issued to foreign workers from 1959 to 1968, classified by type of occupation

Year	Category of permit			Total
	Seasonal workers	Non-seasonal workers	Frontier workers	
Skilled and semi-skilled workers				
1959	70,866	74,447	30,519	175,832
1960	80,199	88,406	33,733	202,338
1961	94,835	104,014	36,491	235,340
1962	100,551	103,174	38,643	242,368
1963	99,914	96,152	41,115	237,181
1964	107,354	91,312	39,744	238,410
1965	105,003	63,490	39,850	208,343
1966	90,331	59,906	42,308	192,545
1967	81,508	57,159	49,186	187,853
1968	75,459	63,782	53,728	192,969
Unskilled workers				
1959	59,191	27,038	11,765	97,994
1960	76,942	49,204	13,381	139,527
1961	100,726	71,936	14,543	187,205
1962	121,908	76,166	15,215	213,289
1963	124,541	68,364	14,904	207,809
1964	133,503	69,247	14,179	216,929
1965	110,719	41,171	14,927	166,817
1966	100,442	37,656	15,784	153,882
1967	94,247	33,442	18,358	146,047
1968	96,510	37,525	18,867	152,902

Year	Percentage of permits issued to skilled and semi-skilled workers			
1959	54.5	73.4	72.2	64.2
1960	51.0	64.2	71.6	59.2
1961	48.0	59.1	71.5	55.7
1962	45.2	57.5	71.7	53.2
1963	44.5	58.4	73.4	53.3
1964	44.6	56.9	73.7	52.4
1965	48.7	60.7	72.7	55.5
1966	47.3	61.4	72.8	55.6
1967	46.4	63.1	72.8	56.3
1968	43.9	63.0	74.0	55.8

Source: La Vie Economique, June 1969.

For the period 1959-1964, the rate of increase in the number of initial residence permits issued to unskilled foreign workers was greater (121 per cent) than for skilled and semi-skilled workers (36 per cent). The result was a drop in the proportion of skilled and semi-skilled workers among total initial permits. But this trend was reversed when the restrictions came into force. The proportion of permits issued to skilled and semi-skilled immigrants went up appreciably, rising from 52 per cent in 1964 to 55 per cent in the following years.

This information says nothing about the occupational advancement of foreigners already employed in Switzerland.

The trend of manpower distribution by industry is shown in Tables 5, 6 and 7, which give a picture of the differential trend by nationality and category of permit.

Generally speaking, it can be agreed that foreign workers have been above all steered towards the lower-paid industries[1] (which does not always mean the least attractive jobs: e.g. the street-cleaning services are mainly manned by Swiss workers). The steering of immigrants in this direction, combined with the restrictions on their geographical and occupational mobility, was to result in different patterns of mobility for the two categories of manpower described above. The mechanism of this will now be studied.

3.2   Mechanism of geographical and occupational mobility

The following are the main factors which have set the trend in the occupational pattern:

- the elasticity of the undifferentiated supply of manpower due to immigration and the geographical and occupational mobility of Swiss workers;

- the trend of employment capacity;

- the changes in the spread of wage rates across industry which have induced shifts in distribution.

In the prevailing climate of economic growth, these three factors have acted in concert, being closely inter-related. The resulting fluidity of the labour market made it easy for entrepreneurs to increase their employment capacity. As this capacity increased, the geographical and occupational mobility of Swiss workers began to operate and labour was distributed in accordance with changes in wage rates throughout industry. (In view of the statistical information available, we shall mainly analyse the secondary sector.)

---

(1) OFIAMT, op. cit., page 89.

TABLE 5

Percentage Distribution of Swiss Workers

		1957	1959	1961	1963	1965	1967	1969	1971
1.	Food, beverages and tobacco	6.5	6.8	6.5	6.9	6.6	7.5	7.6	7.5
2.	Textiles	9.8	8.1	8.3	8.1	7.2	5.9	5.5	5.2
3.	Clothing and linen	8.0	7.6	6.7	6.2	5.8	4.1	4.9	4.4
4.	Capital goods	1.3	1.4	1.6	–	–	–	–	–
5.	Timber and woodworking	6.2	6.3	6.1	5.6	5.6	5.1	4.9	5.1
6.	Paper	2.9	3.0	2.9	2.9	2.8	2.5	2.4	2.3
7.	Printing and bookbinding	5.1	5.6	5.8	6.6	6.8	7.0	7.2	7.2
8.	Leather and rubber	1.1	1.1	0.9	1.7	1.7	1.8	2.0	2.1
9.	Chemicals	5.2	5.7	6.1	5.0	6.7	7.7	8.3	8.9
10.	Cement and cement products, bricks and tiles, earthenware and ceramics, etc.	2.9	3.0	2.8	2.9	3.0	2.7	2.6	2.6
11.	Metals	11.7	11.9	12.0	13.3	13.1	13.2	13.2	13.3
12.	Mechanical engineering, process plant, and precision instruments	28.6	27.9	28.2	27.9	28.0	31.1	30.8	31.8
13.	Clocks, watches and jewellery	11.7	10.6	11.1	11.9	11.8	10.8	10.0	9.4
14.	Musical instruments	0.3	0.3	0.3	0.3	0.3	0.1	0.1	0.1

Source: La Vie Economique, September factory survey.

TABLE 6

Percentage distribution of foreign workers
holding a residence permit

	1957	1959	1961	1963	1965	1967	1969	1971
1. Food, beverages and tobacco	4.5	4.4	4.9	6.2	6.4	6.8	6.6	6.9
2. Textiles	16.6	19.8	13.3	12.4	11.5	10.8	10.6	9.5
3. Clothing and linen	16.6	17.7	15.1	14.7	14.9	14.9	13.5	12.1
4. Capital goods	0.7	0.8	1.3	-	-	-	-	-
5. Timber and woodworking	5.9	5.6	6.6	5.8	5.4	4.9	4.5	4.4
6. Paper	1.6	1.7	2.1	2.5	2.5	2.4	2.3	2.3
7. Printing and bookbinding	1.7	2.6	2.2	3.0	3.0	3.0	2.9	3.2
8. Leather and rubber	1.3	1.4	1.4	2.2	2.4	2.3	2.4	2.5
9. Chemicals	1.4	1.4	1.7	2.2	2.6	3.4	4.3	3.6
10. Cement and cement products, bricks and tiles, earthenware and ceramics, etc.	5.2	5.4	5.1	5.1	5.0	4.7	4.5	4.5
11. Metals	14.5	13.3	15.0	14.6	14.7	14.3	14.7	14.7
12. Mechanical engineering, process plant, and precision instruments	27.0	27.2	26.6	25.7	25.0	26.1	26.9	26.9
13. Musical instruments	0.2	0.2	0.3	0.3	0.3	0.1	0.1	0.0

Source: La Vie Economique, September factory survey.

TABLE 7

Percentage Distribution of Foreign Workers
holding a Permanent Settlement Permit

	1957	1959	1961	1963	1965	1967	1969	1971
1. Food, beverages and tobacco	6.3	6.3	5.3	5.4	5.1	4.6	5.0	4.8
2. Textiles	14.0	13.4	12.3	10.8	9.6	7.9	7.2	7.4
3. Clothing and linen	13.6	12.6	11.5	9.4	9.2	8.4	8.5	8.3
4. Capital goods	0.7	0.7	0.8	-	-	-	-	-
5. Timber and woodworking	6.3	5.8	5.8	4.7	5.0	4.0	4.5	4.5
6. Paper	2.7	2.7	2.4	2.4	2.3	2.2	2.0	2.2
7. Printing and bookbinding	4.7	4.4	4.9	5.2	5.4	5.2	5.5	5.3
8. Leather and rubber	1.5	1.4	1.3	1.8	1.9	1.8	2.1	2.4
9. Chemicals	4.6	4.7	4.8	4.5	4.7	5.0	5.3	5.0
10. Cement and cement products, bricks and tiles, earthenware and ceramics, etc.	3.8	4.0	3.8	3.8	3.4	3.1	2.9	3.0
11. Metals	11.2	10.6	11.9	13.2	13.5	13.8	13.8	14.7
12. Mechanical engineering, process plant, and precision instruments	21.7	25.3	27.2	31.2	34.4	37.4	35.8	35.9
13. Clocks, watches and jewellery	8.1	7.1	7.1	6.7	4.3	5.9	6.6	6.4
14. Musical instruments	0.2	0.3	0.3	0.3	0.3	0.1	0.1	0.1

Source: La Vie Economique, September factory survey.

3.2.1 Role of the wage structure

Wage differences have to be considered from two angles(1):

(1) The factors which explain why there are wage diffe-
    rences between industries. Why does a particular
    industry pay higher or lower wages than another?
    Briefly, this means explaining the rank of the
    various industries according to their order of
    importance. This order of importance is determined
    by various factors, including: the level of skill
    of its manpower, the industry's level of concentra-
    tion, technical progress, labour productivity,
    actual and expected profits, the proportion of costs
    attributable to labour as compared with total costs,
    the structure of the product market, the structure
    of the labour market, the substitutability of the
    factors of production, differences in geographical
    location and the level of trade union membership.

(2) The factors which explain why wage differences between
    industries increase or diminish over the course of
    time. The fundamental element in these variations is
    naturally the situation prevailing on the employment
    market (tight or fluid). In a period of full employ-
    ment, wage differences tend to be reduced, whereas
    they widen when underemployment makes its appearance.

Manpower movements occur according to the greater or
lesser wage difference between industries. Such movements may
in fact be regarded as guided by relative wages. Wages are
certainly not the only factor taken into account when a worker
decides to change his job, but it may be assumed that if he does
so deliberately he is trying to improve his earnings. This has
been proved by various surveys(2).

The part played by interindustrial wage differences in
allocating manpower comes out clearly when we analyse the relationship between changes in these differences and the state of
the employment market as a whole.

---

(1) D. Maillat, "Structure des salaires et immigration" (Wage
Structure and immigration), Dunod, 1968, and D. Maillat,
"Structure des salaires entre branches d'industrie et
mobilité de la main-d'oeuvre", (Wage structure between
industries and labour mobility), Revue économique et
sociale, 3, 1970.

(2) O.E.C.D., "Wages and labour mobility", 1965, pages 63 and
64

The mechanism whereby differences in wage levels cause transfers of manpower is a complicated one. Briefly, it can take two forms: workers may be induced to change their jobs either by differential wage increases or by existing differences in wage rates between one industry and another(1).

(1) On the first assumption, it is considered that a relationship exists between the wage rise in one or more particular industries and the labour movement towards those industries. This is the "market thesis" which assumes that wages, just like other costs, are determined by variations in labour supply and demand. For instance, in the short term, wages increase in industries where the demand for labour is rising because of the inelasticity of labour supply; they fall relatively in industries where labour demand drops or remains stationary because of the immobility of the work force. Apart from the fact that it is unrealistic to think that the interindustrial wage spread responds mechanically to variations in employment, several researches have shown that variations in labour demand are not always the cause of wage movements. In other words, manpower movements occur which in many cases do not necessitate a change in the wage differential. Hence the second assumption.

(2) Under the second assumption (called the job vacancies thesis) no relationship is found between differential wage rises and manpower movements but between wage levels and manpower movements. Under this assumption, when wage differences between industries are too great, even though the exact extent cannot be determined, workers leave the lower-paid industries for the better-paid industries, on condition of course that jobs are available in those industries. Insofar as wages influence the mobility of workers, the latter move from the lower-paid to the better-paid industries when wage differences between industries cross a certain threshold.

All in all, it is the latter assumption which best explains events in Switzerland.

When the labour market becomes tight, shifts of manpower arising from wage differences between industries lead to efforts by the industries with the lowest wage rates to come into line. Before the labour market becomes tight, the industries paying low wages do nothing to change their position on the wage-rate ladder as they are still able to hire workers at the rates they offer. But as soon as difficulties appear on the labour market, they have to take steps in order not to lose their workforce.

---

(1) O.E.C.D., "Wages and labour mobility", op. cit.

3.2.2 Trends in wage differences between industries in Switzerland

We have used the October wage and salary statistics published by the OFIAMT, in which wages are taken as meaning the average hourly earnings of blue-collar workers and salaries as meaning the average monthly pay of white-collar workers.

In order to provide a common basis of comparison, twelve of the seventeen industries covered by the statistics have been taken, namely:

1. Cement and cement products, bricks and tiles, earthenware and ceramics, etc.

2. Food, beverages and tobacco

3. Chemicals

4. Clothing and capital goods

5. Printing trades

6. Metals and metalworking

7. Clocks, watches and jewellery

8. Textiles

9. Paper and leather

10. Craft trades and miscellaneous

A coefficient of variation has been used for measuring the trend in wage and salary spreads.

(a) Trend of wage spreads

During the first period, from 1949 to 1957/1958, wage spreads widened and reached their maximum span in 1958, after which came a period of contraction lasting until 1964. In 1961/1962, the wage spread index rose above its starting value recorded in 1949/1950, and from 1964 onwards the spread alternately widened and narrowed by small amounts.

In order to facilitate studying this trend, the different industries have been classified according to their place on the wage-rate ladder because an industry's place on this ladder is a good indicator of its behaviour when faced by wage increases arising from changes in the demand for labour. The different wage levels attained by each industry are in fact a reflection of their unequal rates of production increase and of their respective stages of development. Obviously, a fully expanding industry will find it easier to offer high wages than a declining industry.

TABLE 8

Wage spread for all manual workers

	1949	1950	1951	1952	1953	1954	1955	1956	1957	1958	1959	1960	1961	1962	1963	1964	1965	1966	1967	1968	1969(1)	1970(1)
Cement and cement products, bricks and tiles, earthenware and ceramics, etc.	94	94	93	93	93	92	93	92	91	91	92	92	94	95	95	97	97	96	97	97	97	99
Food	93	93	93	94	94	94	95	95	95	95	95	95	95	96	95	95	95	95	94	95	94	95
Chemicals	103	103	102	103	103	105	107	107	107	107	106	107	106	104	108	108	109	111	112	110	114	113
Clothing	99	99	98	97	98	98	98	97	97	96	98	97	97	96	95	96	95	95	94	95	96	97
Printing trades	112	113	115	115	115	114	113	113	114	116	117	117	113	112	110	111	112	110	111	113	109	107
Metals and metalworking	98	98	98	99	99	99	100	100	100	102	101	100	102	103	102	102	101	100	100	100	102	103
Clocks and watches	119	119	120	122	123	122	121	123	123	123	119	118	118	114	115	109	109	109	110	107	107	102
Textiles	96	96	97	96	96	96	95	95	93	93	93	92	92	92	91	91	91	91	90	90	92	93
Timber and woodworking	89	89	88	87	87	86	87	86	86	86	87	87	88	91	92	94	94	94	94	95	98	98
Paper and leather	98	98	97	98	96	97	96	95	97	97	98	98	98	98	97	99	100	100	100	102	100	100
Other	101	101	100	100	99	99	99	98	97	97	97	98	99	100	101	101	101	101	101	101	93	93
Coefficient of variation	8.5	8.6	9.1	9.5	9.7	9.5	9.3	10.1	10.2	10.3	9.6	9.5	8.6	7.2	7.5	6.4	6.7	6.7	7.2	6.8	6.8	5.8

Source: La Vie Economique, October wage and salary survey.

(1) These figures are no longer absolutely comparable with those for earlier years owing to a change in the weighting coefficients and the amended classification.

TABLE 9

Salary spread for all white-collar workers

	1949	1950	1951	1952	1953	1954	1955	1956	1957	1958	1959	1960	1961	1962	1963	1964	1965	1966	1967	1968	1969	1970
Cement and cement products, bricks and tiles, earthenware and ceramics, etc.	101	102	101	101	101	100	100	100	101	101	101	101	101	103	103	104	104	104	105	105	104	105
Food	101	101	100	100	100	99	100	99	100	99	100	100	99	100	100	99	100	101	100	100	95	97
Chemicals	107	107	107	107	107	106	106	104	104	105	105	105	105	106	107	108	108	108	110	109	112	112
Clothing	98	98	98	97	97	97	97	96	96	96	96	96	96	95	95	95	94	94	94	94	94	94
Printing trades	100	100	101	102	102	103	103	104	104	103	104	103	103	102	102	103	103	104	103	103	103	100
Metals and metalworking	100	101	101	101	101	102	102	102	103	103	103	103	104	104	103	102	102	101	102	102	102	101
Clocks and watches	103	104	104	106	106	108	107	109	108	106	105	104	103	101	101	99	99	97	98	97	98	95
Textiles	98	98	98	98	98	97	97	96	96	96	96	96	96	95	95	95	96	95	94	95	95	96
Timber and woodworking	92	92	91	91	91	91	92	92	93	92	93	94	93	95	95	97	97	97	98	98	98	98
Paper and leather	106	107	106	105	104	104	103	103	103	104	104	105	104	104	104	104	103	103	102	103	101	102
Other	90	90	90	90	91	91	92	91	91	92	93	93	94	94	94	95	94	94	93	94	97	96
Coefficient of variation	4.9	5.2	5.2	5.4	5.3	5.3	4.8	5.3	5.0	4.8	4.6	4.4	4.3	4.2	4.2	4.1	4.3	4.6	4.8	4.5	5.0	5.0

Source: La Vie Economique, October wage and salary survey.

Industries have been divided into two groups, as follows:

- Group I: clocks and watches; printing trades; chemicals; metals and metalworking

- Group II: paper and leather; clothing, textiles, food, cement and cement products, bricks and tiles, earthenware and ceramics, etc; timber and woodworking.

By over-simplifying, Group I may be said to include the "high-wage" industries and Group II the "low-wage" industries.

Up to 1958, wage differences kept widening because wage increases were greater in the Group I industries than in Group II, but in 1959 the trend was reversed and from 1964 onwards the differences widened and narrowed more or less alternately.

(b) Trend of salary spreads

Salary spreads did not follow the same trend for male as for female employees. For men, they widened slightly up to 1956/1957 and then narrowed, to become steady in 1964. For women, the reverse happened and the spread narrowed up to 1959, after which it widened.

But it should be noted that interindustry salary spreads among white-collar workers keep within very narrow limits. It should be remembered that this category of labour is relatively homogeneous, especially as regards nationality, since few foreigners have been given white-collar jobs. For this reason, we shall only study the trend in the interindustry spread of manual workers' wages.

The explanation may be found by comparing variations in the wage spread with the situation on the employment market. Insofar as wages induce workers to change their jobs, they will tend to leave the less well-paid industries for the better-paid industries when the difference in wages reaches a certain point and provided employment capacity increases, i.e. that there is a demand for labour.

There is no doubt that employment capacity in Switzerland has grown rapidly under the combined effects of a strong overall demand, an abundant supply of labour and an attractive relative price for labour. The heavy demand for labour which has been a feature of the Swiss economy stems from a rapid self-feeding increase(1) in employment capacity and reflects a "labour-intensive" trend. (Let us proceed on this assumption for the moment and analyse it in more detail below.)

_____

(1) See Böhning, op. cit., pp. 7 and 11.

The changes in the structure of employment in the manufacturing industries have been determined by the movement of
Swiss workers (geographical and occupational mobility) and by
the ways in which foreign workers have been placed.

3.2.3 Orientation of geographical and occupational mobility

(a) Orientation of immigrants

In the period preceding 1960, immigration was usually of
the demand-pull type and foreign workers only came in when there
was an actual demand for labour, i.e. when jobs had been created
and not filled by Swiss workers or had fallen vacant on the
departure of the latter (substitution immigration).

In placing immigrant workers, however, preference was
generally given to certain job categories over others, as we
explained when speaking of non-competing groups.

As regards manufacturing industry in Switzerland,
immigrants were directed mainly to the textiles, clothing and
metals and metalworking industries during the period between
1950 and 1960.

In 1950, 64.5 per cent of the foreigners working in manufacturing were employed in Group II industries, i.e. in "low-
wage" industries, and 24 per cent in metals and metalworking
alone, so that a mere 11 per cent of the foreign labour force
was working in the better-paid industries.

By 1960, the proportion of foreign workers in Group II
industries had fallen to no more than 52.5 per cent. The
shortfall as compared with 1950 had been taken up by metals and
metalworking, which now employed 39.5 per cent of all foreigners
in manufacturing industry. The remaining 7.5 per cent were
working in Group I industries.

By 1970, the percentage of foreigners in Group II industries had fallen below 50 per cent. Metals and metalworking
took 42 per cent and other Group I industries 15 per cent.

During this period, the percentage of foreigners in the
total work force of an industry was usually higher in the
Group II industries than in Group I. The trend followed by
this percentage gives a good idea of foreign penetration into
the various industries. The percentage in Group I was below
average (Table 10).

At the beginning of the period under study, the distribution of foreign workers, apart from metals and metalworking,
tended to favour the Group II industries and it was also in
these industries that the percentage of foreign workers in the
total work force was highest. Subsequently, as employment
capacity increased, foreigners arriving were divided between
the Group II industries and metals and metalworking. By 1960,

TABLE 10

Foreign workers as a percentage of total manpower

		1957	1959	1961	1963	1965	1967	1969	1971
1.	Food, beverages and tobacco	16	15	25	36	38	32	32	32
2.	Textiles	30	38	42	48	50	48	51	49
3.	Clothing and linen	34	37	50	58	62	65	59	60
4.	Capital goods	13	13	27	-	-	-	-	-
5.	Timber and woodworking	20	19	32	38	38	34	34	34
6.	Paper	14	14	25	34	36	34	35	35
7.	Printing and bookbinding	10	12	16	23	24	20	21	22
8.	Leather and rubber	23	24	40	45	46	40	40	39
9.	Chemicals	8	8	13	23	22	20	24	26
10.	Cement and cement products, bricks and tiles, earthenware and ceramics, etc.	30	31	44	51	51	47	48	47
11.	Metals	24	22	35	40	42	37	38	38
12.	Mechanical engineering, process plant, and precision instruments	20	19	30	36	37	32	34	34
13.	Clocks, watches and jewellery	7	5	14	20	23	23	27	28
14.	Musical instruments	16	17	30	36	37	24	24	23

Source: La Vie Economique, September factory survey.

TABLE 11

Swiss and foreign active population by economic sector in 1960 and 1970

	Primary sector				Secondary sector				Tertiary sector			
	Swiss		Foreign		Swiss		Foreign		Swiss		Foreign	
	Male	Female	Male	Female	Male	Female	Male	Female	Male	Female	Male	Female
1960	242,226	93,217	17,484	936	782,890	239,269	203,708	67,447	467,754	413,178	49,700	84,480
1970	167,327	52,488	8,456	1,022	780,434	233,810	324,549	113,182	590,752	523,274	101,795	108,050

Source: Cuénoud, op. cit., p.22 (provisional figures).

this latter industry alone employed 40 per cent of the foreign
workers in manufacturing. In short, Group I industries other
than metals and metalworking employed relatively few foreign
workers. Foreign penetration was therefore greater in Group II
industries since the ratio of foreigners to the total work
force was always above average.

The lowest percentage of foreign workers is thus to be
found in those industries where employment capacity has
increased most.

(b) Orientation of Swiss workers

The most significant factor during this period is not so
much the increase in the number of foreign workers as the movement of Swiss workers between the various manufacturing
industries and between sectors.

The Swiss transferred from the primary and secondary
sectors to the tertiary sector - with immigration speeding up
the process - and, within the secondary sector, from Group II
industries to Group I. Moreover, their geographical mobility
was high, which is in itself an indication of the mobility
between sectors and between industries.

(1) Mobility of Swiss workers between sectors

As already mentioned, the geographical and occupational
mobility of foreign workers is restricted. The mobile workers
are the Swiss and foreigners with permanent settlement permits,
the behaviour of the latter being usually the same as for Swiss
workers.

By and large, the movement of Swiss workers has been away
from the primary sector and, to a lesser extent, the secondary
sector towards the tertiary sector (Table 11). Table 11 shows
that between 1960 and 1970 the Swiss active population employed
in the secondary sector fell and that the increased numbers in
this sector were attributable to immigrants(1).

The movement of Swiss workers into the tertiary sector
following the growth of employment capacity in that sector
cannot be explained entirely by economic considerations. Social
position and standing played a decisive part and there was also

---

(1) Further details concerning the dynamics of the sector trend
will be found in a very interesting study presented by
C. Cuénoud (BFS) to the Population Group of the Société
suisse de statistiques et d'économie politique (November
1972). Longitudinal analysis shows that there was a negative balance between 1960 and 1970 for almost all the
50-60 age-group of the Swiss male population in the secondary
sector. This underlines the extent of the transfer of Swiss
active persons from the secondary to the tertiary sector.
In short, immigrants alone provided for the entire increase
in the secondary sector.

a by no means negligible psychological factor, namely the security of employment which workers in the tertiary sector usually enjoy. It is often argued that wage differences are not a major factor in attracting workers to the tertiary sector, but nevertheless the wage rates given in the October wages survey for trades in the tertiary sector show that pay in that sector compares favourably with pay in the secondary sector:

- the wages (hourly earnings) of workers in public transport, electricity supply and commerce are higher or comparable (commerce) with the highest wages paid in manufacturing industry. The situation in private transport is less satisfactory and wages here are nearer the bottom rungs of the wage ladder;

- both male and female white collar workers obtain higher monthly salaries in electricity supply than those in Group I industries and salaries comparable with the latter in banking and insurance. Their pay is average in public transport. It is lower than the Group II industries in private transport and commerce.

It should also be noted that tertiary-type jobs are continually increasing in the secondary sector, especially in industry, and that these jobs are usually held by Swiss workers. Security of employment is also an important factor here as, in the event of a recession, employers are more prone to pay off workers employed directly on the production line.

Moreover, although a good many Swiss have moved into the tertiary sector, it is equally certain that most new Swiss workers entering the labour market for the first time have avoided the secondary sector and taken work in the tertiary sector or, more usually, jobs of a tertiary type. There are even signs that the younger workers are tending to steer clear of industrial occupations, so that we are faced with the "tertiarisation" of Swiss labour. This trend must soon lead to the aging of the Swiss active population structure in the secondary sector.

This movement of Swiss labour towards the tertiary sector has of course created a considerable need for labour in the primary and secondary sectors. The vacuum left behind by the departure of Swiss workers from the secondary sector has been so great that its employment capacity has increased and, as we have already seen, it was foreign workers who replaced the departing Swiss.

In a sense, immigration has played the role which would normally fall to technical progress in smoothing the way for Swiss workers into the tertiary sector(1). However, under

_____

(1) Cuénoud notes in the above-mentioned study that entries to the tertiary sector are spaced out to quite an advanced age, which demonstrates the evident attraction of this sector for all age-groups.

normal circumstances, the movement to the tertiary sector is
due to the shortage of jobs in the secondary sector because of
the recessive nature of technical progress. In Switzerland,
the movement has been voluntary and facilitated by immigration,
which has stimulated geographical and occupational mobility.

Although movement from the secondary to the tertiary
sectors is a long-term process, the trend seen in Switzerland
is somewhat abnormal since the employment pattern of Swiss
labour has developed ahead of the pattern of production. This
explains why foreign labour has become a structural necessity
and marks the essential difference between the period from 1950
to 1960 and the period from 1910 to 1930.

In conclusion, it can be claimed that the prevailing
situation on the labour market has speeded up the normal transfer of Swiss labour from the primary and secondary sectors to
the tertiary sector.

(2) Mobility in manufacturing industry

The mobility of labour between sectors has repercussions
within the secondary sector, where it is found that Swiss workers
are leaving the lower-paid industries for Group I industries,
unless they can find jobs in the tertiary sector.

In fact, we find that foreign penetration is accompanied
by falling numbers of Swiss workers in several industries and
that these numbers are falling despite the fact that employment
capacity is rising. The number of Swiss workers has thus generally dropped in Group II industries and risen in Group I
industries.

While the movement from the secondary to the tertiary
sector may be explained by pyscho-sociological rather than
economic factors, it seems that inside the secondary sector
economic factors assert themselves to the full, in particular
wage differences between industries, and that Swiss workers as a
whole have in fact taken advantage of the situation and left the
lower-paid for the higher-paid industries.

3.2.4 Effect of the wage spread on the redistribution of labour in manufacturing industry

(a) Period 1949-1959

Since the end of the war, and more especially from the
beginning of the fifties, every industry has taken on foreign
workers since they all need them for the jobs at the lower end
of the occupational ladder. We assume that Swiss worker movements were few in number at that time. The small span of the
interindustrial wage spread offered little inducement to change
from one industry to another, especially as the employment
capacity of Group I industries was only just beginning to grow.
But soon the mechanism which has governed labour movements was
to make its appearance once and for all.

Increasing employment capacity in all industries necessitated the recruitment of more workers. But Swiss workers were less and less interested in the Group II industries so that the latter were finally no longer able to find the extra Swiss workers required. Gradually, they even lost some of their national labour force. However, this did not interfere with their output as they replaced their lost home labour and even increased their total labour force by taking on foreign workers who were prepared to work for the prevailing wage rates.

The abundant labour supply was responsible for wage rises being lower in Group II industries than in Group I. The wage spread between industries therefore broadened.

The broadening of the wage spread then induced Swiss workers to leave Group II industries for Group I or the tertiary sector. This inducement was still further strengthened by psycholigical factors including a certain measure of xenophobia.

It was in fact very feasible for Swiss workers to leave Group II industries since Group I industries raised their employment capacity more quickly, both in absolute figures and percentagewise.

As Group I industries, apart from metalworking and engineering, employ a smaller work force than Group II, they were understandably able to satisfy their labour requirements by mainly recruiting home labour.

These industries were able with a fairly broad wage spread to raise the number of new jobs and were therefore in an excellent position to attract Swiss workers wishing to earn more. In fact, during this period, the best way of increasing one's real income was to transfer to a Group I industry and Swiss workers apparently did not overlook this factor. In addition to direct wages, most Group I industries offer frequently substantial fringe benefits which are better than those offered by Group II industries.

Thus, between 1949 and 1959, the job vacancy mechanism seems to have had a preponderant effect on the geographical and occupational mobility of Swiss workers. When the wage spread became sufficiently broad, i.e. about 1952/1953, the departure of Swiss workers from Group II industries gathered speed. During this period, the wage spread was due mainly to the behaviour of the low-wage industries. The continual higher-than-average wage increases in Group I industries were certainly not attributable to the desire to increase the supply of home labour but were rather due to other factors connected with the markets for products (e.g. profits). Thus, there were no unusual wage increases in Group I industries.

During this period, Group II industries were able to employ "cheap" labour and could therefore keep their wage costs within reasonable limits. This advantage certainly made up for

those disadvantages due to the shortage of skills among the
foreign labour force and to the cost of on-the-job training for
future semi-skilled workers.

Group I industries, for their part, were able to recruit
Swiss workers at wages which were definitely higher than those
paid in Group II industries but did not exceed their possibilities as the abundant labour supply prevented any excessive
claims being made. They were also able to capture semi-skilled
and skilled workers so that their training costs were not too
high and they had no need to have recourse to over-qualification.

Finally, the possibilities Swiss workers had of changing
from one industry to another in the context of the broadening
interindustrial wage spread was conducive to the maintenance of
"industrial peace" unaccompanied by any excessive wage charges
for employers.

In conclusion, during the period 1949-1959/1960, the
labour supply was very abundant thanks to immigration and the
geographical and occupational mobility of Swiss workers. This
factor entailed different wage increases according to which of
these categories firms obtained.

These different wage increases caused the interindustrial
wage spread to broaden and this, combined with the greater
employment capacity of Group I industries, was the cause of the
faster movement of Swiss labour to these industries. Foreign
manpower was relatively less mobile owing to the legal restrictions on its geographical and occupational mobility and to the
recruitment policy of Group I industries, which preferred to
take on home workers.

(b) Period 1959-1960/1964

The fluidity of the labour market could only last as
long as the geographical and occupational mobility of Swiss
workers was sufficient to meet the demand from Group I industries.
Tightness began to appear on the employment market in 1960 and
was aggravated by the inflation which was a feature of the Swiss
economy at that time. It was also then that the results of the
increasingly permanent nature of immigration (result of the
self-feeding process) began to be felt. This situation was to
give an ever greater impetus to Swiss economic growth and to
draw labour away from private industrial production. Increasing
requirements as regards infrastructure had to be met, and
especially housing for immigrants, who were tending more and
more to bring their families with them. Seasonal workers also
become pseudo-seasonal workers.

During this period, Swiss workers moved mainly towards
the tertiary sector.

Group II industries therefore gradually lost their home
labour force. About 1960, there were not very many more Swiss
workers who wished voluntarily to change to another industry,

especially as Group II industries which could not allow all of their home workers to go had to react in order to keep some of them. Some of these industries were therefore obliged to speed up their rate of wage increase and to bring their terms into line with those of Group I industries.

Efforts were of course made at that time to increase the participation of potential national workers (older workers, women, etc.), but these were not sufficient.

Working hours, for their part, fell on the whole, but this reduction was largely tempered and even compensated for by overtime.

Because of this reduction in geographical and occupational mobility and because of the small success met by policies for increasing participation, the number of Swiss workers increased in only the following two Group I industries during this period: the printing trades and chemicals. Apart from these exceptions, the number of Swiss workers fell in all other industries, the reduction being particularly striking in Group II industries.

The situation on the employment market was such that firms signed mutual agreements that they would not "steal" each others' labour force.

Because of a general increase in demand, employment capacity continued to grow, to such a point that the mobility of Swiss workers was no longer sufficient to meet the demand for labour. In these circumstances, it became necessary to amend immigration policy and make it less selective(1). Foreign workers were henceforth to be recruited by all industries, although no change was made to the principles governing their movements.

This policy introduced a certain measure of flexibility into the labour market which was nonetheless very different from the situation previously obtaining, since as a result of the gradual reduction in the geographical and occupational mobility of Swiss workers, the new labour supply was to consist practically entirely of foreign workers for all branches of manufacturing industry. This new situation was to be the cause of the narrowing of the interindustrial wage spread. Thus, the Group II industries were obliged to raise their wages in order to attract immigrants for whom their need was increasing more than ever. The wage increases as from 1959-1960 in most Group II industries were higher than average, while at the same time the increases in Group I industries were slower. The industries where the increases were lower than average (clothing, food) were those which lost and would continue to lose most Swiss workers.

_____

(1) See V. Lutz "Manodopera straniera e livelli salariali interni con particolare riferimento alla situazione svizzera", Moneta e Credito, 64, 1963, pages 497-566.

(c) Period 1964-1970/71

On 1st March, 1963, the Federal Council restricted the entry of foreign manpower, and as a result of this policy the labour market became tight and the wage spread narrowed to less than it had been in 1949. However, the tightness of the employment market was relaxed until 1964 since foreign workers could always replace Swiss workers leaving certain industries.

As from 1965, the trend of the interindustrial wage spread bears the mark of both immigration (twin-ceiling system) and cyclical policy.

During the cyclical showdown in 1966-1967, the spread tended to remain narrow or, to be more exact, it followed a zigzag pattern. This trend well illustrates the expectations of the various industries as regards changes in immigration policy and more especially for a policy combining the internal liberalisation of foreign manpower, as well as their concern to keep their Swiss labour force. Wage rises in the various industries therefore followed quite a complex pattern. They no longer obeyed the same logic as previously or, in other words, the behaviour of industries within each group was no longer identical. The different wage increases partly followed the trend of employment capacity.

On the whole, an adjustment procedure came into operation whose purpose was to keep wage differences on an even keel. Hence the zigzag trend of the wage spread: as soon as wages increase in certain industries and the spread broadens, a readjustment movement may be observed in other industries. This results in a higher wage increase than previously[1].

It must in fact be noted that the "twin-ceiling" system considerably reduced workers' possibilities of geographical and occupational mobility, while at the same time the supply of new labour was also reduced. In these circumstances, it is normal that the wage spread should remain narrow since all employers wish to keep their labour force; but it is also normal that industries which need more labour should tend to raise their wages.

The "twin-ceiling" system has restricted geographical and occupational mobility, and even though a certain mobility has been established under this system, it has not concerned a sufficient number of workers to justify wage increases. But the new system introduced in March 1970 should in theory permit greater

_____

[1] See also the arguments by A.A. Rossi and K. Schiltknecht, "Uebernachfrage und Lohnentwicklung in der Schweiz", op. cit., pages 247 and 252.

geographical and occupational mobility(1). Thus, the "twin-ceiling" system was abolished and the obstacles to the mobility of foreign workers relaxed both as regards occupational mobility (change of trade) and geographical mobility (movements from one canton to another). In these circumstances, it is not impossible that all Swiss wages will fan out again.

A number of points should be considered in order to assess the trend of future geographical and occupational mobility and the role of the wage spread in the reallocation of employment:

1.   This mobility will mainly affect foreign workers. It will depend on the number who have lived for three consecutive years in Switzerland, and are therefore able to change their job or canton, and also on the attraction of higher wages for these workers.

2.   The policy of the cantonal commissions responsible for distributing the cantonal quotas can be decisive. If these commissions allocate the new residence permits to dynamic firms, the interindustrial wage spread will tend to remain narrow. If, on the contrary, new foreign workers are steered to the lower-paid industries, the spread will probably tend to broaden.

---

(1) This was what in fact happened. Thus, in the annual survey of the situation in Switzerland in 1972, the O.E.C.D. considers (pages 12 and 13) that interindustrial labour shifts were on the increase. "On the basis of simple indices attempting to quantify this phenomenon, there seems to have been a faster degree of workers' mobility in both 1970 and (especially) in the first nine months of 1971 than in 1968 or 1969. The same seems to have been the case if total (and not just workers') employment is considered. As for the direction of these shifts, it is less easy to be precise. In 1970, the largest declines in workers' employment were all recorded in sectors ranking lowest in a scale constructed on the basis of hourly wage earnings. Similar, though less marked, falls have taken place in the first half of 1971. Strong increases in employment, on the other hand, are not uniformly to be found among high-wage sectors. The chemical, printing and rubber industries, which rank 1st, 2nd and 3rd respectively in terms of wages, attracted workers, but so too did the construction sector, though hourly earnings in this branch are relatively low. The longer duration of the working week in building implies, however, that in terms of weekly earnings its rank among the twenty most important branches is perhaps 7th or 8th (against 15th on the basis of hourly earnings)".

3.   Insofar as there has been some liberalisation of the
geographical and occupational mobility of foreign manpower, wage
movements and interindustrial mobility will probably depend on
the extent to which the production apparatus has been changed in
the various industries as a result of labour restrictions. The
trend of employment capacity and therefore the demand for labour
will depend on such changes. For instance, if the production
apparatus has been sufficiently altered to become more capital-
intensive, with economies on labour therefore, manpower movements from one industry to another will be limited, not because
the workers do not want to change their jobs but because the
industrial branches do not offer more jobs. It is therefore the
trend of employment capacity following changes in the production
apparatus which becomes decisive when analysing manpower
movements.

4.   Consequences of manpower supply policy

As we said at the start, Switzerland's immigration policy
has enabled it to dispense with a growth policy or a counter-
cyclical policy, foreign manpower having acted as a regulator
of economic activity for many years and as an indispensable
growth factor in the sense that it has prevented the formation
of bottlenecks.

A process which was thought to be temporary became
indispensable to the working of the system and to the pattern
of employment. As soon as the parties concerned realised that
the machinery could seize up, they gave it their earnest
attention, but their thinking was confined to the possibility
of obtaining more and more labour and to the problem of the
worsening quality of that labour. The secondary consequences
which were to become important were only rarely considered
before 1965.

The fact is that to deal with this continuing migration
and its mounting consequences would have required adopting an
adequate counter-cyclical policy much sooner and even a growth
policy, or preferably a structural policy.

The migratory phenomenon therefore had various consequences
which must be now looked into. In dealing with them, we shall
leave out the sociological aspects, in particular the assimilation problem and the xenophobic reactions which led to the
famous Schwarzenbach initiative (20th May 1969, rejected by
popular vote on 7th June 1970 by 654,844 against 557,517), and
shall consider the effects of the process on the structure of
employment (shortage of Swiss workers in certain industries,
orientation of Swiss workers towards the tertiary sector, large
numbers of foreign workers in industry, etc.), and then its
effects on the inflationary process and on the growth of community requirements, and lastly its impact on the pattern of
productive organisation (trend of production factor combinations).

4.1   Inter-industrial pattern of employment

It is possible to correct the effects of immigration on
the cost of living or on the balance of payments by means of an
adequate counter-cyclical policy, but the structure of employment raises a different problem since the stage has been reached
where several Swiss industries would run into serious difficulties if a certain amount of foreign manpower was not available
to them (Table 10). Due to past immigration policy, all
industries have not been penetrated equally by foreign labour
and it is not possible to correct rapidly the existing mal-
distribution of foreign labour between industries. It looks as
though the Swiss economy will long continue to depend on foreign
workers, the more so as those industries which employed but few
foreign workers before 1960 (chemicals, clocks and watches,
printing trades) now employ considerably larger numbers of these
workers. This phenomenon is not peculiar to the secondary
sector but also applies to the tertiary sector. It is in fact

increasingly the case that while the foreign labour force subject to control is falling in most secondary sector industries
(with the notable exception of building and construction) it is
rising in such branches as health, personal services and for
trade staff.

The stoppage of immigration caused the labour supply
renewal mechanism to seize up and at the same time reduced the
fluidity of the market. An increase in the Swiss active population cannot be counted on to re-establish this fluidity but
rather the geographical and occupational mobility of foreign
workers who are now practically free of any discrimination as
regards the jobs they can take. However, such movements can
evidently only benefit the more attractive industries, while
the others will always have more difficulty in renewing their
labour force. In most cases, the problem can only be solved by
changing the structure of the productive apparatus. For the
time being, however, the struggle to obtain labour will remain
keen and result in wage increases, in the absence of which it
will in time become impossible to find workers to take certain
relatively badly paid jobs(1). It remains to be seen whether
this will come about naturally or whether more direct measures
will be necessary.

4.2 Inflation

Before 1960, immigration seemed rather to have the effect
of curbing inflation because foreign manpower kept the labour
market fluid and many immigrants did not bring their families
with them; but after 1960 the problem arose in a new form.
Overall demand was growing, the wage spread was already beginning to narrow (meaning that the "low-wage" industries were
raising their wage rates) and the percentage of foreign workers
was becoming large in certain industries. What was more surprising, but reflected the disturbance in the productive
apparatus at that time, was that the massive arrivals of
foreigners were only one more sign of the tightness of the
employment market and the pressure on the productive apparatus.
The tertiary sector also was developing. Foreign workers'
families were arriving in increasing numbers. Infrastructure
investment which had been delayed until then had to be carried
out in roads, housing and schools. As a result of internal
migration towards the main urban centres, the housing market
came under very strong pressure. All of these factors helped
immigration to snowball.

However, it would be a mistake to regard immigration as
being alone responsible for inflation. Certain qualifications
are necessary. This is the opinion of Rossi and Thomas(2), who

(1) W. Böhning, op. cit., page 8.

(2) Rossi and Thomas, op. cit., pages 763 and 764.

say that, after 1958, "almost without exception, this increase in the rate of inflation has been attributed to an expansion of aggregate demand. In particular, it is maintained that this increase in aggregate demand started with an investment boom and was reinforced by increases in private consumption.

As far as the determinants of the expansion of aggregate demand are concerned, it is held that this was the result of factors whose origin was outside the Swiss economy - in particular the importation of money capital and labour. One view is that the investment boom of the sixties was a consequence of the inflow of capital from abroad and the resultant fall in interest rates. An alternative view is that the boom was the result of an expansion in investment demand caused by the need for a widening of productive capital to keep it in line with a labour force which was rapidly expanding because of increased immigration. Supporting this view is the argument that in the second part of the postwar period a rapid increase in government expenditure was necessary to re-establish a certain equilibrium between the needs of the increased population and the available social capital.

Expansions in private consumption are also regarded as chiefly a consequence of immigration. It is maintained that, at first, the average immigrant, with his high rate of saving and remittances abroad, contributes more to aggregate supply than to aggregate demand. However, once the immigrant's family joins him, the ratio between his contribution to aggregate supply and his contribution to aggregate demand must necessarily fall. To this must be added the influence on aggregate consumption of the increase in the size of the non-working proportion of the immigrant population, which accompanied the increase in total immigrant manpower".

In short, the faster pace of inflation in Switzerland "can be attributed to a cumulative process, whereby an increasing population results in an increased demand for both consumption and investment goods which in turn leads to upward pressure on wages and prices and an increasing tightness in the labour market. The steadily increasing demand for labour creates more job opportunities and this in turn causes yet further immigration".

In their model, these two authors make immigration play an anti-inflationary role: "An increase in aggregate demand for final goods leads to tighter labour market conditions. This in turn encourages greater immigration, swells the total labour force, thus easing conditions in the labour market. The rate of wage and price inflation is therefore lower than it would be in the absence of immigration"(1). And to conclude, "it appears that divergencies between the rates of increase of real GNP and average productivity (output per man) are important

(1) Rossi and Thomas, op. cit., page 768.

factors in determining the rates of wage and price inflation in Switzerland. When real GNP grows faster than average productivity, both the rate of inflation and the level of immigration rise, although the increase in immigration acts as a braking force on the wage and price rises. However, when average productivity growth exceeds that of real GNP, the inflationary tendencies are curbed and the level of immigration is stabilized and eventually reduced."(1)

One must therefore be wary of seeing too direct a link between immigration and inflation. The flow and volume of migration are in fact only the manifestation of a long process which has steered the productive apparatus and therefore the cost structure(2).

Under the weight of strong aggregrate demand, the system for allocating foreign workers broke down and thereby dismantled the unwritten wages policy which had operated so far. It was then that the inadequacy of the capital/labour mix became apparent and probably also the scale of production. We shall continue our researches by analysing these factors.

4.3   Effects on the capital/labour mix(2)

As we have seen, the labour supply was a decisive factor in the dynamics of Swiss economic growth.

The plentiful supply of labour has without a doubt set the trend for the capital/labour mix and for the size of production units, and has consequently determined how much labour and capital should be employed.

It can be claimed that the labour market policy followed in the fifties amounted to some extent to indirectly establishing a differentiated wage policy.

In other words, up to 1958/60, wages increased with productivity in each industry. In manufacturing industries as a whole wages went up by about 3 per cent a year between 1949 and 1960 and for the same period the increase in productivity per man/hour was, according to various sources, 2.5 to 3.5 per cent.

The increase in earnings in general was higher than average in Group I industries and lower than average in Group II industries and it is precisely this dissimilar develppment that has broadened the inter-industrial wage spectrum.

---

(1)   Rossi and Thomas, op. cit., page 785.

(2)   See W. Böhning's chapter, op. cit., on this problem, pages 51 et seq.

As a result the less dynamic industries have benefited considerably to the extent that they have been able to keep wage increases in step with the growth in their own productivity and not with the growth in average productivity or with productivity in the most dynamic industries.

Seen against this background, in what way has immigration policy, through its effect on aggregate manpower supply, influenced developments in the factor mix and therefore employment capacity.

Developments and improvements in the supply of jobs depend upon the mix of the various factors of production that firms adopt as a result of socio-economic pressures.

Though Switzerland found itself in a growth situation at the end of the Second World War it was feared that the recovery would be short-lived and the psychological climate that this produced had a considerable influence on the behaviour of entrepreneurs with regard to the expansion of the production facilities necessary to meet the vigorous demand on the home market and the even more vigorous demand from abroad. It is important to remember that the volume and nature of aggregate investment depends upon industry's view of what the future holds. European reconstruction called for substantial investment and Switzerland's resources were in great demand since her production facilities had not suffered during the war.

In response to demand at home and abroad industry was very quickly working at maximum capacity and output had to be increased by stepping up the labour force and expanding production capacity.

The first of these two processes absorbed manpower in great numbers and all available Swiss reserves were very quickly taken up (full employment of indigenous manpower). This was why, even at that early date, a quota of foreign manpower had to be imported for some industries. However, increasing the workforce was only a very short-term method of increasing output and industry very quickly had to expand its production resources in order to meet the growing demand.

Decisions on investment were taken at a relatively early date, probably prior to 1950. At that time Switzerland had not fully recovered from the shock of the war and the future was viewed with pessimism. There was no shortage of economists and others prophesying that an economic crisis was imminent and undoubtedly there was very little elasticity in industry's forward planning. This psychological climate was hardly one in which entrepreneurs would be likely to take the risks involved in new investment requiring a change in the mix of factors of production.

Thus, to meet the continuing need for increased output, production resources were almost invariably expanded without alteration to the original factor mix. In other words the new production units perpetuated the old techniques with, at the most, small-scale rationalisation and innovation.

Contributing to this was the fact that manpower was plentiful, the economy was buoyant (with prices going up steadily) and thus a constant decline in marginal productivity in terms of value could be accepted (in such circumstances the countries able to increase their production most rapidly are those with the biggest manpower resources).

At the core of the problem, therefore, was the capital/labour mix. But using more, or less, labour or capital naturally varies with the sector involved (industry, agriculture, construction, services, etc.) and thus the effect of immigration on the relative proportions of labour and capital may have been very different from sector to sector. Too broadly-based a study of the situation might lead to incorrect conclusions. It is possible, for example, to form a rough picture of what happened in the secondary sector, but it is more difficult to analyse the services sector in which productivity, as is known, is low, and in which the situation in Switzerland was highly conducive to expansion in view of its attraction for indigenous manpower. This tertiary sector (including tourism) is certainly responsible to no slight extent for the increasing expansion in the total number of jobs in the Swiss economy.

It may therefore be assumed as a working hypothesis that immigration has been a major incentive for retaining the existing structure of production resources(1) not only from the technical viewpoint but also in terms of maintaining the social structure (type of ownership, management system). The latter point is important since there is no doubt that immigration has made it possible to postpone changes in scale of production which, in most cases, entail changes in social structure.

But it would be wrong to regard immigration as the only factor affecting the labour/capital mix: there are several structural features in Swiss production resources that need to be considered:

- The structure of Swiss industry (mainly small and medium-sized enterprises) is conducive to investment of the "capital-saving" type;

- Swiss industry is regarded traditionally as labour-intensive;

(1) D. Maillat, Structure des salaires et immigration, op. cit., p. 95; O.E.C.D. Economic surveys, Switzerland 1967, p. 11; M. Hagmann, Les Travailleurs étrangers, chance et tourment de la Suisse, p. 80.

- Another factor is the cyclical situation and the entrepreneur's tendency to react quickly to the pressure of demand. This applies to many firms and in particular export-oriented firms anxious not to lose their markets. In this context, "capital-saving" investment offers much more flexibility for increasing output. It must not be forgotten that a relatively long time may elapse between deciding to use new techniques and being in fact in a position to use them and during this time there can be no corresponding increase in sales. Major changes of this kind more often than not mean the relocation of plant, new staff, changes to the internal chain of command, etc. Thus Swiss industry, export-oriented by force of circumstance, is obliged to remain extremely flexible and avoid crippling capital investment. The fact is that a firm planning large-scale technical improvements in its production resources and therefore compelled in many cases to make substantial fixed investment in order to increase its scale of production to the necessary level, takes a grave risk, since, as long as it is in activity there are difficulties in the way of changing its production processes. This is why the risks involved in large-scale fixed investment in a country exporting specialised products act as a disincentive to capital expenditure and result in production being broken down into small units providing a certain capacity for absorbing cyclical fluctuation;

- A further factor is the family ownership of many firms and the obstacle that this presents for a policy of amalgamation or concentration to achieve economies of scale;

- The fact that it is only recently that Switzerland has become interested in an agreement with the E.E.C. may also have helped to delay the process of adjustment through which changes to the industrial structure of the country might be made.

    As a general principal, therefore, it must be considered that Switzerland has to be able to show considerable flexibility in industrial adjustment in relation to foreign trade and this explains why the capital/labour mix is designed to secure this flexibility. By avoiding over-large production units and applying a sort of generalised sub-contracting system, Switzerland has absorbed cyclical fluctuations with comparative ease. Moreover, a conservative attitude with regard to excessive fixed investment has kept acceleration under tight rein and has helped to prevent any deterioration in the balance of payments position.

    In spite of the foregoing, there is no denying that, on the whole, immigration has been "capital-saving" even if only because it has helped to provide labour for various existing firms and has helped others to be set up, in cases where this

would not have been possible without a plentiful manpower
supply. But if the mechanism of the situation is to be properly
understood it would be wrong to consider only the special
cases; the study needs to be conducted at individual industry
level since not all industries or firms have reacted in the
same way.

A preliminary principle which may be assumed at this
point is that the degree to which a factor of production is
plentiful or otherwise affects its relative price and thus con
ditions the attitude of entrepreneurs towards its possible use.
In the present case manpower is the factor in plentiful supply.
It is therefore likely that firms wishing to lower their production costs or to hold them at the lowest possible level will
employ more manpower than capital in relative terms. The
capital/labour mix will therefore be of the capital-saving
type. Other parameters (technological progress in particular)
affecting development in production functions also need to be
taken into account, the basic idea being that the introduction
of technological advances has been delayed by the plentiful
manpower supply(1).

It should be noted that "capital-saving" and "labour-
saving" factor mixes are not mutually exclusive. It is in fact
rare for an investment to reduce the cost of only one factor
since this would imply zero substitution elasticity. In the
most general case absolute but unequal savings are achieved in
both factors. The question is therefore whether the automation,
rationalisation, etc., which industry claims to have introduced,
has meant relatively greater economies in manpower than in
capital. A further question is whether these technical advances
that have been introduced have increased the elasticity of substitution.

Elasticity of substitution is important because it helps
to establish the extent to which changes in the relative prices
of factors of production lead to a quickening or slowing down
in the rate of increase in productivity deriving from technological progress itself.

A further important factor in determining the labour/
capital mix is the initial decision. In other words, thought
must be given to the circumstances in which it is right to use
the production function in the analysis. Generally this can
be used for purposes of taking an investment decision. Because
each technique calls for different capital equipment, the
choice between the various technologies must be made before the
investment is committed. Once the decision on technique has
been taken and the investment made, analysis in terms of the
production function is no longer applicable. Throughout the
life of the equipment, substitution between factors of production

(1) The opposite view is taken in F. Schaller, Le rôle de la
     main-d'oeuvre étrangère dans l'économie suisse, op. cit.

can only be short-term; it is limited by the nature of the
equipment. It is not until the equipment has to be replaced
that analysis in terms of the production function becomes
applicable again. Thus the choice between the various techniques
defined by the production function applies only to entrepreneurs
having to make investment decisions with regard to new or
replacement equipment.

Generally the decision is governed by:

- the cost of capital (rate of interest)
- the cost of labour (wage rates)
- the cost of capital goods.

The most important relation, in fact, would appear to be
that between the cost of labour and the cost of capital equipment.

During the period 1949-69 the increase in the index of
nominal wages in relation to the index of domestic capital
formation has been of the order of 52 per cent (Table 14). In
the long term, therefore, there seems to have been a slight
tendency for the substitution of capital for labour. Nevertheless, it is important to note that the trend of the labour
cost/capital cost ratio is not linear. It is only from 1963
that it showed a clearcut tendency to increase. During the
period between 1959 and 1963, the annual growth rate in this
ratio was practically zero and the same is true of the period
between 1954 and 1958. The index remained at about 110 from
1954 to 1958 and then increased to 115/120 between 1959 and
1968. Thereafter, the gap has increasingly widened. It may
therefore be concluded that up to 1963 the relative costs of
labour and of capital were roughly the same and there was therefore little incentive to substitute one for the other.

Admittedly the labour cost index/capital cost index ratio
provides no breakdown of investment as between extensions and
equipment. This breakdown is, however, possible from 1958
onwards. From that year on the curves for the labour cost index/
construction cost index, labour cost index/machinery and equipment cost index and labour cost index/capital formation cost
index ratios have a similar profile to the aggregate relationship. These curves show that, up to 1963, the relative costs
of labour and of construction investment were stable. The same
applies to machinery and equipment investment except that the
cost in this case begins to increase from 1960 on. There is
therefore no reason for altering our earlier conclusion that
there was little incentive, up to 1963, to substitute capital
for labour. It was only after this date that wage increases
gave rise to substitution trends since it was only then that
the labour cost/capital cost ratio altered in any marked manner.
From the examples quoted it can be seen that in Switzerland
improvements in productivity resulted from a slow process of
substitution of capital for labour as a result of the gradual
changes in the relative prices of these factors and it is the

fact that the improvement in productivity stemming from the substitution process is relatively slight which explains why labour productivity has increased very slowly in Switzerland compared with other industrial countries.

Thus the steps which firms have taken to increase their level of mechanisation and the partial automation in existing structures to which this has led has produced only very slight improvements in labour productivity.(1) Substitution of this type therefore has a relatively negligible effect on cost trends since its labour-saving effect is also very slight.

The retention of the traditional structure made it difficult to do better. It is a known fact that savings in all factors are mostly the result of economies of scale (which are necessary for investment projects representing major technological advances).

In short, improvements in labour productivity depend primarily on technical progress and economies of scale, and less on substitution of factors of production.

This theoretical argument would appear to be largely true in relation to the Swiss economy and particularly in the secondary sector. It confirms that restricting immigration would call for a considerable change in the scale of production. Industrial concentration appears to be the best way of improving the productivity of all factors of production and such processes (changes in the scales of production, rationalisation at industry level) are now taking place. This is why it is now being said in Switzerland that production resources are being "restructured in depth".

At this point another problem arises and that is the use to be made of production capacities based on the old formula and now becoming obsolescent because of immigration restrictions. The case is pertinent since many firms are complaining that they cannot use their full production capacity for lack of manpower (quite apart from the cyclical downswing). The truth is that many firms will have to substitute capital for capital. Structural investment will probably have to slow down and machinery and equipment investment accelerate in order to provide the necessary substantial increase in labour productivity. This is because the substitution measures taken when manpower was still plentiful cannot be extended in time.

_____

(1) Whilst new technologies may be introduced to replace existing equipment during the life of a firm, in practically every case this process is less effective and more costly than building them into a new plant. In the extreme case it may be absolutely impossible to use new and old techniques together; this applies when the improvements made by the new technologies call for changes of scale (so that in many cases there is no alternative but to retain the traditional labour/capital mix).

TABLE 12

CAPITAL COST INDICATORS (from national accounts)

	1949	1950	1951	1952	1953	1954	1955	1956	1957	1958	1959	1960	1961	1962	1963	1964	1965	1966	1967	1968	1969
1. Consumption expenditure on goods and services	100	99.7	104.1	107.1	106.8	107.7	109.3	111.2	113.7	116.4	115.7	116.8	118.7	123.7	127.3	132.1	136.9	142.9	149.1	153.3	157.6
2. Gross domestic capital formation	100	91.8	100.7	105.4	102.7	101.6	104.0	107.5	111.8	114.8	114.9	119.3	126.9	133.9	143.7	150.0	154.3	159.6	162.6	165.1	169.2

Indices for the following rows are on base 1958 = 100:

	1958	1959	1960	1961	1962	1963	1964	1965	1966	1967	1968	1969
2. Gross domestic capital formation	100	100.1	103.9	110.6	116.6	125.2	130.7	134.4	139.0	141.6	143.8	147.4
3. Construction	100	100.1	111.9	118.0	126.3	132.0	135.7	140.2	142.9	145.2		149.8
4. Machinery and equipment	100	101.2	105.4	114.0	121.4	131.3	137.7	141.8	145.5	147.2	148.8	154.9
5. Fixed asset formation	100	97.9	104.2	108.1	112.1	117.6	121.2	124.5	130.8	135.4	139.2	141.3

Source: La Vie Economique

TABLE 13

WAGE INDICES

	1949	1950	1951	1952	1953	1954	1955	1956	1957	1958	1959	1960	1961	1962	1963	1964	1965	1966	1967	1968	1969
6. Blue-collar workers (earnings)	100	101	105	108	109	111	114	119	124	129	133	140	149	160	173	187	201	217	220	242	257
(1958 = 100)										100	103	108	116	124	134	145	156	168	179	188	199
7. White-collar workers (salaries)	100	101	105	108	110	112	115	120	125	129	133	138	145	155	164	176	188	202	216	228	242
(1958 = 100)										100	103	107	112	120	127	136	146	157	167	177	188

Source: La Vie Economique, October survey of wages

TABLE 14

RATIOS: Wage indices/capital cost indicators

	1949	1950	1951	1952	1953	1954	1955	1956	1957	1958	1959	1960	1961	1962	1963	1964	1965	1966	1967	1968	1969
6/2	100	110.0	104.3	102.5	106.1	109.3	109.6	110.7	110.9	112.4	115.8	117.3	117.4	119.5	120.4	124.7	130.3	136.0	141.5	146.6	151.9

Indices for the following rows are on base 1958 = 100:

	1958	1959	1960	1961	1962	1963	1964	1965	1966	1967	1968	1969
6/2	100	102.9	104.4	106.3	107.1	110.9	110.9	115.7	121.0	125.9	130.5	135.1
6/3	100	102.9	103.1	105.0	106.2	109.7	114.8	119.9	124.8	129.2		132.9
6/4	100	101.9	102.9	101.3	102.1	102.1	105.2	109.8	115.6	121.2	126.0	128.6
6/5	100	105.3	104.1	106.8	110.6	114.0	119.5	125.1	128.5	131.7	134.7	140.9

5.   Conclusion

     One objective conclusion from the above considerations is
that immigration has been an important factor in the flexibility
of Swiss production resources. It has allowed rapid short-term
adjustment of small-size units of production, which have been
able to tap this source of labour to respond quickly to the
pressure of demand. The importance of this role of immigration
has been heightened by the fact that the indigenous active population has been increasing at a very slow rate. This point is
made in a general way by J.L. Reiffers(1), who writes: "...it
seems clear that a country whose own active population has
ceased to increase and which is made up of economic units
aspiring to a higher level of well-being (and therefore exhibiting
a consumption behaviour directed at a continuously higher product level) cannot do without a supply of imported labour.
Even though it may be argued that the immigrant consumes more
than he produces (which is highly debatable) and that his use
necessitates considerable investment (which is true in theory
but rarely in practice) these costs will be unimportant compared
with the indirect benefits of immigration, whose essential
advantage is that it releases the economy from the constraints
of over-employment". The restrictions on immigration will now
rob the Swiss economy of this flexibility particulary since the
government does not have the necessary machinery to regulate
aggregate demand. This raises the question of the long-term
growth of the Swiss economy. In view of the direction already
taken in terms of the labour/capital mix when the labour market
was still flexible, new growth thresholds will now have to be
crossed in conditions in which the labour market will be tight.
The structural changes that this implies "will be largely dic-
tated by the ease of capital-labour situation(2)". Whilst
operations of this kind are now in progress(3), it is also

_____

(1) J.L. Reiffers, op. cit., p. 184.

(2) O.E.C.D., Economic Surveys, Switzerland, 1972, p. 10

(3) "It should not be forgotten in this context that though the
     supply of labour will not rise much in the future, the
     capital stock has increased substantially and will, in all
     likelihood, continue to grow rapidily. The share of gross
     investment in Switzerland has been, and is, among the
     highest in O.E.C.D. countries. This implies that, even with
     low investment growth, annual additions to the capital stock
     are sizeable. The upward investment spurt of the last few
     years has, of course, reinforced this tendency. It is true
     that a relatively large share of gross investment has, lately,
     been devoted to replacement of obsolete equipment but it can
     be argued that, in the specific post-1965 Swiss conditions,
     replacement investment represents to a large extent, in any
     case larger than in the past, a net addition to the capital
     stock. This is mainly a consequence of the abrupt change in
     factor availabilities which has led to shifts in factor mixes
     and implies that the machinery which at present replaces
     worn-out equipment is likely to embody the latest capital-
     intenive techniques". (O.E.C.D., Economic Survey,
     Switzerland, 1972, p. 48)

probable that other adjustments will take place including the transfer abroad of a number of productive activities(1).

These comments, read together with the results of our study, indicate the extent to which immigration has become part of the mechanism of the Swiss economic system. Perhaps too extreme a use has been made of immigration policy in order to facilitate the structural modifications that are necessary for sustained economic growth since it is difficult to see how over-employment bottlenecks are going to be obviated without an additional supply of labour.

Possibly, as we have pointed out, investment may be shifted abroad. Whilst this would appear to provide a solution to some problems, in the long run Swiss economic growth could well be jeopardised since the firms moving their productive activities abroad will certainly not be those lacking initiative and vigour. All this clearly shows that immigration policy alone is not a full answer to the problem and that what is required is a real policy for economic growth including, in particular, an industrial policy since this is the only way to take a progressive option on the future. An approach of this kind will certainly be difficult in a country which still hesitates to give its government the cyclical policy instruments to regulate overall demand.

(1) O.E.C.D., Economic Studies, Switzerland, 1972, p. 10.

BIBLIOGRAPHY

1. ARDENTI J.C. et REICHENBACH J.P.,
   Estimation de la fonction de production CES pour la Suisse,
   Revue suisse d'économie politique et de statistique, 4/1972,
   p. 575-588.

2. BAHRAL, Uri,
   The Effect of Mass Immigration on Wages in Israel,
   Jerusalem, 1965.

3. BELTRAMONE A.,
   La mobilité géographique d'une population, Ed. Gauthier-
   Villars, Paris, 1966.

4. BFS,
   Quelques données démographiques, 1960-1970, Doc. trav.
   72.02, Berne, février 1972.

5. BRAUN R.,
   Sozio-kulturelle Probleme der Eingliederung italienischer
   Arbeitskräfte in der Schweiz, Rentsch, Erlenbach-Zürich,
   1970.

6. CASTLES S. et KOSACK G.,
   Immigrant workers and class structure in Western Europe,
   Oxford University Press, 1973.

7. Council of Europe
   Report on the demographic and social pattern of migrants
   in Europe, especially with regard to international
   migrations. (MM. Livi-Bacci et M.H. Hagmann) 2nd European
   demographic conference, 1971.

8. DANIELI L.,
   Labour scarcities and labour redundancies in Europe by
   1980: An experimental study, Dipartimento statistico
   matematico, Firenze, 1971.

9. FOEHL C.,
   Stabilisierung und Wachstum beim Einsatz von Gastarbeitern,
   Kyklos, vol. XX, 1967.

10. GIROD R.,
    Travailleurs étrangers et mobilité sociale en Suisse,
    Revue économique et sociale, mai 1966, p. 149-171.

11. GNEHM A.H.,
    Ausländische Arbeitskräfte, Vor-und Nachteile für die
    Volkswirtschaft, Haupt, Bern, 1966.

12. HAGMANN M.,
    Les travailleurs étrangers, chance et tourment de la
    Suisse, Payot, Lausanne, 1966.

13. HOFMANN-NOVOTNY, H.J.
    Migration, Ein Beitrag zu einer soziologischen Erklärung,
    Stuttgart, 1970.

14. HUGH-JONES E.M., Ed.,
     Wage structure in Theory and Practice, North Holland
     Publishing Company, Amsterdam, 1966.

15. HULTMANN C.W.,
     Factor Migration: Trade Theory and Growth Centers,
     International Migration, No 3, 1970, p.130-137.

16. JOEHR W.A. et HUBER R.,
     Die konjunkturellen Auswirkungen der Beanspruchung aus-
     ländischer Arbeitskräfte. Untersuchungen mit Hilfe eines
     Simulationmodelles der schweizerischen Volkswirtschaft,
     Revue suisse d'économie politique et de statistique, no 4,
     1968, pp. 365-610 et no 1, 1969, pp. 3-92.

17. JONES K. et SMITH A.,
     The Economic Impact of Commonwealth Immigration, Cambridge
     University Press, London, 1970.

18. KAYSER B.,
     Cyclically determined homeward flows of migrant workers,
     OCDE, 1972.

19. KAYSER B.,
     Manpower movements and labour markets, OCDE, 1971.

20. KALBACH W.E.,
     The Impact of Immigration on Canada's Population, Dominion
     Bureau of Statistics, Ottawa, 1970.

21. KINDLEBERGER C.P.,
     Europe's Postwar Growth, The Role of Labour Supply,
     Harvard University Press, 1967.

22. KINDLEBERGER C.P.,
     Emigration and Economic Growth, Banco nazionale del Lavoro,
     no 74, 1965.

23. KNESCHAUREK F.,
     Perspectives de l'évolution de l'économie suisse jusqu'en
     l'an 2000, Population et activité, ST-Gall, 1969.

24. Kommission für Konjunkturfragen, Anhänge zum Bericht Ziele,
     Mittel und Träger der Konjunkturpolitik, Bern, sept. 1971.

25. KRUSE A.,
     Der deutsche Arbeitsmarkt und die Gastarbeiter, Schmollers
     Jahrbuch, no 4, 1966, p. 423-434.

26. KRUSE A.,
     Volkswirtschaftliche Aspekte des Gastarbeiterproblem,
     Volkswirtschaftliche Korrespondenz der Adolf-Weber Stiftung,
     no 7, 1966.

27. LAMBELET J.C. et SCHILTKNECHT K.,
     On the importance of an elastic supply of foreign Labor
     and Capital, University of Pennsylvania, Discussion Paper
     no 236, May 1972 (roneoed).

28. LUTZ V.,
     Manodopera straniera e livelli salariali interni con parti-
     colare riferimento alla situazione suizzera, Noneta de
     credito, 1963.

29. MAILLAT D.,
     Research on the economic effects of the employment of
     foreign workers: the case of Switzerland, OCDE, (Working
     document), April 1974.

30. MAILLAT D.,
    Structure des salaires entre branches d'industrie et
    mobilité de la main-d'oeuvre, Revue économique et sociale,
    no 3, 1970.

31. MAILLAT D.,
    Structure des salaires et immigration, Dunod, Paris, 1968.

32. MARSHALL A.,
    Labour force immigration in the Netherlands, Nederlandse
    economische Hogschool, 1972, roneo-ed

33. MERX V.,
    Struktur und Flexibilität des Arbeitsmarkts in der BR-
    Deutschland unter dem Einfluss der Beschäftigung auslän-
    discher Arbeitnehmer, Köln 1972.

34. MISHAN E.J. and NEEDLEMAN L.,
    Immigration: Some Long Term Economic Consequences,
    Economica Internazionale, vol. XXI, nos 2 et 3.

35. OFIAMT,
    Le problème de la main-d'oeuvre étrangère, Berne 1964.

36. OECD,
    Expenditure trends in OECD countries, 1960-80, July 1972

37. OECD,
    Wages and Labour Mobility, Paris, 1965.

38. OECD,
    Economic Survey, Switzerland, various years.

39. REIFFERS J.-L.,
    Le rôle de l'immigration des travailleurs dans la croissance
    de la République fédérale d'Allemagne, 1958-1968, ILO, 1970.

40. ROSSI A.A. et SCHILTKNECHT K.,
    Uebernachfrage und Lohnentwicklung in der Schweiz. Eine
    neue Hypothese, Kyklos, vol. XXV, 1972, p. 239-253.

41. ROSSI A.A. et THOMAS R.L.,
    Inflation in the Post-war Swiss Economy - an Econometric
    Study of the Interaction between Immigration and the Labour
    Market, Revue suisse d'économie politique et de statistique,
    4, 1971, p. 761-790.

42. RUESTOW H.-J.,
    Gastarbeiter-Gewinn oder Belastung für unsere Volkswirt-
    schafts? Wirtschafstdienst,no 12, 1965

43. SALOWSKY H.,
    Gesamtwirtschaftliche Aspekte der Ausländerbeschäftigung,
    Beiträge des deutschen Industrieinstituts, Heft 10/11, 1971.

44. THOMAS B.,
    Migration and Urban Development, London, 1972.

45. WEBER L.,
    Etude pour une politique conjoncturelle en Suisse, Thèse
    Lausanne, 1971, 256 p.

46. WITTMANN W.,
    Wachstum- und Konjunkturaspekte des Fremdarbeiterproblems,
    Wirtschaft und Recht, 1962.

OECD SALES AGENTS
DEPOSITAIRES DES PUBLICATIONS DE L'OCDE

ARGENTINA – ARGENTINE
Carlos Hirsch S.R.L.,
Florida 165, BUENOS-AIRES.
☎ 33-1787-2391 Y 30-7122
AUSTRALIA – AUSTRALIE
B.C.N. Agencies Pty. Ltd.,
161 Sturt St., South MELBOURNE, Vic. 3205.
☎ 69.7601
658 Pittwater Road, BROOKVALE NSW 2100.
☎ 938 2267
AUSTRIA – AUTRICHE
Gerold and Co., Graben 31, WIEN 1.
☎ 52.22.35
BELGIUM – BELGIQUE
Librairie des Sciences
Coudenberg 76-78, B 1000 BRUXELLES 1.
☎ 13.37.36/12.05.60
BRAZIL – BRESIL
Mestre Jou S.A., Rua Guaipá 518,
Caixa Postal 24090, 05089 SAO PAULO 10.
☎ 256-2746/262-1609
Rua Senador Dantas 19 s/205-6, RIO DE
JANEIRO GB. ☎ 232-07. 32
CANADA
Information Canada
171 Slater, OTTAWA. KIA 0S9.
☎ (613) 992-9738
DENMARK – DANEMARK
Munksgaards Boghandel
Nørregade 6, 1165 KØBENHAVN K.
☎ (01) 12 69 70
FINLAND – FINLANDE
Akateeminen Kirjakauppa
Keskuskatu 1, 00100 HELSINKI 10. ☎ 625.901
FRANCE
Bureau des Publications de l'OCDE
2 rue André-Pascal, 75775 PARIS CEDEX 16.
☎ 524.81.67
Principaux correspondants :
13602 AIX-EN-PROVENCE : Librairie de
l'Université. ☎ 26.18.08
38000 GRENOBLE : B. Arthaud. ☎ 87.25.11
31000 TOULOUSE : Privat. ☎ 21.09.26
GERMANY – ALLEMAGNE
Verlag Weltarchiv G.m.b.H.
D 2000 HAMBURG 36, Neuer Jungfernstieg 21
☎ 040-35-62-501
GREECE – GRECE
Librairie Kauffmann, 28 rue du Stade,
ATHENES 132. ☎ 322.21.60
ICELAND – ISLANDE
Snaebjörn Jónsson and Co., h.f.,
Hafnarstraeti 4 and 9, P.O.B. 1131,
REYKJAVIK. ☎ 13133/14281/11936
INDIA – INDE
Oxford Book and Stationery Co.:
NEW DELHI, Scindia House. ☎ 47388
CALCUTTA, 17 Park Street. ☎ 24083
IRELAND – IRLANDE
Eason and Son, 40 Lower O'Connell Street,
P.O.B. 42, DUBLIN 1. ☎ 01-41161
ISRAEL
Emanuel Brown :
35 Allenby Road, TEL AVIV. ☎ 51049/54082
also at :
9, Shlomzion Hamalka Street, JERUSALEM.
☎ 234807
48 Nahlath Benjamin Street, TEL AVIV.
☎ 53276
ITALY – ITALIE
Libreria Commissionaria Sansoni :
Via Lamarmora 45, 50121 FIRENZE. ☎ 579751
Via Bartolini 29, 20155 MILANO. ☎ 365083
Sous-dépositaires:
Editrice e Libreria Herder,
Piazza Montecitorio 120, 00186 ROMA.
☎ 674628
Libreria Hoepli, Via Hoepli 5, 20121 MILANO.
☎ 865446
Libreria Lattes, Via Garibaldi 3, 10122 TORINO.
☎ 519274
La diffusione delle edizioni OCDE è inoltre assicu-
rata dalle migliori librerie nelle città più importanti.

JAPAN – JAPON
OECD Publications Centre,
Akasaka Park Building,
2-3-4 Akasaka,
Minato-ku
TOKYO 107. ☎ 586-2016
Maruzen Company Ltd.,
6 Tori-Nichome Nihonbashi, TOKYO 103.
P.O.B. 5050, Tokyo International 100-31.
☎ 272-7211
LEBANON – LIBAN
Documenta Scientifica/Redico
Edison Building, Bliss Street,
P.O.Box 5641, BEIRUT. ☎ 354429 – 344425
THE NETHERLANDS – PAYS-BAS
W.P. Van Stockum
Buitenhof 36, DEN HAAG. ☎ 070-65.68.08
NEW ZEALAND – NOUVELLE-ZELANDE
The Publications Officer
Government Printing Office
Mulgrave Street (Private Bag)
WELLINGTON, ☎ 46.807
and Government Bookshops at
AUCKLAND (P.O.B. 5344). ☎ 32.919
CHRISTCHURCH (P.O.B. 1721). ☎ 50.331
HAMILTON (P.O.B. 857). ☎ 80.103
DUNEDIN (P.O.B. 1104). ☎ 78.294
NORWAY – NORVEGE
Johan Grundt Tanums Bokhandel,
Karl Johansgate 41/43, OSLO 1. ☎ 02-332980
PAKISTAN
Mirza Book Agency, 65 Shahrah Quaid-E-Azam,
LAHORE 3. ☎ 66839
PHILIPPINES
R.M. Garcia Publishing House,
903 Quezon Blvd. Ext., QUEZON CITY,
P.O. Box 1860 – MANILA. ☎ 99.98.47
PORTUGAL
Livraria Portugal,
Rua do Carmo 70-74. LISBOA 2. ☎ 360582/3
SPAIN – ESPAGNE
Libreria Mundi Prensa
Castelló 37, MADRID-1. ☎ 275.46.55
Libreria Bastinos
Pelayo, 52, BARCELONA 1. ☎ 222.06.00
SWEDEN – SUEDE
Fritzes Kungl. Hovbokhandel,
Fredsgatan 2, 11152 STOCKHOLM 16.
☎ 08/23 89 00
SWITZERLAND – SUISSE
Librairie Payot, 6 rue Grenus, 1211 GENEVE 11.
☎ 022-31.89.50
TAIWAN
Books and Scientific Supplies Services, Ltd.
P.O.B. 83, TAIPEI.
TURKEY – TURQUIE
Librairie Hachette,
469 Istiklal Caddesi,
Beyoglu, ISTANBUL, ☎ 44.94.70
et 14 E Ziya Gökalp Caddesi
ANKARA. ☎ 12.10.80
UNITED KINGDOM – ROYAUME-UNI
H.M. Stationery Office, P.O.B. 569, LONDON
SE1 9 NH, ☎ 01-928-6977, Ext. 410
or
49 High Holborn
LONDON WC1V 6HB (personal callers)
Branches at: EDINBURGH, BIRMINGHAM,
BRISTOL, MANCHESTER, CARDIFF,
BELFAST.
UNITED STATES OF AMERICA
OECD Publications Center, Suite 1207,
1750 Pennsylvania Ave, N.W.
WASHINGTON, D.C. 20006. ☎ (202)298-8755
VENEZUELA
Libreria del Este, Avda. F. Miranda 52,
Edificio Galipán, Aptdo. 60 337, CARACAS 106.
☎ 32 23 01/33 26 04/33 24 73
YUGOSLAVIA – YOUGOSLAVIE
Jugoslovenska Knjiga, Terazije 27, P.O.B. 36,
BEOGRAD. ☎ 621-992

Les commandes provenant de pays où l'OCDE n'a pas encore désigné de dépositaire
peuvent être adressées à :
OCDE, Bureau des Publications, 2 rue André-Pascal, 75775 Paris CEDEX 16
Orders and inquiries from countries where sales agents have not yet been appointed may be sent to
OECD, Publications Office, 2 rue André-Pascal, 75775 Paris CEDEX 16

OECD PUBLICATIONS, 2, rue André-Pascal, 75775 Paris Cedex 16 - No. 33.095 1974
PRINTED IN FRANCE